THE BIBLE UNDER ATTACK

Three papers read at the 1977
Conference of the British Evangelical Council

EVANGELICAL PRESS

EVANGELICAL PRESS
P.O. Box 5, Welwyn, Hertfordshire, England

© Evangelical Press 1978
First published September 1978

ISBN 0 85234 123 7

Cover design by Peter Wagstaff

Printed in Great Britain by
Stanley L. Hunt (Printers) Ltd., Rushden, Northamptonshire

Contents

Foreword	5
The Inerrancy of Scripture *Hywel R. Jones*	9
Creation and Evolution *Edgar H. Andrews*	32
Our Times and their Lessons *Iain H. Murray*	59

Foreword

It is a privilege to be asked to write a foreword to this book since, as General Secretary of the British Evangelical Council, I was largely responsible for arranging our Council's Silver Jubilee Conference in Westminster Chapel, London, where the three addresses here printed were first presented under the overall theme which is the title of this book, *The Bible Under Attack*.

Such a theme could hardly have been more appropriate to the occasion, nor more relevant to the contemporary scene. It was appropriate to the occasion for this reason. When the World Council of Churches was formally constituted at Amsterdam in 1948 there were some evangelical church leaders who saw that it was not enough simply to oppose such an unscriptural ecumenicity; what was needed was a positive alternative in line with biblical principles. To meet this very need our Council was formed four years later, its aim being to promote fellowship, understanding and mutual co-operation between evangelical churches which were united in their belief in the fundamental doctrines of the historic, orthodox Christian faith. Those doctrines were spelt out in a commonly accepted doctrinal basis, the first clause of which affirms belief in 'The inerrancy of the Holy Scriptures as originally given, their verbal inspiration by God and their supreme authority as the only rule of faith and conduct'. Any ongoing attack upon the Bible is therefore a matter of vital concern to the many hundreds of gospel churches who now belong to our Council.

That the Bible was under attack once more, not only in the secular world, but even among so-called evangelicals, had become all too evident during the year preceding our conference. Dr. Ralph Martin, formerly a lecturer at the London Bible College, had publicly attacked Dr. Harold Lindsell's book, *Battle for the Bible*, in which Dr. Lindsell argues that 'a belief in biblical inerrancy was an essential mark of the true evangelical: if this were lost, other vital truths were soon lost also'. Subsequently, the General Secretary of the Evangelical Alliance had in effect claimed that the inerrancy of Scripture was not a matter of essential belief, but one where evangelicals could hold conflicting views. Our Executive Council felt this was a challenge that could not be ignored and was grateful to one of its own members, Hywel Jones, for facing it so helpfully, in the first of the addresses printed here.

But the Bible had also been under attack in the secular world of education, for during the year a County Education Authority had been widely reported as having dismissed the Head of Religious Education in a large comprehensive school for refusing to teach children that the biblical account of creation was folklore and a 'collection of myths and legends'; and his dismissal had been upheld, on appeal, by an industrial tribunal. Not least because of that, but also because of the unbiblical beliefs of so many professing evangelicals at this very point, we asked Edgar Andrews to address our conference on *Creation and Evolution*. His diagnostic, yet positive and challenging approach to that subject will, I am sure, be as much appreciated by readers of this book as it was by those who first heard it.

It was equally appropriate and timely for Iain Murray to take as his subject, at one of our conference evening rallies, *Our Times and their Lessons*. His penetrating analysis of the cause of the gospel and the state of the kingdom of God during the preceding quarter-century gave us much serious food for thought. However we were at the same time made to see the way in which the living God, the God of the Bible, had been at work and were encouraged as well as challenged to trust and serve Him faithfully in the coming days.

My prayer would be that the readers of this book, as well as those of us who first heard its contents, may not only be confirmed in our belief in the Bible, but may also thereby be encouraged to have faith in, and to live in obedience to the living God of the Bible, who 'is able to do exceedingly abundantly above all that we ask or think according to the power that worketh in us', that 'unto Him' there may be 'glory in the church by Christ Jesus throughout all ages', this one included, 'world without end, Amen'.

July 1978   ROLAND LAMB

About the Authors

Hywel R. Jones, M.A. is a graduate of the Universities of Wales and Cambridge where he studied Hebrew and Theology respectively. He is at present minister at Grove Chapel, London, and also lectures at London Theological Seminary.

Edgar H. Andrews, B.Sc., Ph.D., D.Sc., F.Inst.P., F.I.M. is Professor of Materials in the University of London and Head of the Department of Materials at Queen Mary College. He is an international authority on the science of large molecules and has had over seventy scientific papers and books published.

Iain H. Murray, B.A. is a graduate of the University of Durham and a minister of the Free Church of Scotland. He is a trustee of the Banner of Truth Trust and editor of *The Banner of Truth* magazine.

I The Inerrancy of Scripture

Hywel R. Jones

Over the past decade or so the doctrine of the inerrancy of Scripture has become more and more generally recognized in the evangelical world as being a current theological issue. Some have deplored this as being yet another of the self-inflicted wounds by which evangelicalism is in danger of losing its life-blood. Others regard it as a necessary means to purify that body from an element which is inimical to its health.

Any survey of evangelical writings over the last ten years will bring to light no lack of evidence to demonstrate that some evangelical scholars, to whose writings many had gratefully if somewhat uncritically turned for help in the conservative–liberal conflict, have been making some surprising and unnecessary concessions to non-biblical scholarship.

Because of the importance of this subject we ought to continue to read the signs of the times with regard to it. However, rather than giving documented evidence from the past, we shall consider two new developments in the controversy and try to evaluate them. In the last twelve months new elements have appeared; the debate has entered a new phase. This feature greatly enlarges the whole subject and the treatment must therefore be extended.

What is the major new factor? It is that a defence of the case against inerrancy has been made public. This has not been done in a formal way, that is by a paper or a book on the subject, but by way of reply to Dr. Harold Lindsell's book *Battle for the Bible*. Various comments and reviews have appeared in the Christian press on both sides of the Atlantic. These indicate an acceptance of the charge that there has been a shift in the way in which evangelicals now refer to Holy Scripture. No longer then do we need to amass evidence in order to argue that there is a real case to be answered. The charge has been accepted; the answer is now forthcoming. We do need, however, to continue to gather evidence because it will show how serious this shift is and how much is really involved in this concept of inerrancy, and safeguarded by this word and this word alone, to the exclusion even of infallibility (though, speaking strictly, infallibility should be regarded as saying all that needs to be said). Now that evidence will appear as various scholars concentrate attention on what they claim Scripture means by what it says. That may appear to be – and it really is – a legitimate approach and concern. We value the words of Scripture for no other reason than the meaning they contain and reveal. What possible hesitation, then, could we have when people say that they are concerned with the meaning of Scripture? This will be taken up later but, very briefly just now, the point that we must be aware of is this: that when the meaning of Scripture is referred to all the intention of the original authors, that intention and meaning can be curtailed by the interpreter to matters essential to faith and conduct and not extended to matters of geography, history and science, etc.

So we turn to consider some published reactions to *Battle for the Bible*. In doing so we shall isolate reasons for no longer speaking of inerrancy and not seek to defend Dr. Lindsell against his critics. Two sources only have been chosen, in order to keep this study within manageable proportions. The first source is a general comment by Dr. Ralph Martin, under the heading 'Letter from America', which appeared in the *Life of Faith* in March 1977. The second is a review by Professor Bernard Ramm of Eastern Theological Seminary, Philadelphia which appeared in *The Reformed Journal* 1976 under the heading 'Misplaced Battle Lines'. We shall then turn to a review article by Mr. Tony Lane, Lecturer in Historical Theology at London Bible College, which appeared in *The Christian Graduate* in March 1977, because it contains a proposal as to the way forward for those who do believe in inerrancy. We shall thus end on a positive note, though in passing it should be said that Mr. Lane does make some statements which resemble those made by the two writers already named. These sources are reasonably accessible to anyone wishing to pursue the matter further.

There are certain differences between Dr. Martin and Professor Ramm on this subject. However, notwithstanding the differences, there is a large area of agreement and so a fairly coherent picture of the 'anti-inerrancy case' does appear. It can be reduced to two main features, each in the form of an objection.

OBJECTIONS TO INERRANCY AS A TERM DESCRIPTIVE
OF HOLY SCRIPTURE

From the sources mentioned I have gathered *five objections*.

1. *Inerrancy and infallibility are synonymous*

Dr. Ralph Martin writes: 'Many of our readers will be wondering why this use of words is so important. "Inerrancy" . . . "infallibility"; there seems to be a distinction without a difference.'

Dr. Ralph Martin's point here is not disputed, though his conclusion is. While infallibility and inerrancy are etymologically and theologically synonymous they are not synonymous in the evangelical world of today. There are those who, while retaining infallibility, do not extend it to everything that Scripture teaches. Inerrancy cannot be handled in this way and so they have had to drop it. An illustration may help here. Because of political changes, and housing development schemes, new atlases and street maps have to be drawn. Our world, however big or small it may be, undergoes changes. The theological map changes too, and terms are like landmarks. New ones have to be invented, and old ones undergo reinterpretation. When inerrancy was identical with infallibility it could be dropped. Today it is not, so it must be maintained.

2. *Inerrancy has no generally recognized meaning among present-day evangelicals*

Dr. Ralph Martin writes: 'For some, inerrancy means the literal meaning of the text of the Authorized Version, and any translation later than 1611 is anathema; for others, the phrase runs "inerrant in the original manuscripts", which, of course are lost forever; and this refinement allows room for the mistakes and corruptions caused by the transmission of the text and scribal variations; still using the term inerrancy are those who wish the term to cover all the affirmative teaching of Scripture (as in the Lausanne document), while other evangelicals draw a distinction between "what the Bible teaches" and "what the Bible touches".' His point is this, that inerrancy means so many different things that it should no longer be used. Now, it must be confessed that there is some truth in this statement. Inerrancy does mean different things to different people and that is to be lamented. The answer to this objection, however, lies along the following line. Is it true that these variations in understanding are *only* to be referred to inerrancy? Is it not also true that infallibility is popularly misunderstood as well? It is, and what is more, infallibility is misunderstood in exactly the same ways as inerrancy is misunderstood. To many, infallibility is bound up with the status of the text of the Authorized Version. To others, it is bound up with that particular translation. Further, infallibility always has been related to the phrase 'as originally given' just as inerrancy has been, and should be. The distinction to which Dr. Ralph Martin refers between 'teaching' and 'touching' involves the meaning of Scripture. It therefore affects infallibility no less than inerrancy. These variations cannot be related exclusively to inerrancy and removed from infallibility. They apply equally to both. And yet, the argument is that because inerrancy is misunderstood in these ways the term should be jettisoned, whereas infallibility is also misunderstood in these exact ways but it is preserved. That is unfair; it amounts to an element of special pleading. Is there any real force in the argument that because a term is popularly misunderstood it should be dismissed? If that is the case, would this objection not also toll the bell for any theological term for which there happened to be a wide degree of latitude in the thinking of the church? It would! Why does Dr. Ralph Martin not consider the possibility that when a term is misunderstood, efforts should be made to have it rehabilitated? Why not explain it? Why not clarify its meaning rather than consign it to oblivion? The answer which springs to mind is that the term is not worth keeping as far as Dr. Martin is concerned. This objection is therefore a pretext, a cover-up.

3. *Inerrancy leads to a misuse of Scripture*

Dr. Ralph Martin writes: 'Excessive defence of the minutiae of Scripture, however well-intentioned and buttressed with all the apparatus of argument, leads to a wrong use of Scripture, as it defines its own role. Why do we need Scripture as the indispensable rule of our faith and practice? . . . Not to provide an encyclopaedia on all manner of things; but to make us wise unto salvation . . . and to equip the servants of God.' (A reference to 2 Tim. 3: 15-17.)

Now the word with which this quotation opens is the word 'excessive' and in considering its significance we ought to remember that it is used here by someone who is out to demolish inerrancy and it voices his reaction against those who are therefore forced to defend it with emphasis. For practical purposes then, the statement may be read as follows: not 'excessive defence of the minutiae of Scripture' but '*any* defence of the minutiae of Scripture', for in real terms this is what it comes to.

Now is that true? Does a defence of the minutiae of Scripture distort its purpose? Theoretically one would have to say that it could, but it must be denied that it has to. It can in the sense that over-emphasis on many doctrines – not just inerrancy – can throw the whole body of truth out of gear. For example, inerrancy is no more culpable on this score than some aspects of eschatology. But inerrancy does not *have* to distort the purpose of Scripture, because it is in accord with the nature and purpose of Scripture. How can it be otherwise? What inerrancy points to and affirms is this: that *whatever* the Bible teaches is true because all of it came from the God who cannot lie. The very verses which speak of the purpose of Scripture (namely 2 Tim. 3: 15-17) contain the words 'all Scripture' or 'every Scripture', neither translation affects the point in any material sense. Which is that 'all Scripture', viewed collectively or extensively; or 'every Scripture', viewed particularly, 'is given by inspiration of God'. Paul also says in Romans 15: 4, 'Whatsoever things were written aforetime were written for our learning.' Inerrancy is co-extensive with inspiration and is its necessary consequence. Whatever the Bible teaches about anything, God wants us to know. Yet some things it tells us are of course less important; for example, chronological, numerological, geographical, cultural data. These are less important in that it is not necessary to believe them in order to be saved, but we must remember that they come to us from the same God who reveals things essential to salvation and we cannot set up a distinction between them in terms of their accuracy when the same unerring God has given them both. Further, matters that are essential to salvation are frequently inextricably bound up with matters that are nonessential. On what basis shall we say that Jonah's three days in the great fish was not actual and yet our Lord's burial was? Any distinction between the one and the other in terms of historical factuality is groundless. This objection again dismisses inerrancy on a pretext. Inerrancy harmonizes with the purpose of Scripture. What God has given to us to know is integrally related to His main purpose in giving the whole of Scripture which is as is rightly said, 'to make us wise unto salvation through faith which is in Christ Jesus' and to furnish us for every good work.

4. *Inerrancy is not in accord with the self-disclosure of God*

The arguments against inerrancy become more and more surprising. This indicates the cruciality of the term. Perhaps this sounds the most staggering of all. It is Professor Bernard Ramm who voices this objection. His point is that there must inevitably be some hiddenness, abasement, and contradiction of the world's thinking in the self-disclosure of God in the Incarnation and the Cross. He says: 'We must also have a doctrine of the Scriptures which is of the same heartbeat as the theology of the Cross . . . God's written word is in the form of humiliation just as the Son of God in His incarnation. It too shares the brokenness, the servanthood, the masking of the divine glory as the incarnate Son . . . Yahweh of the Old

Testament leads a hidden, mysterious existence for He alone will be worshipped and adored. And we dare not betray the nature in which Yahweh encounters man.'

That smacks of neo-orthodoxy. It is in line with Brunner's doctrine of the divine incognito, in which the humanity of both Jesus and Scripture is so presented as to demean their greatness, and to invite even contempt. It has a fatal effect on the reality and knowability of deity.

In answer to this statement, two points need to be made:

(a) Insistence on inerrancy is not in conflict with the human element in Scripture, and to pay due emphasis to the human element does not involve the recognition of fallibility or error. This is to say that true humanity is not necessarily linked with fallibility. Real humanity is not inextricably bound up with the fact of error. Adam was truly human but not fallible before he fell. So was, and is, and ever will be the Lord Jesus Christ. The deity of Jesus Christ is truly, gloriously but mysteriously compatible with His full humanity. The humanity of Scripture is not incompatible with its being divinely inspired and inerrant.

(b) The inerrancy of Scripture does not militate against the truth of the ineffability of God. All it affirms is that whatever is revealed is accurate and true. It does not amount to a claim that the Bible is exhaustive truth. There are, and it tells us so itself, things that are not yet revealed. When these secret things are revealed at the Last Day, however, that which has been revealed in the Bible, because it is true, though it be supplemented, will not be corrected. It will rather be consummated. We shall not find a different God, we shall not find different facts, we shall not find a different Jesus Christ. We shall find more that is in accord with what we now know. Therefore, while maintaining inerrancy, we remember that though this Bible is the Word of God it is not God, and the old charge of bibliolatry is in reality a fiction to anyone who has come to know the God of whom the Bible speaks. It is because this Book has confronted a soul with God that it is so regarded and prized and used to that end. Inerrancy is not in conflict with the ineffability of God. While Scripture points us to itself, it points us through itself to the One who gave it – God, in Christ, and by the Holy Spirit.

5. *Inerrancy is neither acceptable nor defensible in the contemporary philosophical and theological context*

If there is a real reason against inerrancy, then this is it. The other four do not amount to a case.

Dr. Ralph Martin writes: 'There is another and more fundamental reason why this is an unsatisfactory expression. It is negative; and is it not a principle of logic that you can never prove a negative?'

Here again is an example of unfair or impartial arguing. Inerrancy is dismissed on the grounds which are equally applicable to infallibility. Both are negative – but of course inerrancy and infallibility are negative only in form; they are positive in meaning and purpose. Now if inerrancy cannot be logically proven because it is negative and therefore must be dismissed, how can infallibility, which is also negative, be proven and so retained? It must be because Dr. Martin wants to keep infallibility and not inerrancy,

THE INERRANCY OF SCRIPTURE

and this because infallibility can, in his mind, be restricted to soteriological and ethical matters. Perhaps it could be replied that since infallibility has lost its opprobrious associations and is becoming theologically respectable, logical proof is not therefore necessary. Let us beware of such rationalizing. In the Roman Catholic Church the indefectibility of the church has been proposed as an alternative for the infallibility of the Pope. Is it not at least conceivable that in the future infallibility will no longer be used with reference to the Scripture but indefectibility take its place? If infallibility can be demonstrated theologically from 2 Timothy 3: 16, so can inerrancy! Both are necessary consequences from the unique authoritative reality of divine inspiration. Inerrancy and infallibility *must* share the same fate or the same glory.

Professor Bernard Ramm develops this objection. He writes: 'Anybody who has lived with biblical criticism through the years knows the clusters of problems we face on every page of Scripture. If we told a logician that there are no errors in Scripture but thousands of problems (not an exaggeration in view of the huge books on Old and New Testament introduction) he would die laughing. We must not have a view on Holy Scripture which, to use a current philosophical phrase, "dies the death of a thousand qualifications".'

Two observations must be made on this statement:

(a) It is incredibly superficial and erroneous, and is so in two respects. Professor Ramm tells us that he believes the history of biblical criticism is the sure guide to the problems of Scripture; the second is that the size of the tomes on biblical introduction is the sure guide to the number of these problems. Any evangelical who has had anything to do with biblical criticism should not need to be convinced that its tendency has been to manufacture problems which have no real foundation in Scripture, and to feed on itself, spinning its own labyrinthine webs, without any real reference to Scripture.

(b) Professor Ramm's more basic point, however, is that the distinction made between a problem and an error is ridiculous, and it makes an utter nonsense of inerrancy. Now he is perfectly aware of the honoured names associated with this distinction, namely A. A. Hodge and B. B. Warfield, for he admits in his review that he read their joint production entitled *Inerrancy* by way of preparation for what he wrote on *Battle for the Bible*. Further he says that Lindsell's position is essentially the same as theirs. He knows then what he is doing. He goes on to say: 'The old debates about original manuscripts are passé; the argument that we can have many problems but are safe if we have no errors is threadbare.'

Why is this outmoded? Why is there no substance in the distinction between a problem and an error? Why is the debate about the original manuscripts outdated and to be ridiculed?

Is there any way of relating the texts we have to what God gave, which all acknowledge He did not preserve in their original given form and in their entirety? Is there any other way of dealing with that distinction than by referring to the original manuscripts and the painstaking search for that text in all its purity from the mass of manuscripts we have concerning those very, very few which are textually doubtful? 'As originally given' is a way of facing difficulties and not losing them; recognizing problems and not dismissing them.

What about the problem of distinguishing between a problem and an error? D. A. Hubbard, the President of Fuller Theological Seminary, in his review of *Battle for the Bible* in *Time Magazine*, caricatured it as 'the gas-balloon theory of theology. One leak and the whole Bible comes down.' To maintain this position, says Dr. Lane, 'presents evangelical theology with a Herculean apologetic task'. In the passage already quoted from Professor Ramm, he himself uses the word 'problem' and not 'error'. If the logician would die laughing at the distinction being made between problem and error, a grammarian would die in despair if it were not made. To fail to maintain the distinction and to denominate massive difficulties as certain errors has been the folly of the higher critics. This is one of the ways in which archaeology has exercised such a positive influence in turning many from the barren philosophical sterility of the old liberal approach to Scripture. Evidence which has appeared later has solved the apparently insoluble. To maintain this distinction is not only necessary but wise. But it is a distinction that can only be maintained by faith, not reason. By maintaining it we are able to say what we believe and why we believe it, while at the same time declaring the limitations of our knowledge. That is why it rubs against reason. We declare that, since God is truth, no facts which will come to light can possibly contradict His Word. To believe in the inerrancy of Holy Scripture is not to lay claim to possess all the answers, much less to having no problems. B. B. Warfield's old statement is as defensible as it is accurate. He said, 'So long as the proper evidence by which a proposition is established remains unrefuted, all so-called objections brought against it pass out of the category of objections to its truth into the category of difficulties to be adjusted to it.'

This adjustment, as he so admirably revealed by his believing scholarship, is not a twisting of the evidence to make it fit, but a painstaking investigation of it according to the accepted principles of historico-grammatical exegesis.

OBJECTIONS AGAINST INERRANCY AS A TEST TO DETERMINE THE ORTHODOXY OF ONE'S VIEW OF SCRIPTURE, AND ALSO ONE'S STANDING AS AN EVANGELICAL

Dr. Ralph Martin refers to those in America and Britain 'who make the decisive test (of whether one is truly evangelical or not) a Christian's affirmation of the inerrancy of Scripture. You will notice,' he continues 'from the way the definition is phrased that the litmus test involves the actual word "inerrancy". No other term will do, on the assumption that any substitute word is weaker and serves only to cast doubt on the Bible.' Accepting this as an accurate enough description of us, we are faced with a question: 'Why this insistence on inerrancy?' Is this an example of blind attachment to a word, for failure to use which we make a man an offender? Or is there a justification for its employment? And is this justification of sufficient magnitude to make the use of the word a matter of imperative necessity?

Dr. Ralph Martin is correct in regarding a view of the Bible as being bound up with being an evangelical.

THE INERRANCY OF SCRIPTURE 23

This is one of its hallmarks. However, for Dr. Ralph Martin to quote Professor F. F. Bruce to the effect that 'to believe in the God who justifies the ungodly is to be evangelical' is for both men an avoidance of the real issue by sleight of speech. It is not possible to believe in the God who justifies the ungodly without in our minds and hearts having some relationship with the Book which tells us who that God is and how He does it. The evangelical has ever identified himself and been known by a particular view and experience of Christ and the Bible. This is essentially one view is it not? It is the Lord guaranteeing the Book and the Book displaying the Lord. Therefore inerrancy can function as a test in both directions, of one's view of Scripture and one's standing as an evangelical (not of whether one is a Christian or not), if it has point with reference to the Bible, for it is only there we find Jesus Christ infallibly presented. Our first step therefore is to investigate inerrancy as pointing to something crucial with regard to the Bible.

What, then, is inerrancy? Dr. J. I. Packer replies: 'Logically its function has been to express a double commitment: first, an advance commitment to receive as truth from God all that Scripture is found on inspection actually to teach; second, a methodological commitment to interpret Scripture according to the principle of harmony.'

Clearly, on this basis, inerrancy is no disposable part of Scripture's nature. It should not therefore be a disposable part of anyone's confession regarding Scripture, who claims to believe in it.

Dr. Ralph Martin makes his position clear in the following way, and in doing so shows us the importance of inerrancy. He says that some evangelicals, no doubt himself included, 'have decided to abandon inerrancy, not because their attitude to Scripture is any less reverent, nor because they doubt its complete trustworthiness and reliability in those matters which it prescribes as all-important.' The all-determining words in that statement are the closing ones, namely 'in those matters which it prescribes as all-important'. That qualification is *the* issue. This is what certain people mean when they speak of the infallibility of Scripture loud and long but never speak of its inerrancy. What they are saying is that the Bible is infallible or inerrant, in a limited sense only. Now, to be fair to them, the only errancy which they allow for is in matters non-essential to faith and conduct. But this shift, this concession is bound sooner or later to erode what one says is infallibly presented. It did so in the Presbyterian Church in the United States at the turn of the century when Professor Warfield contended with H. P. Smith over what was then termed 'limited inspiration'. Professor Warfield referred to H. P. Smith (note this) as 'a moderate man of strong evangelical spirit', yet he contended with him because he saw that the concession made on what was non-essential to salvation would be followed by concessions on matters essential, as subsequent history proved.

Now, Professor Ramm ridicules Dr. Lindsell's assertion that to surrender inerrancy is equivalent to the ultimate surrender of everything. He says: 'Lindsell is claiming too much for a view of Scripture. We can have some first-rate heresies by surrendering other doctrines too, such as the Trinity, the Incarnation and the Atonement.' But not one of these doctrines is the source of all the doctrine. Scripture is! This surprising statement shows a complete failure to realize what Scripture really is. It is the source book for all doctrines. Failure to maintain this principle, as we should, will vitiate the whole. Inerrancy, which is the necessary consequence of plenary and verbal inspiration is a test of the orthodoxy of one's view of Scripture and in the contemporary evangelical world it is the test.

Secondly, does inerrancy have any bearing on one's standing as an evangelical? It does, because it is no more than a description of Holy Scripture *in the light of the Lord's teaching about it*. Therefore, our view of it reflects and has repercussions on our view of Him. The Lord does not permit the use of Scripture's purpose to distinguish between the infallible and the errant in the Old Testament. He believed in the inspiration of Moses, David, Isaiah, the creation by God, Adam and Eve, Cain and Abel, the flood, the ark, the destruction of Sodom and Lot's wife, the manna, the serpent of brass, the widow of Sarepta, Naaman. He places His imprimatur on it all as the Son of God who is the Truth, whose words will not pass away when heaven and earth have. He places His imprimatur on these statements no less than on others which are essential to salvation.

How then can we call Him Lord and not believe all He said? Was He no more than a child of His time, adopting the common mistaken view on these matters? This kenotic view of Christ may enable some to speak of errors without impugning His dignity. But on what basis do we then give credence to His other remarks? Was He in error and knew it, yet said these things? Was He in error and did not know it when He said them? Who wants either alternative? These suggestions are the voices of unbelief in a divine Christ, in an incarnation of God.

THE WAY AHEAD

Having examined reasons presented in favour of dispensing with the term inerrancy, and rejected them, we now turn briefly to the other matter referred to earlier in this paper. We do so via the main burden of Mr. Tony Lane's review article on *Battle for the Bible*.

Mr. Lane confesses a belief in inerrancy, and a concern over the evidence Dr. Lindsell has presented. However, he also expresses concern over Dr. Lindsell's reaction to those facts, as he believes this is 'itself . . . one of the causes of the drift from orthodoxy', and 'will ironically force many down the very slippery slope from which it purports to be defending them'. Mr. Lane believes this will happen because the book deals with a secondary aspect of Scripture, namely inerrancy, to the almost total exclusion of the primary one, namely inspiration; and, secondly, because of 'the naive concept of error' reflected in the book, in the interpretation of Job 38: 7, and the harmonization of the records of Peter's denials.

While accepting unreservedly that to uphold inerrancy does not demand that we regard the Gospels as presenting verbatim accounts of what the Lord actually said, much less literalistic interpretation of any Scripture (as distinct from the literal meaning) a query may be raised as to whether this twofold critique of Dr. Lindsell's presentation of inerrancy forms a sufficient basis for Mr. Lane's claim that we need 'a doctrine (of Scripture) which will not repeatedly provoke defection'. By this is meant 'a fresh statement of orthodoxy which retains our essential belief in the divine origin and truthfulness of Scripture while incorporating newer insights into its humanity'. This will mean 'an orthodox doctrine of Scripture for the 1970s and 1980s'. Mr. Lane believes that the way to do this is via 'the concept of intention. We are committed to the truthfulness of Scripture but only in the sense *intended* by its authors.'

It is to an examination of this concept of intention that we turn, and we shall first of all clarify what is involved in it, and then offer some cautionary remarks with regard to it.

Some clarification of the concept of intention is necessary because it is often difficult to take exception to the language used. What is more important than the original meaning of any Scripture? Is this not bound up with historico-grammatical exegesis? Would not the expression 'as originally intended' therefore be synonymous with 'as originally given'. It would not, and it is not. The latter refers to the actual Scriptures themselves; the former to their meaning at any point, which meaning we have to discover. Therefore 'as originally intended' includes the interpreter and so a subjective element enters in; whereas 'as originally given' excludes all except the sixty-six books themselves. When the latter is confessed, something fixed is referred to which spans the ages; the former can change from generation to generation, and because there is no utterly objective standard, there can be no final confession of what is genuine and what is false. The focus will ultimately shift from God's Word to man's interpretation. Some questions will indicate how this will work out.

How did the author of Genesis 1-3 intend us to view its details? As factual statements? Or pictorial representations? Did Jesus intend to affirm the Davidic authorship of Psalm 110 when He quoted from it, or the authorship of Isaiah by the eighth century Isaiah of Jerusalem when He quoted from it? When He referred to Jonah in the fish for three days and three nights did He intend us to believe that He believed these things to be factual? Now an up-to-date example of this kind of approach can be found in G. C. Berkouwer's book *Holy Scripture*. He refers to the time-boundedness of Scripture, the time-relatedness of Scripture. By way of example he refers to the statements in 1 Corinthians 11 regarding womanhood. This is what he says: 'Paul . . . did not in the least render timeless propositions concerning womanhood. Rather, he wrote various testimonies and prescriptions applicable to particular . . . situations against a background of specific morals and customs of that period.'

Now we are not suggesting that Scripture should not be integrated with its situation. The meaning of the words is bound up with their meaning at the time in which they were used. Scripture abounds in illustrations of this. There are references to contemporary culture and so on. But on what basis can it be said that this is what Paul is doing in 1 Corinthians 11 when he goes back to creation and not to contemporary Greek culture or to Jewish culture? When he speaks about the man being the head he goes back to creation. The strange thing is this, that Berkouwer proceeds within

THE INERRANCY OF SCRIPTURE

a few pages of that statement to refer to what the apostle teaches in 1 Corinthians 7 about marriage and remaining unmarried and there, quite rightly, he says that there is a time-relatedness in the teaching of the apostle. We know there is, Paul tells us so. He speaks of the present distress, of time being short and because of what he foresaw it was better not to marry. But where is the example and where is the proof of time-relatedness in 1 Corinthians 11? It is not there. Why import it then? It is because of the present ecclesiastical and theological distress on the subject in question. However, it is of the utmost importance that in considering the use made of the concept of intention as a hermeneutical principle that a distinction be made between those who use it and dismiss inerrancy, and those who use it while maintaining inerrancy. With the former we must engage in debate over the nature of Scripture; with the latter we must discuss the meaning – the full meaning – of any given Scripture. If this distinction is not made and acted on then the nature of Scripture will be forgotten in a study of its meaning, and will run the risk of being lost as the supreme and ultimate confession of the genuineness, or otherwise, of any interpretation.

The following cautionary remarks are now offered as a sincere contribution to the study of the use of 'intention', not only as an exegetical exercise, but as an element in any confessional statement regarding the nature of Scripture.

1. Did the authors of the Old Testament fully understand the meaning of their writings? Daniel clearly did not (Dan. 12: 8-9), and all the prophets had very limited understanding in comparison with the

full revelation, yet that is what they prophesied and recorded (1 Pet. 1:11-12). If our principle of intention is related to the intended meaning of the human authors, then how can we get beyond their ignorance, or partial knowledge?

2. The concept of intention needs the doctrine of verbal inspiration to supplement and anchor it if we are to have a genuine Word of God in the words of men. There are two reasons for this:

(*a*) An interpreter could assent to 'intention' and yet play havoc with biblical expressions in his pursuit of their intended meaning. He can say that what any writer intended is in effect only what *he* wants to affirm.

(*b*) Who can guarantee that the intentions of any biblical writer were accurately expressed in what he wrote? We have no way into his mind but through his statements.

In each of the above cases we are by 'intention' led away from Scripture and not to it.

3. It is therefore accepted that the various language forms in Scripture must be investigated, and inerrancy commits us to this. The words are crucial for they contain and convey the meaning. Some statements are factual, others are pictorial. Some are to instruct, others to illustrate. Here is the way forward for those who believe in inerrancy. It is fully consonant with inerrancy, and we only contend for an inerrant Scripture because we want to know *all* that God wants us to know.

Inerrancy is a proper test of one's view of Scripture, and one's standing as an evangelical. In the present situation it is an imperative one. It is not something to

THE INERRANCY OF SCRIPTURE

be scorned as intellectually foolish, nor is it the manifestation of special pleading, fear, or a refusal to face facts. It is a strong apologetic position on the Bible, uniting event and record, occurrence and interpretation.

Inerrancy must be maintained. To drop it will leave one immediately with less than a whole Holy Bible, and less than a whole divine–human Saviour and Lord. What it leaves us with will itself diminish, and sooner than we think. The church will have neither the Christ of God nor the Word of God. This is no strife about words to no profit. The inerrancy of Scripture is an integral part of the pattern of sound words (i.e. health-giving and health-preserving) which we are to hold fast, and of the delivered faith for which we are to agonize.

II Creation and Evolution

Edgar H. Andrews

As I considered how I should approach this subject, two alternatives presented themselves to me. The first, which I have rejected, would have been to rehearse the growing case against an evolutionary interpretation of life and nature. It might have been more enjoyable to have adopted that approach, since we could possibly have had an entertaining 'knock-about' session at the expense of the theory of evolution. But there are two reasons why I rejected that approach. The first is that there already exists a growing body of readily available literature presenting the arguments and the evidences against an evolutionary interpretation of the universe. There are a few books which I should perhaps mention at this point. One is the excellent booklet by Sylvia Baker entitled *Bone of Contention* and a second is written by myself and entitled *Is Evolution Scientific?* These are suitable to give to non-Christians and indeed were written for that purpose. There are more weighty books like *The Genesis Flood* by Morris and Whitcomb, with which I am sure many of you are already familiar. The Newton Scientific Association has a series of pamphlets and leaflets on the various subjects which pertain to evolution and creation. In addition to this there is a considerable literature, most of it technical and originating in the

CREATION AND EVOLUTION

United States, which provides, probably for the first time, a scientifically respectable reply to the evolutionary theory.

There is, however, a second and more fundamental reason for taking a different approach to our subject today. I believe we have to raise the level of our discussion beyond the arguments for and against evolution, important though they are. We have to deal with the root of the problem. We are faced with a philosophical problem and we shall never make progress in this particular battle whilst we stand around the edges of the subject simply sniping at our opponents. We have to come to the heart of the matter which, as I hope will emerge from what I have to say to you, is not basically scientific at all, but philosophical and theological.

This more philosophical approach is necessary because unless we understand and proclaim the theological framework of our understanding of nature, of life and of creation, we shall not provide anything positive. It is all very well to be purely negative and to say, evolution cannot have happened because of this and that and something else. It is quite simple to demonstrate that certain aspects of the theory of evolution are plainly incredible, but that is not sufficient. What we must do in our debate with the world around us is provide a positive alternative to evolution. It is within that larger and more positive framework that we must operate, preach and teach.

What I have to say can be considered under two headings. Firstly, the attack and secondly, the answer. Although this analysis is very simple the matters that we are dealing with are weighty indeed.

THE ATTACK

I want to suggest that the attack comes to us from four directions.

The Materialistic World

First of all, it comes from a materialistic world-view. It comes from a concept of creation and all that it contains, of time and life and human history that is materialistic. Many would say that the view to which I refer is scientific but I would reject that submission. I believe it is materialistic rather than scientific.

What is this materialistic world-view which constitutes the first source of attack upon the biblical doctrine of creation? It is one with which we are all too familiar. In a sense it is unnecessary for me to rehearse it because it comes to us from the mass media, from popular literature, from newspapers and magazines, from radio and television. It features in our school lessons and our school books, our university courses and our university texts. It is an attempt, which in the minds of most men is successful, to explain the phenomena of life and man, and indeed the entirety of nature, in terms of the operation of scientific law alone.

This materialistic world-view must begin, of course, with some origin which it cannot explain; a genesis in which the entire universe came into being in some catastrophic and unimaginable explosion – the so-called 'big bang'. According to this idea the universe as we know it now, the stars, the galaxies and the earth (as a tiny speck of dust amongst this cosmic turmoil) are but the fragments and the debris of that primordial catastrophe. This account of the universe tells us how

CREATION AND EVOLUTION

stars evolved and how they go through a life cycle in terms of billions of years. It looks back to the 'big bang' which occurred something like 6,000,000,000 years ago and concludes that the earth itself is a cinder, the result of a subsequent supernova explosion, which is perhaps four thousand or four thousand five hundred million years old. This view pictures the earth cooling down gradually until some of the processes we know today began to operate. The processes of solar irradiation and lightning discharge are supposed to have produced, from small and simple molecules in the earth's atmosphere, larger organic molecules. These molecules were washed down into the seas and rivers of the earth and there they became increasingly concentrated. In this concentrated form they joined together to form larger molecules, and eventually these larger molecules separated from the aqueous medium in which they were dissolved. They became encapsulated and, in some way which even the evolutionists do not yet attempt to explain, were transformed into the first living cell. This then began to multiply and duplicate and acquire the ability to undergo genetic variation. Upon that genetic variation there operated a process of natural selection until from that first tiny spark of life, there arose the whole order of living things and, to crown it all, man himself.

This is the world-view which (let us not deceive ourselves) the vast majority of men and women in our Western society accept today. Of course there are features of this view which we as Christians cannot accept and I want to list those features in case we are misled at this point.

Why can we not believe this world-view? Why

can we not accept this picture, this materialistic scheme, of how things came to be? Well, the *first* and most obvious reason is that *it leaves no place for God.* God is totally unnecessary either as a concept or as an agent within this process. It is true that many Christians claim that this world-view is essentially correct except that it leaves out the meaning and the purpose that God can provide. So they attempt to graft the idea of God on to this materialistic picture of the universe. But as I hope we shall see, you cannot superimpose God on such a picture. There is an innate conflict, an intrinsic irreconcilability, between the concept of God and this materialistic view. If you want to build God into your view of the world, then you must *begin* with God. You cannot add Him as an afterthought, because if you try to do so He becomes dispensable to anyone who does not like the idea of God. And, as we know from our understanding of Scripture, the human heart in general does not like the idea of God. Romans 1 explains this perfectly clearly. Man did not like, and does not like, to retain God in his knowledge.

We all need an interpretation of the world around us, for it is quite intolerable for a thinking creature like man to live without some answer to the 'why' of our existence. It is therefore very attractive to the human heart, in its sin, rebellion and blindness, to accept a theory of being that dispenses with God. It is no use our saying, 'Oh no! You *must* have God to provide meaning'. They will say, 'No thank you! We can provide meaning from other sources and in other ways. We will do without God because our materialistic description and world-view is perfectly adequate.'

CREATION AND EVOLUTION

So not only do we reject this world-view because it has no place for God, we also reject it because, *secondly, it satisfies the unregenerate human heart*. It provides for that heart a place of escape from the challenge of the concepts of creation and Creator, from the implication that there is a God who made us and to whom we are answerable.

There is a *third* reason why we, as Christians, must reject this view, and this is that *the Bible tells us perfectly plainly that creation is a finished work*. Creation is not an ongoing process which is still to be observed today, it is a completed work. The evolutionary view begins with the evolution of the universe, proceeds onward to the origin of life by chemical evolution and then to biological evolution. Indeed it goes on, in the minds of many people, to the concepts of directed and man-controlled evolution. The view that evolution gives us, therefore, is that of an unfinished and ongoing process. But the Bible states perfectly plainly that God saw the things which He had made and declared them not only good, but complete and perfect. We are told that on the seventh day He rested from all His labours. Creation was finished.

Now we must not allow the evolutionists to confuse us at this point. They will say, 'But we can demonstrate that evolution is going on today. We can point to this variation and that variation in this species and that species and we can show you that evolution is an active process observable today.'

What they are really pointing to is *variation* not evolution. Now it is quite evident that the Bible teaches variation because, just to quote a single point, all the varieties of the human race, black, white, red, yellow skins and all the racial variants amongst men have been caused by variation during the descent of the human race from Adam. The Bible does not say that God created half a dozen different types of human being. He created one. He created one man and one woman and from that single pair have descended all the varieties, the pygmies, the giants, the Eskimos and the Negroes, the Caucasians and so on. Thus the Bible provides for a tremendous amount of variation within a kind. (We must not fall into the trap of identifying the 'kinds' of Genesis with the scientifically defined species of today.) Of course there is variation, and when people quote such things as the industrial melanism of moths as evidence for evolution, it is nothing of the kind. It is simply an example of variation. Within the limits of that variation, natural selection may well operate. We have no quarrel with that idea. The quarrel is with the concept that all living kinds have arisen from a single original form by a process of mutation and natural selection. That is what we must reject on biblical grounds.

A *fourth* reason why we must reject this materialistic world-view is that *evolution works in the opposite direction to the processes that we see operating in Scripture*. Evolution is ever upward, from imperfection to perfection and from simplicity to complexity. In contrast, the Bible demonstrates a creation that was originally perfect and complete and infinitely complex, and the only direction of change is that of deterioration. There has been sin. There has been a degradation of God's original perfect creation. There has been a downward movement, not an upward movement. I find it impossible to reconcile those two opposites.

CREATION AND EVOLUTION

Then, *fifthly*, we must reject this materialistic worldview, because *there are specific conflicts with the Word of God*. People often suggest that evolution tells roughly the same story as the Book of Genesis but such a claim will not stand up to close examination. To cite one example only, Genesis makes it clear that life arose first on earth (plants), not in the sea as evolution claims.

Atheistic Philosophies

I have spent a considerable time on the materialistic view of nature because, in a sense, it is the most basic direction from which attack comes. The next two directions of attack I am going to deal with very briefly. The second is that of atheistic philosophies. Whether we are thinking of atheistic communism, scientific humanism, or other such systems of thought, these philosophies differ from the basic materialistic view which I have just been describing in that they positively attack the Christian gospel and its concept of God. Anything that smacks of the supernatural they have vowed to destroy. Whereas materialism ignores God, atheism attacks God. In one sense the exponents of atheism are more easy to deal with, because they have the intelligence to see that man is essentially a religious being. They recognize that man must have his religion. Whether you call it communism or humanism or, to quote Sir Julian Huxley, 'religion without revelation,' even the atheist must have a religion. These atheistic philosophers are deliberately trying to replace the old supernatural religion with a new religion, and they know it and admit it. In their new religion there is a new deity, the deity of human reason. There are new processes, new methods of worship, and new means of promulgating the atheistic gospel.

We can therefore meet these people on their own ground because it is a question of one ideology against another. As I said before, this makes atheism considerably easier to deal with than the sheer dead weight of materialism.

Attacks from within Christendom

The third direction from which attack comes is from within Christendom. We are all familiar with the way in which Satan's attack on the early church was first from without, then from within, and then once more from without, and so on. In this biblical tradition, unhappily, we have to defend the Scriptures from attacks originating within Christendom. I do not need to elaborate upon this because it is not my subject here and will be considered elsewhere. The fact that much of Christendom has abandoned a belief in the inspiration and authority of Scripture is self-evident and known to us well. Once you have rejected the doctrine of the inspiration of Scripture, then the creation stories and their contradiction of the evolutionary outlook become irrelevant. All you have to do is to choose those parts of the Bible which you can accept and reject the rest. Thus the Bible has been totally set aside by the majority of our professing Christian churches as a source of reliable authority in matters of faith, practice and revelation.

Attacks from Conservative Evangelicals

I want to spend more time on the fourth direction

from which the attack comes and one which gives me much greater cause for concern. That is the attack upon the doctrines of Scripture that comes, unwittingly, from within the conservative evangelical camp. I want to spend time on this because I might be 'treading on toes' here and I feel I have to justify what I am about to say.

Attacks upon the Bible from within the conservative evangelical camp? Is that conceivable? Well, unfortunately I believe it is, especially in this area with which we are now concerned. I want to review this matter briefly by looking at a number of publications which I believe are either key to the matter, or reflect current opinion amongst evangelicals. Some of these books, I believe, have been formative. That is to say, they have directly influenced evangelical thinking in the matter. Others are not important in that respect but simply reflect the current mood.

One which I believe to have been formative is a book by Bernard Ramm entitled *The Christian View of Science and Scripture*. Published in 1955, it is a scholarly book and therefore carries great weight. I want to quote one or two of the commendations of this book from the dust jacket, because I think we shall then see how dangerous such a book can be. This danger arises because the book, along with its erroneous teaching, contains much which is good and wholesome and true and because it is written as a sincere attempt to reconcile the conflicts between science and religion and to bury them for ever.

Dr. Wilbur Smith apparently wrote of this book: 'The most important discussion of the problems involved in the vast and difficult subject of modern science and the ancient scripture that has appeared in this country for the last fifty years. It is the truly epochal work, *The Christian View of Science and Scripture* by my friend Bernard Ramm. It is the only book that I know of by an evangelical scholar today that can favourably be compared with the masterly learned works in this field which were produced in the latter part of the nineteenth century. This truly remarkable volume is the best that our evangelical world has yet produced in our day.'

Dr. Harold Ockenga of Boston says: 'Sane, objective, constructive, scholarly and biblical, it fearlessly faces the provincialism of fundamentalism whilst sternly adhering to the great fundamentals of the Faith.'

Dr. Billy Graham writes: 'While I have accepted the verbal inspiration of Scripture by faith, Dr. Ramm's book strengthens my intellectual acceptance. He gives logical and conclusive reasons for the hope that is within us. While I cannot say that I can agree with every point, I must commend it as the outstanding book that has come into my hands in the last few months.'

I could provide you with further quotations, but I think these are sufficient to show that this book was widely accepted by the Christian public and by Christian leaders at the time of its publication. Indeed, it was hailed as a profound expression of evangelical belief, yet when we come to examine what the book teaches we find profound departures from conservative theology. Here are one or two extracts. Naturally I am picking the particular passages which illustrate my point, but they are none the less telling for that.

CREATION AND EVOLUTION

'Hyper-orthodoxy' (which I believe describes my own position) 'does not believe its platform to the hilt. It is willing to retain faith in the Bible no matter what the scientists say. But would they really believe the Bible if at every point the Bible and science conflicted?' The implication here is, plainly, that we are only allowed to believe the Bible as long as it is in agreement with science. If we carry on believing the Bible when it appears to conflict with scientific theories we are called 'hyper-orthodox'.

Here is just a single but typical sentence: 'We also have reliable knowledge of millions of years of geological history; exhaustive researches have been made.' So he accepts, without any question or discussion, the geological time scale that is presented to us by uniformitarian geology.

Ramm quotes, with favour, C. W. Shields: 'Take the Bible without astronomy and there would remain the infinite and absolute Jehovah enthroned in the skies of our little planet as the only scene of his abode.' I refute that totally. I do not agree for one moment that this is the picture the Bible gives of God. Even Solomon declared, 'The heaven, and the heaven of heavens cannot contain Thee.' I do not see there the parochial view of God that Shields ascribes to the Bible. The quotation continues: 'But bring the two together (i.e. Scripture and astronomy) and at once the Author of Scripture becomes the Author of Nature with all His revealed attributes in full manifestation. . . . Astronomy thus yields overwhelming evidence in favour of real religion.' Now, I understand the sincerity of the writer in penning these words. I understand what he is driving at and I sympathize with it to some extent.

But he is treading on extremely thin ice because the implication is that revelation needs to be bolstered up, supported and evidenced by science. That is the slippery slope down which I believe these writers have begun to slide and from which it is very difficult to escape.

Here is another quotation from the same book: 'The book of nature and the Word of God emanate from the same infallible Author and therefore cannot be at variance; but man is a fallible interpreter and by mistaking one or both of these Divine Records he forces them often into unnatural conflict.' You notice that the book of nature and the Word of God are both 'Divine Records'. They are put on a par, on an equal level, so that one is not to be preferred or advanced beyond the other. This surely is a denial of the evangelical doctrine of Scripture and the teaching of Romans 1 concerning the inability of fallen man to comprehend the 'book of nature'.

The attitude to the miraculous in this book is frankly that of escapism, an attempt to explain away that which is miraculous, although the author constantly pleads a totally different attitude. The geological record as presently interpreted is preferred to the historicity of the Book of Genesis. Ramm rejects a literal interpretation of Genesis 1 and he also rejects any possibility of the universality of the flood: 'The universality of the flood,' he concludes after a long argument, 'simply means the universality of the experience of the man who reported it.' This is a plain contradiction of numerous Scriptures, for example, Genesis 6: 7 ('I will destroy man . . . from the face of the earth; both man, and beast, and the

CREATION AND EVOLUTION

creeping thing, and the fowls of the air; for it repenteth Me that I have made them'). See also Genesis 6: 13, 17; 7: 4 ('Every living substance that I have made will I destroy from off the face of the earth'); 7: 21-23; 8: 21; 2 Peter 3: 6.

Well, there is a book commended by Christian leaders in glowing terms, which has, I believe, profoundly influenced evangelical Christian thought.

In 1959 another book was published. It marked the centenary of Darwin's *Origin of Species* and it is entitled, *Evolution and Christian Thought Today*, edited by Dr. Russell Mixter of Wheaton College. Again we find the same tendencies. This historicity of Genesis is rejected in such terms as these: 'Before we examine this material it is of the utmost importance that the nature of biblical language be understood. Biblical language is not the precise language of modern day science. It is popular, phenomenal and oftentimes poetical. Thus we are not to look for intricate detail but for basic underlying principles. It is also well to be reminded that the Bible's main aim is to tell us who made the universe and not how it was made.' I wonder how the writer can substantiate a claim of that sort in the light of the relevant Scriptures. He continues: 'These remarks apply particularly to the early chapters of Genesis for recent researches into ancient literature assure us that these passages are not to be interpreted literally but poetically or allegorically.'

On the origin of life we find that the authors (and this is a volume edited by the professor of Zoology at Wheaton College, Illinois) give complete credence to the concepts of chemical evolution which, as a scientist, I have no hesitation in rejecting totally: 'It does mean that reputable scientists do have faith that life arose from inanimate matter through a series of physico-chemical processes no different from those we can observe today. If Christians cannot accept this at least as a legitimate hypothesis there will inevitably be conflict at this point.' Well, the writer speaks truly enough there!

Under the heading 'A Christian view of the origin of life' we read as follows: 'Many devout Christians have found little difficulty in accepting the evidence for the age of the earth presented in an earlier chapter, and the gradual development of living forms to be discussed in subsequent chapters, regarding this as an illustration of God's use of natural forces in a process of continuous creative activity.' To me, that sounds exactly like the materialistic world-view I have first described. It is certainly not a 'Christian view of the origin of life'.

I want now to come to another book. In 1965, the Inter-Varsity Fellowship published a book of essays entitled *Christianity in a Mechanistic Universe*, edited by Professor MacKay. In this book, there is advanced what is called 'the principle of complementarity'. This was not an original idea, but I believe the book brought it forward, and made the Christian public aware of it in a new way and with new force. Now although the people who wrote this book are true Christians, and I consider them brethren in Christ, I must nevertheless say that the doctrine of complementarity is to my mind one of the most mischievous teachings in the whole of this debate.

Very simply, complementarity suggests that there are two distinct and self-consistent descriptions, or

CREATION AND EVOLUTION

explanations, of the universe and of nature: the theological and the scientific. On one side we have a scientific description of the universe which is totally self-consistent and complete and in which the concept of God is irrelevant and unnecessary. On the other side, we have the theological interpretation and explanation of life which we find in the Bible. Now they say that both are true and the whole truth can only be obtained by holding the two as separate but complementary views of the universe.

Once again those involved in advancing these views are sincerely attempting to solve some of the problems and resolve some of the conflicts between Christianity and science. Why should we disagree with them? What is wrong with complementarity?

The *first* fault that I find with this view is that it encourages the construction of a world-view without God, as an alternative to the biblical world-view. It deliberately encourages the construction of the materialistic philosophy that I referred to earlier. It says, 'Yes by all means construct an account of creation and of life and of being that ignores God, but remember that when you have done this, it is only one of two complementary views.' The illustration is given of a painting. You can describe that painting either in terms of the artist's intentions and the message that he is seeking to convey, in terms of the subjective influence and impact it has upon the viewer, or you can describe it in scientific terms. You can analyse each point of the picture and specify its chemical composition and thereby give a total and complete and perfect description of the picture in terms of scientific formulae without any reference to the purpose of the artist or its subjective or aesthetic effect upon the viewer. This is a very persuasive illustration, a very persuasive argument. But we must not, we dare not, encourage the construction of a godless world-view. For having constructed that world-view it will be accepted by those around us, and when we say, 'Just a minute, you have to have the other view as well' their reaction will be, 'No thank you very much; we are quite happy with this'.

The *second* fault I find with complementarity is that it suggests that science *is* a self-contained system, and I would deny that that is true. I am a scientist and I earn my living and my reputation by the practice of science but I would state in the strongest possible terms that science is not self-contained. Science offers only half an explanation of nature, because whilst it is possible to explain all kinds of phenomena and observations in terms of scientific law, it is quite *impossible* to explain *scientific law* in terms of science itself! That is what I mean when I say that science is only half an explanation. To suggest that in some way a scientific description of the universe is complete and can stand in its own right as a self-contained system of thought is, in my opinion, quite false.

Thirdly, the principle of complementarity leaves the doctrines of creation, providence and the miraculous in a kind of limbo, because it has divorced and separated the spiritual from the material. Perhaps we could recognize in this divorce a latter day gnosticism, but that might be unkind. But it certainly leaves us with nowhere to put the doctrines of providence and creation, as is evident from the quotations I have given you. The complementarians are really at a loss

CREATION AND EVOLUTION

to know what to do with the doctrine of creation and they dare not mention the doctrine of providence or miracles, because these doctrines involve interaction between the two 'spheres' which complementarity so assiduously separates.

The faults, then, of our evangelical brethren who subscribe to these views may be summed up as follows. They have, first of all, a tendency to see science and revelation as parallel, equivalent or alternative views of the universe instead of ceding superiority to revelation. Secondly, their view discounts entirely the biblical testimony on the shortcomings of human wisdom. It seems to me that they have not read 1 Corinthians 1 and 2. They give an almost unbelievable degree of credence to anything that is said or stated or claimed in the name of science. They yield the ground before it is even disputed. They forget that science itself is an interpretation of observations and that those interpretations are subject to the fallibility of fallen human nature. The facts of observation generally are not disputed. The interpretations we put upon those facts are, and indeed should be, hotly disputed whenever those interpretations contradict the doctrines of the Word of God. Finally, they fail to understand the nature of science and the nature of the miraculous. We shall return to that in just a moment.

THE ANSWER

We turn now to my second heading, that is The Answer. I want to be positive at this point since up till now I have been, to some extent, destructive. You will remember that Nehemiah had to clear away the rubbish before he could start building the walls of

Jerusalem; similarly there is always a destructive work to be done on false or mistaken ideas before we can start rebuilding with sound ones. But, as I said at the beginning, it is not sufficient for us to be destructive. It is not sufficient just to snipe at our opponents in this matter. We have to answer in a positive way. We have to present, positively and strongly, the biblical viewpoint as a complete theory of being that will satisfy the keenest intellects, will give a proper place to scientific investigation, will recognize in science a great source of benefit to mankind, but will not elevate science or any other form of human intellectual endeavour to the same level as revelation.

So then, what is our answer? I believe *first of all* that we (and I am addressing fellow Christian workers, ministers of the gospel, and indeed all Christians) must return again to a clear and unequivocal proclamation of the superiority of revelation to reason. I feel that we have too often been ashamed to challenge from the Scripture the views that I have just been criticizing. We have tried to avoid them. We have welcomed ideas such as complementarity because they seemed to separate the contestants and eliminate the conflict, and in spite of the unbiblical character of these ideas we have been content and comfortable with this situation. But we have to return to the attack. We have to return to a clear and unequivocal declaration that revelation is superior to reason.

We have to take up those considerable passages of Scripture that, starting with the doctrine of the Fall of man, point to the unreliability of human reason and therefore of any materialistic system or world-view based upon human reason. 'Where is the wise? Where

CREATION AND EVOLUTION

is the scribe? Where is the disputer of this world? Has not God made foolish the wisdom of this world?'

Now in doing this we must avoid the charge of being obscurantists. We are not dismissing human reason and wisdom. Remember how Paul goes on in 1 Corinthians 2 to say, 'Howbeit, we speak wisdom'. Paul is very quick to indicate that he is not setting reason and rationality aside. 'Howbeit we speak wisdom'; but it is not the wisdom of this world. It is a wisdom in which human rationality and intellect work upon the data of revelation to lead us to a deeper knowledge of God. It is quite evident from a cursory reading of the New Testament that we are not trying to set reason aside, or oppose reason, or say that faith is irrational. God forbid! It is quite evident that the use of rational argument in Scripture is itself a denial of that accusation. What we are saying is that reason must bow to revelation. We are saying that you can only have one ultimate authority (and here I am following the arguments so powerfully presented by Dr. J. I. Packer in his book *Fundamentalism and the Word of God*). Either that authority is revelation, and human reason must bow to revelation where it cannot reconcile that revelation with its own limited, fallen insights; or else we must make human reason the final court of appeal, and where human reason cannot comprehend or reconcile the statements of Scripture then Scripture must give way. You cannot have it both ways, yet I feel that some of our dear brethren whose views I have been quoting are guilty of trying to do so. They are trying to have an inspired and authoritative revelation but they are only prepared to have it as long as they can understand it in every detail, in every particular and reconcile every observation and interpretation of science with that revelation.

We must recognize that science itself is a series of interpretations, as I have argued more fully elsewhere in my booklet *Is Evolution Scientific?* We must not accept as the final word what scientists say, what they theorize, and what they *deduce* from the facts of observation. So often scientists have to go back and retract what they have said and reinterpret the facts. We do not dispute the facts, but we very often and very properly dispute the interpretations that are sometimes placed upon those facts. In a sense the scientist is open to exactly the same accusation that is hurled at the 'hyper-orthodox'. That is to say, his facts may be correct but his interpretations wrong. The Bible is true but our interpretations are wrong, they say. We interpret it literally when it should be interpreted poetically or allegorically. Well, exactly the same kind of accusation can be laid at the door of science. Scientific theories are interpretations of the facts, not the facts themselves. Wherever those interpretations are made in the absence of a regenerate and enlightened mind, they will inevitably fall short of the whole truth.

Secondly, we must proclaim the biblical doctrine of nature in greater depth. I am going to coin a phrase (I think I am coining it rather than borrowing it) namely, 'the theology of science'. Do we have a theology of science? And if we do not, why not? After all, every aspect of human experience is subject to its own branch of theology. We have, for example, a theology (that is simply to say a God-centred view or interpretation) of history, do we not? We proclaim

CREATION AND EVOLUTION

that history is the unfolding of God's purposes. And yet there is no greater factor in human life and education today than science. It is one of the foremost thought-modes, bodies of knowledge and areas of human endeavour of our time. I feel, therefore, that we have failed as evangelicals by not going to our Bibles to work out a theology of science. We tend to think that since it is not religion or theology, we are not concerned with it in the teaching of Christian doctrine. We consider science to be simply irrelevant. I sympathize, of course, with those ministers and preachers who have had no scientific training, but let us face the fact that the majority of young people today get a reasonably adequate exposure to the basic concepts and approaches of science and, unfortunately, to the wholly false idea that science and faith are incompatible. We need, therefore, a theology of science.

I believe that a very simple and a clear theology of science can be deduced from the Scriptures. I would point you to such verses as Colossians 1:17 and Hebrews 1:2 and 3, where we are told that Christ, the second Person of the Trinity, upholds all things by the word of His power and that 'by Him all things consist' or hold together. With those two verses alone, together perhaps with Acts 17:28 and the great teachings of the doctrine of providence in the Old Testament, we can construct a theology of science. We can point out that the scientific laws to which all science is ultimately reduced, *are* the word of God's power. That is, I believe, what the Bible means by the statement that He upholds all things by the word of His power. This verse refers to the rules or laws which operate in nature and by which this 'scientific' world is seen to work. The laws of science are the commands of God operating moment by moment. In Him we live and move and have our being and so also does all life and all material existence. By this biblical reasoning we provide an underpinning for science, a reason for science, a basis for science, an explanation of science. And immediately, far from separating science from religion, and a scientific world-view from a theological world-view (as the doctrine of complementarity seeks to do) we bring them together, we unite them, we synthesize them into a single grand and glorious picture of a sovereign God who, in total immediacy, is Ruler of heaven and earth. We must understand that science is derivative from God. If we do that we shall provide ourselves with a positive framework in which we can reinterpret science in a biblical and God-centred manner.

The *third* part of my answer follows from the second. We must reinstate the rationality of the miraculous in our preaching and teaching. One of the most tragic things about these books that I have been quoting is that although they pretend to accept the Scriptures as being inspired, and would accept fully the miracle of the resurrection of Christ, they bend over backwards to explain away every other miracle that they possibly can, in terms of naturalistic and scientific occurrences. We must not be ashamed of the miraculous; we have to realize that the whole gospel is based upon the miraculous. 'If Christ be not risen from the dead,' says Paul, 'then is your faith vain and our preaching is vain; ye are yet in your sins.' We must stop being apologetic about the miraculous element in Scripture.

It seems to me that most of this discussion arises because Christians who pretend to accept the Bible as infallible, are ashamed of the miraculous element in it and so, of course, they must dispute the historicity of Genesis. Only by saying that creation was miraculous can you substantiate and support the historicity of Genesis, and we are afraid to do it. We are frightened of being considered superstitious. But let us realize that the supernatural and the miraculous lie at the very heart of our gospel and we must not be ashamed to proclaim them.

I said that we must reinstate the rationality of the miraculous. What exactly do I mean by this? I think that much of our embarrassment over the miraculous comes from a failure to understand our Bibles on the subject. So often evangelicals have interpreted the miraculous in terms of God's *intervention* in the natural order. We have painted a picture of a universe that runs and operates according to scientific law, with God remote and external to that universe. In this false view, God has left the universe running smoothly according to scientific principles and only interferes from time to time to produce miraculous events. Well, of course, this makes God nothing more than a meddler.

The theology of science to which I have just referred leads us to a completely different view of miracles, namely the concept that God is present now, upholding all things by the word of His power; that every operation of scientific law is the present-tense purpose and design of God. This concept opens the way for a rational understanding of the miraculous. As long as we think of God as someone standing outside the material universe, occasionally coming in just to interfere, we shall not have a very persuasive doctrine of the miraculous. If however, we recognize that the *normal* processes of scientific law are a manifestation of the presence and activity of God ('for in Him we live and move and have our being'), we find that the miraculous is no longer an act of intervention at all. We find rather that the miraculous is qualitatively exactly the same thing as the non-miraculous!

Let me explain what I mean by giving you an illustration. Every morning of every working day I travel from my home in Hertfordshire to my office in London University. If some observer watched my travelling habits, he would very quickly be able to deduce the 'laws' or rules which control my travelling. He would observe that Mondays to Fridays at a certain time each morning I leave my home and make my way to the railway station. I catch a certain train and I follow a certain route to my office. He might observe that this does not happen two mornings a week, and so on. Thus by gathering data he would construct a law which describes my behaviour. This is analogous to the way a scientist might construct a law describing the behaviour of atoms or molecules or electrical discharges or any other scientific phenomenon. But occasionally, when there is good reason for it, I travel by car. Very rarely do I do this, but there may be some special reason for needing a car in London and so I travel by car. This breaks my habit of travelling by train. It is an exception to the rule that the observer has so carefully constructed and written down. That is like a miracle happening which contravenes, or sets aside for a moment, localized in time and space, the normal operation of scientific law.

The point I want to bring home is this: that even though I usually travel by train there is each morning the positive decision, conscious or unconscious, to use one or other mode of transport. Just because ninety-nine times out of a hundred I travel by train, it does not mean that my journey by train does not represent a conscious decision each morning to do so. So, qualitatively, travelling by train or travelling by car are really quite identical. They both represent the outcome of conscious decision on my part. It is only quantitatively that one seems so different from the other, because I nearly always travel by train and only rarely by car.

Like all illustrations, no doubt this one has serious inadequacies, but I think it helps us to understand the nature of the miraculous. When normal scientific law operates it does so by the conscious, moment by moment, purpose and decision of God, because God is continually upholding all things by the word of His power. When a miracle occurs, it represents just the same kind of conscious decision by God as that which is normal. Namely, a decision that what is normal should be set aside for that which is extraordinary.

We must stop being ashamed of miracles. We must preach the miraculous as an integral and necessary part of our precious gospel.

CONCLUSION

In this brief review, I have suggested that the attack upon the Bible comes not only from without, from an unbelieving and materialistic world, but also from within. Evangelical Christians, faced with the undoubted problems and challenges of scientific theory, have given the wrong answers. Attempting to defend the inspiration and inerrancy of Scripture they have, instead, been driven into untenable compromises which, at best, smother the Bible's true teaching on creation, providence or miracles, or, at worst, blandly contradict it. Perhaps the main reason for this unhappy state of affairs is that theologians and scientists alike have been afraid to criticize 'the sacred cow' of science.

It is our responsibility to change this state of affairs. Science is not infallible. It is not even always clever. Like all fields of human endeavour it contains within its broad boundaries both the excellent and the second-rate, and we must learn to distinguish between them.

Specifically I have suggested three ways in which we should approach the task of reconstructing the philosophical framework of our Christian view of nature. We must reassert the superiority of revelation over reason. We must work out and teach a biblical theology of science. And we must reinstate the miraculous and providential works of God as both essential to our gospel and acceptable to the rational mind. May God grant us the wisdom and energy to set about these tasks.

III Our times and their lessons

Iain H. Murray

Every period of church history has its own characteristics: like the tide in the Thames, there are many variations between high and low water. The world is full of changes and to each generation of Christians there comes afresh the duty of discerning the signs of the times.

At the outset it is necessary to pinpoint two dangers which are involved in considering this subject.

First, in speaking of the spiritual conditions of our times it has to be remembered that our judgements are bound to be affected by the limited and partial nature of our vision. The impact of the gospel in churches, in universities, and in the wide variety of branches of Christian work, tends to show striking variations. We do not see the whole and therefore we must be slow in making generalizations. If all of us could share with one another the knowledge we each have of the contemporary situation we should no doubt have many surprises, but even then our information would still be very incomplete. It is well to remember that the prophet Elijah in his day fell into a considerable misjudgement over the strength of God's cause and in this respect, as in others, he 'was a man subject to like passions as we are'.

Secondly, there is considerable danger that in trying to assess our spiritual condition we may enter a province which belongs to God alone. There is much that is secret and hidden in God's providential ruling of the church and it is not for us to pronounce with certainty on the work of God. Certain preachers in the church at Corinth were busy, as it appeared, in building the kingdom of Christ, but in reality, says Paul, they were working not with the precious stones of enduring truth, but with 'wood, hay, stubble'. Similarly, in our day large claims are sometimes made about what is being done for Christ or about what the Holy Spirit is doing in certain movements. But Paul's warning is that the real verdict is not now: 'Judge nothing before the time, until the Lord come' . . . 'Every man's work shall be made manifest: for the day shall declare it, because it shall be revealed by fire; and the fire shall try every man's work of what sort it is' (1 Cor. 4: 5; 1 Cor. 3: 13).[1]

These are the dangers, yet at the same time there are the strongest reasons why we should seek a true understanding of the state of Christian witness in our own day.

1. It is a scriptural duty. Self-examination is laid upon professing Christians, individually and corporately. The Old Testament records that at a troubled period in the history of Israel the children of Issachar were commended because they 'were men that had understanding of the times, to know what Israel ought to do' (1 Chron. 12: 32). The prophets often rebuked the people of Israel because they failed to discern the signs of the times and Jesus condemned the religious leaders of the Jews for the same reason (Matt. 16: 3).

2. The desire to know more of the state of the work of Christ at large is an important aspect of Christian piety. If we are real Christians we cannot

---

[1] For a valuable exposition of this passage see R. L. Dabney's *Discussions*, Vol. 1, pp. 551ff.

OUR TIMES AND THEIR LESSONS 61

bury our heads in the sand or live in a corner, we are bound to be concerned about spiritual affairs beyond our own homes and congregations.

3. I think it can be argued that the justification for the existence of the British Evangelical Council is closely related to this question of understanding our times. Let me explain what I mean. In the year 1846 the Evangelical Alliance was formed and for 120 years it represented the interests of almost all the evangelicals in this country. But some ten years ago a considerable number of men ceased to look to the Evangelical Alliance as a means of expressing their fellowship with other evangelicals and instead they became identified with the B.E.C. The justification for that step was not that the Evangelical Alliance had changed, it was that the times had changed. In 1846 members of the Evangelical Alliance agreed to view their denominational differences as secondary – such differences, for instance, as those relating to church government or baptism – but the fact is that at that date all these denominations were Protestant and all held to the Bible as the rule of faith. In 1966 the denominational position was almost unrecognizably different, and it is no wonder that action was required different from that of 1846. In other words, we must take the action which is most appropriate to the needs of the day in which we live, and that we cannot do unless we know and understand the times.

Certainly there are dangers in trying to judge our times, but there are greater dangers in making no assessment, in simply drifting with events, without knowing where we are or where we are going. In the first issue of a magazine called *Church and Nation* (the magazine of the new Uniting Church of Australia, which is a large ecumenical grouping of Methodists, Congregationalists and Presbyterians) the editor made this extraordinary admission: 'For years we uniting Christians have been busily shovelling the coals of organic unity into the locomotive of the church. At last the engine has moved off. Now we must recognize that we do not know whether it is heading in the right direction.'

We may assert that we are not ecumenical, but this does not mean that we are automatically preserved from this same mistake. To be preserved we must discern the times. We must have a sense of direction. We must know the state of the tide.

FEATURES OF OUR TIMES

As we take up this subject I want, in the first place, to draw your attention to three features of our times which seem to me to be of major importance.

1. We live in a day when the character and results of liberalism in the church have been thoroughly exposed. About a hundred years ago a new influence came into almost all the Protestant churches of our country. It was introduced by religious leaders who claimed to speak in the name of intellectual progress and of biblical scholarship. These men did not deny the Bible[1] and they did not reject evangelism. They

[1] That is to say, they did not deny it in plain terms, but a radically changed view of the Bible was inherent in liberalism. This change claimed to have the interests of Christianity as its justification; for example, H. E. Ryle in his liberal work *The Early Narratives of Genesis*, 1892, wrote in the Preface: 'They, indeed, have been fortunate in their experience who have not known an instance in which antagonism or indifference to religion has been fostered by the rigid refusal, on the part of well-meaning Christian parents and teachers, to admit the possibility of an alternative to the traditional interpretation of this portion of Scripture.' One parent guilty of such 'rigid refusal' was H. E. Ryle's own father, John Charles Ryle.

OUR TIMES AND THEIR LESSONS

simply professed that new light and new understanding was becoming available to be possessed by the church: they believed that the form in which Christianity was presented to men required some modifications whereby the church would win the approval of the majority of thinking people to a greater extent than ever before. It was claimed that many obstacles to faith which troubled non-Christians would be removed and that, with the adjustments which they proposed, the church of the twentieth century would command great influence in the world.

This was liberalism. When it first appeared there were some who declared that it was a different religion from biblical Christianity: C. H. Spurgeon, for example, left the Baptist Union over it, but the great majority adopted a more 'charitable' attitude. After all, some men of liberal views appeared to be devout Christians, and perhaps good might result from their new approach.

We are surely in a position to see today that this decision in favour of tolerance was a disastrous turning point in church history. Liberalism was disguised unbelief. Its general tendency was to present a deity who is not the God of the Bible, not the living God, not the God who sends unction, dew and blessing upon the church. And consequently the effect of liberalism has been desolation. This has been the century of spiritual catastrophe. Vast numbers of church buildings today stand empty and derelict, and buildings once thronged with congregations are now used as warehouses or garages. Thus we see a little of what liberalism has done. The cause and effect ought to be as clear as daylight: disbelief in Scripture encourages spiritual carelessness, and spiritual carelessness leads to spiritual death. Richard Baxter once wrote: 'I observed, easily, in myself, that if at any time Satan did more than at other times weaken my belief of Scripture and the life to come, my zeal in religious duty abated with it, and I grew more indifferent in religion than before. . . .'

Indifference to religion is the great characteristic of our age and the principal cause lies in what happened in the church at the end of the last century. Liberal theology as a system falls under the terrible condemnation which Christ proclaimed in Matthew 23: 13: 'Woe unto you, scribes and Pharisees, hypocrites! for ye shut up the kingdom of heaven against men: for ye neither go in yourselves, neither suffer ye them that are entering to go in.'

There is only one thing to add on this point. To accuse liberalism of having dismantled historic Christianity is not the language of blind prejudice: the fact is that in their private discussions some of the men who introduced this new influence revealed that they understood very well what was happening. Take, for example, one of the best-known liberals at the beginning of this century, Dr. Marcus Dods, once Principal of New College, Edinburgh. In a letter written to a friend on January 8, 1902, Dods wrote: 'I wish I could live as a spectator through the next generation to see what they are going to make of things. There will be a grand turn up in matters theological and the churches won't know themselves fifty years hence. It is to be hoped some little rag of faith may be left when all's done. For my own part I am sometimes entirely under water and see no sky at all.'[1]

[1] *Later Letters of Marcus Dods*, 1911, p. 67.

OUR TIMES AND THEIR LESSONS

Dod's anticipations were correct. From what was happening in 1902 he could see what the state of the church was likely to be in 1952. The church at large has reaped what its fathers have sown and the consequences of liberal theology are before the eyes of all. Never at any time since the early part of the eighteenth century has the church had so little influence upon the masses of the people. A careless world is a sure consequence of an unbelieving church.

2. We have been witnessing in recent years what may be called the break-up of evangelicalism, that is to say, of the type of evangelicalism which was predominant throughout the first half of this century. To explain what I mean let me illustrate. Many of you can remember that twenty-five or thirty years ago large evangelistic meetings and campaigns were a regular part of the religious life of this city – they were held in many places, sometimes in Central Hall, Westminster, or in the Albert Hall, even in Westminster Abbey at the time of the Festival of Britain. What has happened to that evangelicalism now? Or think of the evangelical weeklies which were then the popular mouthpieces of evangelicalism, *The Christian*, and *The Life of Faith*. What has happened to them? One has gone and the other is struggling to survive.

You will recognize that I am referring to the evangelicalism which was traditional in this country from the late Victorian period until the 1950s and 1960s. I do not want to refer to its defects but let me remind you of some of its merits. It believed that men's souls are lost and that conversion is an indispensable necessity for every individual who will enter the kingdom of God. It believed in holiness of life. It believed in prayer. It believed in preaching, and it taught separation from the world.

Some of the things it did *not* teach are equally significant: it did not teach that we must at all costs be 'relevant' and 'modern'; it did not teach that, to be effective, evangelistic campaigns require the support of liberals or Roman Catholics; it did not teach young people that they could be Christians and yet go to theatres or cinemas for their pleasure and entertainment.

My assertion is that this kind of evangelicalism has been breaking up. If we can still use the word, the evangelicalism of 1977 is not the evangelicalism of 1953. There is a new evangelicalism. It has perhaps more reputation for 'scholarship', it may have more acceptance with non-evangelicals than was enjoyed by the former evangelicalism, but it is less concerned to prepare men for eternity, less concerned with prayer, less concerned about the dangers of doctrinal compromise and less concerned with what used to be called 'worldliness'. Beneath the umbrella of the term 'evangelical' there has been a massive change in the climate of opinion. Some of the best-known contemporary evangelical papers and magazines would have had a small market among evangelicals if they had written in 1950 what they are writing now. Similar changes are to be seen in a number of the Christian Unions in the universities. Certainly the picture is varied; in some university Christian Unions there is much that is encouraging, but disturbing features are also apparent. Numbers of students attending C.U.s are larger than twenty years ago but there is reason to think that prayer meetings are frequently smaller. Evangelistic meetings used to be a main part of the term's programme in a Christian Union: in many cases that is no longer true today. And it is in harmony with this change of climate that we now have the phenomena of dances and concerts being introduced in some leading Christian Unions.

The former evangelicalism is breaking up![1]

3. In the last twenty-five years we have seen a considerable recovery of the heritage of historic Christianity. Something has happened which has enlarged and deepened the faith of many Christians, especially among the younger generation.

C. H. Spurgeon in his *Autobiography* describes how as a boy he wandered into an old darkened room in his grandfather's manse at Stambourne, Essex, and began to discover the contents of the leather-bound books which lined the walls. Something similar has occurred in the lives of thousands of people in recent years. Perhaps through preaching, perhaps through the Evangelical Library, perhaps through conferences or just through buying a book, many have been led to a deeper understanding of the Word of God.

I mentioned that the evangelicalism of twenty-five years ago had defects. One of the greatest of these was that its roots did not go back far enough. It gave little or no attention to the great heritage of historic Christianity. Books such as Bishop Ryle's *Christian Leaders of the Eighteenth Century* were neglected, if not almost unknown. The Reformers and the Puritans

[1] From another direction the charismatic movement, emphasizing the 'deadness' of the church as an institution and the need for all the miraculous gifts of the apostolic era, is accelerating this break up. Although in some respects a reaction against the former evangelicalism, the charismatic movement is also a child of it.

were practically forgotten by the average evangelical. In liberal circles it was worse. I was brought up in the English Presbyterian Church, a church which was nominally committed to the Westminster Confession of Faith, but in years of listening to sermons I never once heard a reference to that Confession nor to the teaching it contains. With a few eminent exceptions, the ministry in England had come to the conclusion that Christianity and the Reformed Faith were two different things. At the time of the First World War Puritan books were thrown out in their thousands for salvage – £12 a ton was the going price for unwanted books – and between the Wars demand for these books scarcely existed. No regular publisher in the country would touch them!

Let me give you an example of what I mean from the life of Arthur W. Pink. Pink was an Englishman converted in his home-town of Nottingham in 1908 at the age of twenty-two. In 1910 he went to the United States and became a pastor and teacher in the Fundamentalist tradition. He was in demand as a speaker and as well as holding various pastoral charges he travelled widely in the States. But then Pink was brought to the same discovery that Spurgeon made in his grandfather's study at Stambourne; he was moved to the depths of his being by the inspiration of the doctrines of grace and the result was that when he came back to minister in this country he was unable to find any church that wanted his preaching. For thirty years from 1922 he published a monthly magazine and yet despite efforts to circulate it in the United States, Britain and Australia, the number of readers was usually below one thousand. When Pink died in

Britain in 1953 he was practically unknown. He could scarcely have believed that the change which we have lived to see could or would come about. Today his writings, which no one wanted, are selling in their thousands and so are many other books with the same outlook.

Here in Westminster Chapel another example springs readily to mind. Some of us were privileged back in the 1950s to sit under the ministry of the Word of God in this building. One characteristic of the congregation in those days was the number of students and young people temporarily in London from many parts of England, and all, with scarcely an exception, spoke of the utter absence in their home districts of the type of preaching which came to mean so much to them here. In the Midlands, in the industrial North, in the West Country, evangelical, Calvinistic, experimental and searching preaching was practically non-existent. But tonight there are not a few preachers here from all parts of the land who are being used to build up congregations in the spiritual tenets of that biblical Christianity which only twenty years ago was so rare! Again, at that date we thought it a wonderful thing to see the hundreds who sat under Dr. Lloyd-Jones' ministry week by week, little believing that within two decades that same ministry would be read across the world by tens of thousands! Only this morning I was handed a paperback by a United States author which begins with the words, 'One of the most exciting signs of our time is the increasing interest in the study of the Word of God, and in the biblical theology of the Reformation'. This is surely true.

Perhaps we live in a day of 'small things'. Certainly there is much to remind us of our failures, and much to humble us profoundly, yet in God's mercy *something* is happening. Let us not err in crediting nothing to God if He does not work in the way we expected. We may, like Elijah, look for 'a great and strong wind' or 'an earthquake', when in the end it is 'a still small voice' which constrains us to worship (1 Kings 19: 11, 12). 'The kingdom of God cometh not with observation' and the tide can turn so silently that we fail to notice it. In a real sense I believe that the tide has turned and this is a feature of our times which we ought to observe.

It may well be that this assertion that we are witnessing a partial recovery of historic Christianity leaves some unimpressed. They may respond: 'It is all very well to speak about the Reformed Faith being preached and read, but what good has it done? What are the results of this supposed resurgence?' I want to suggest that there are some important lessons which men are in the process of learning. Perhaps we once supposed that these lessons would not take us long to learn, but God's providence is teaching us otherwise.

SOME LESSONS

1. We are learning that our activity and our use of means cannot build the church unless God Himself undertakes the work. No amount of energy expended by us is of any use if we work alone. Because men in the church at Corinth failed to see this they were occupied with human instruments rather than with God, so that Paul had to rebuke them with the words: 'Who then is Paul, and who is Apollos, but ministers

by whom ye believed, even as the Lord gave to every man? I have planted, Apollos watered; but God gave the increase. So then neither is he that planteth any thing, neither he that watereth; but God that giveth the increase' (1 Cor. 3: 5-7).

Surely this is not a simple lesson to learn! We are born with a sinful self-sufficiency in our hearts, and even after we are converted we are prone to forget that by our energy alone we can accomplish nothing of enduring value. The hall-mark of the Reformed Faith is that its doctrines break down self-sufficiency. They teach us that God alone is the author of every spiritual blessing – our calling, our conversion, our faith, our position in Christ, these are all His gifts as Paul demonstrates so clearly in his first letter to the Corinthians. God works by choosing 'the weak things of the world to confound the things which are mighty; And base things of the world, and things which are despised, hath God chosen.' If we are Christians this is equally true of us: God did not love us because of what we are nor because of what we might do for Him. 'What hast thou that thou didst not receive?'

When we are brought to believe the doctrines of grace it must affect increasingly our attitudes and our priorities. The matter of first importance is no longer our activity, for we know we could be busy seven days a week in Christian 'work' and still accomplish nothing. Our *first* need is to obtain the help of God. In the Gospels we do not read that Christ said much to the disciples about how to preach, or how to evangelize; but how frequently He spoke to them about their praying! How often the apostle Paul implores the churches to help him by interceding with God –

that he might be given boldness, that he might receive 'the supply of the Spirit of Jesus Christ', that he might be enabled to preach as he ought to preach!

Is it not possible that as Christians many of us are far too active in public? Activism is the spirit of our age and it has penetrated into the church. The temptation for ministers is to have an incessant round of engagements, to be constantly preaching, taking meetings or sitting on committees. And for all Christians there is the danger that public activities of one kind or another all but monopolize the time we give to matters spiritual. Even on Sundays time for *private* spiritual devotion can be entirely crowded out.

In American periodicals there is some interesting discussion of this phenomenon at the present time. No church in the world has ever been so highly organized for evangelism as many churches are today in the United States, but with all the activity there seems to be an increasing recognition that something is wrong. In one area recently, for example, 178 churches took part in an intensive series of meetings and 4,106 decisions for Christ were recorded. Yet out of this number only 3 per cent became church members! The question is being rightly asked whether this is the outworking of the Great Commission or of the Great Commotion?[1]

I believe it could be argued that when the church was eminently used by God, there was much more emphasis on private and family religion, much less emphasis on organized activity and meetings than there is now. But the striking thing is that when public activity was less it achieved more. I was recently

[1] See *Eternity*, September, 1977.

reminded of this by reading in the diaries of Charles Calder of Ferintosh, in Easter Ross. During Calder's ministry, in the late eighteenth century, Ferintosh was a centre of spiritual light and power: from that church waves of blessing reached across the Scottish Highlands. Yet Calder's church appears to have had nothing except Sunday services and a far larger proportion of Calder's time was spent in private than is customary today among ministers. J. C. Ryle draws this general lesson from the lives of the eminent preachers of the eighteenth century: 'Our Evangelical forefathers had far fewer means and opportunities than we have . . . but the few weapons they used, they used well. With less noise and applause from man they made, I believe, a far deeper mark for God on their generation than we do, with all our conferences, and meetings, and mission rooms, and halls, and multiplied religious appliances. Their converts, I suspect, like the old-fashioned cloths and linens, wore better, and lasted longer, and faded less, and kept colour, and were more stable, and rooted, and grounded than many of the new-born babes of this day. And what was the reason of all this? Simply, I believe, because they gave more attention to *private* religion than we generally do.'[1]

My case is that there is a doctrinal reason behind this difference. Our activism has been too often the product of a defective understanding of Scripture. We sorely needed the recovery of a theology which puts God first and shows the absolute necessity of the work of the Holy Spirit. No one could be more profoundly mistaken than the person who imagines that questions of doctrine and theology are simply theoretical matters

[1] *Holiness*, 1900, p. 432.

which have no urgent bearing on living the Christian life. The truths which teach us to 'cease from man whose breath is in his nostrils' and to make our end the glory of God are powerful truths.

I do not say that we have yet learned this lesson but in God's mercy I believe many are being helped to learn it. Understanding this certainly changes a man's priorities. Less than 200 years ago the church in this country stood on the threshold of a great missionary expansion and William Carey, in 1792, summarized the attitude which lay behind that expansion with some memorable words. Carey's slogan did not begin with the phrase, 'Attempt great things for God,' it had a different starting point. The starting point is not what we plan to do but what God must do, 'Expect great things from God!' Have faith in Him, cry to Him and then, in His strength, 'Attempt great things for God!' A whole theology lies behind the order of Carey's words.

2. There is a second lesson which I believe we are having to relearn at the present time. It is that faithfulness to God is our *first* obligation in all that we are called to do in the service of the gospel. In the chapter to which I have already referred, 1 Corinthians 3, Paul is speaking of the building of the church, and the overruling principle which is laid down he states in 1 Corinthians 4: 2: 'It is required in stewards, that a man be found *faithful*.' Servants of Christ, he says, have different work to do, some have to plant, others have to water, but *faithfulness* towards God is the rule for all: when Christ comes we shall be judged not by the results we achieved but by obedient labour rendered in God's cause. 'Every man shall receive his

own reward according to his own *labour*.' Christ says to us what He said to His church in Smyrna, 'Be thou faithful unto death, and I will give thee a crown of life.'

We are all exposed to temptations which would lead us to lower the importance of faithfulness in our scale of values. One of the most subtle of these temptations comes to us in this way: if we are true Christians and especially if we are ministers of the gospel we long to see spiritual success, we want to see conversions, and we are dismayed at the thought of being fruitless or barren. Now these are highly spiritual feelings – to be found in complacency and ease in a day like this is great sin! – but for these very reasons we are exposed to an influence which comes to us and says, 'What good is all your so-called faithfulness to Scripture when you have so few results? Nothing seems to happen in your churches. But look at these other Christians – they don't claim to be "reformed" or anything like that, but what success they have! Isn't there something wrong with your doctrine when it achieves so little?'

It is very likely that we shall all hear this kind of statement today. There has been a reviving of the doctrines of grace across the world, but in response to this some people are saying, 'It is all very well for these young preachers to stand apart from modern evangelism and criticize "decisionism", but what are they doing? How many sinners do they bring to repentance?'

My present concern is not to answer that charge, but to point out that unless we are on our guard the temptation which comes to us when we hear such statements is to wonder whether perhaps purity of doctrine is not so important after all. But the temptation has to be resisted. The world wants to judge everything by results. Can a man fill a church? Who is most successful? And how can we be equally successful? This is not the biblical yard-stick, which is 'that a man be found *faithful.*'

If *success* is to be the yard-stick what sort of judgement must be formed of that large company in Scripture who went out of this world in circumstances which illustrated how little success they saw? 'Others had trial of cruel mockings and scourgings, yea, moreover of bonds and imprisonment: They were stoned . . . were tempted, were slain with the sword: they wandered about in sheepskins and goatskins; being destitute, afflicted, tormented; (of whom the world was not worthy). . . .' Or think of the long history of the church. If the English reformers had been primarily concerned with success they would have given up altogether. What success did William Tyndale see before his execution? Very little! What did the 288 men and women see of success who were burned to death in the reign of 'Bloody' Mary? What about the 2,000 ejected Puritans of 1662 and the pioneer missionaries who had to toil for years before they saw conversions? If some present observers had seen William Carey in India at the end of the eighteenth century they might well have said that he was another of these 'dead young Calvinists' – five-and-a-half years at Mudnabatty and not a single Indian convert!

Perhaps many of us have been at fault. We have tended to speak of the doctrines of grace as though they were a guarantee of success. That is not true. But it is the doctrines of grace that make a man go on and endure – 'plod' was Carey's term – even when success is not visible. Shadrach, Meshach and Abednego said to Nebuchadnezzar, 'Our God whom we serve is able to deliver us from the burning fiery furnace. . . . But if not, be it known unto thee, O king, that we will not serve thy gods, nor worship the golden image which thou hast set up' (Dan. 3: 17, 18). So we ought to say, 'God is able at this present hour to send mighty deliverance and blessing to His church, *but if not*' – supposing the days get darker, supposing no revival comes, supposing a storm of persecution breaks upon us – must we then sit down and bemoan our unhappy lot? No! 'But if not, we will not be the servants of men, by God's grace we shall still seek to be faithful and obedient.' We have no business to act as though we intend only to be joyful and zealous if God makes us reapers in the harvest. We know that His Word shall not return unto Him void. The times and seasons are in God's hands, and supposing we do not see a great awakening in our life-time, eternity is before us and God says to His servants as He said to Daniel: 'Go thou thy way till the end be: for thou shalt rest, and stand in thy lot at the end of the days.'

This is a great lesson to learn and it can be said to God's glory that there are men who are learning it. I think, for example, of a man who went eleven years ago to a mission charge in one of our cities in the North-East. For eight years he laboured, he preached the truth, and yet things got worse, rather than better; the temptation was strong to give up and his testimony is that if it had not been for the doctrines of grace he would have done so. Now he has lived to see sound conversions and the beginning of much brighter days.

Two weeks ago I read a letter from a man who has been a missionary for thirty years in Japan. His great concern is for the salvation of souls, but recently his support from one church was cut off because this church had discovered that he was not preaching the universal atonement of Arminianism. The missionary's response to this was that he would rather die than change his preaching. Or again, let me give you one other instance from the latest prayer letter of a missionary who went out many years ago to Brazil. There he and his wife continue to serve a small congregation in a town far up the Amazon. While they see little fruit at present, another church in the same town is full, and recently, he writes, this church 'after only some ten days of meetings was reporting a fantastic number of "decisions".' But his letter also contains news of an incident which shows the difference between these two churches. A teenage girl in the missionary's congregation was abducted by a young man. When this young man at length came back, the girl's father, who was a deacon in the missionary's church, insisted that they be married. The missionary refused on the grounds that the young man had declared he had no intention of living with the girl; whereupon the pastor of the other congregation readily performed the ceremony and added the deacon and his daughter to their numbers. But sadly, as anticipated, 'it has proved to be but a paper marriage'. 'Perhaps,' writes the missionary, 'the Lord is teaching us not to look to numerical success for our strength and joy, but to depend for this upon Him.'

We do well to long for spiritual prosperity, but in the meantime there is a great lesson to learn, 'that a man be found faithful!'

3. In the last place I can only touch briefly on what I believe is the primary lesson we need in this age. It is that our vision of God must be controlled not by what we *see* in the world but by what Scripture authorizes us to *believe*. The God revealed in Scripture is 'the great and mighty God', with whom 'is terrible majesty' – the Creator, Preserver, and Judge of all men. But amidst the moral and spiritual confusion of our times, when men scorn the idea that the God of the Bible is the living God, we are prone (like the psalmist in Psalm 73) to allow the state of the world to affect our judgement. We begin to think in terms of God's absence or inactivity. Only the revelation of God in Scripture can deliver us from that error. In an age of abounding evil, when men called 'evil good, and good evil', Isaiah declared, 'The whole earth is full of His glory' (Isa. 6: 3). Paul, surveying the sin of the Roman world, sees divine activity – God's dominion and power – 'For the wrath of God is revealed from heaven against all ungodliness and unrighteousness of men' (Rom. 1: 18).

We must *begin* with the revelation of God in Scripture and only in that context does the urgency of man's need appear. His state before God is one of condemnation and the true inspiration for all evangelism must begin with this knowledge. The salvation announced in the gospel is no cheap and easy solution for the problems of man's temporal happiness; it is deliverance from the wrath of 'Him which is able to destroy both soul and body in hell' (Matt. 10: 28), and deliverance by a means which will enlarge our conceptions of divine justice and grace to all eternity.

Surely at no point is our spiritual weakness more apparent than in the poverty of our knowledge of God. Acts 9: 31 describes the churches of the apostolic era: they had conscious joy in the Holy Spirit, they were blessed with growth, and these are things of which we all often speak; but how much do we know of the *first* characteristic of those Christians? 'Then had the churches rest throughout all Judea and Galilee and Samaria, and were edified; and *walking in the fear of the Lord*, and in the comfort of the Holy Ghost, were multiplied.'

Our lack of this fear is proof of our detachment from Scripture and for this there is only one remedy. From her darkest hours the church rises as she lives, by faith – faith in Calvary, faith in the Resurrection, faith in the abiding realities of Pentecost and of the kingdom of God! Elisha's servant at Dothan, surrounded by the horses, chariots and the great host of the king of Syria, judged the Lord by 'feeble sense' and cried to Elisha, 'Alas, my master! how shall we do?' The truth of the prophet's reply remains unchanged, 'And he answered, Fear not: for they that be with us are more than they that be with them. And Elisha prayed, and said, Lord, I pray thee, open his eyes, that he may see' (2 Kings 6: 15-17).

May God grant us grace thus to pray that we might see and know afresh the answer of Scripture. Then, come what may, we will continue to sing,

God is our refuge and our strength,
in straits a present aid;
Therefore, although the earth remove,
we will not be afraid.

Y0-CVH-357

DISCARDED

PENGUIN AFRICAN LIBRARY AP19
Editor: Ronald Segal

African Trade Unions
IOAN DAVIES

IOAN DAVIES

African Trade Unions

Penguin Books
BALTIMORE · MARYLAND

Penguin Books Ltd, Harmondsworth, Middlesex, England
Penguin Books Inc., 3300 Clipper Mill Road, Baltimore 11, Md, U.S.A.
Penguin Books Pty Ltd, Ringwood, Victoria, Australia

First published 1966
Copyright © Ioan Davies, 1966

Made and printed in Great Britain by
C. Nicholls & Company Ltd
Set in Monotype Plantin

This book is sold subject to the condition that
it shall not, by way of trade or otherwise, be lent,
re-sold, hired out, or otherwise circulated without
the publisher's prior consent in any form of
binding or cover other than that in which it is
published and without a similar condition
including this condition being imposed on the
subsequent purchaser

Contents

	Editorial Foreword	7
	Introduction	10
1	Economic Development and the Changing Social Structure	15
2	The Colonial Experience (Labour Policies of Britain, France and Belgium)	31
3	Industrialization and Race in South Africa	53
4	The Rise of Trade Unionism in Africa	72
5	Trade Unions and Political Commitment Before Independence	95
6	Towards an African Working Class	114
7	Trade Unions and Governments – (i) In Opposition	135
8	Trade Unions and Governments – (ii) Socialism and the One-Party State	152
9	The Politics of International Trade Unionism	188
10	Labour and Economic Development	219
	Further Reading	233
	Glossary	245
	Index	251

Editorial Foreword

The purposes and functions of trade unionism differ in time and space. The proper object of a trade union in the United States at the moment may well be the winning of wages as high and working conditions as congenial as the shrewd conduct of industrial struggle allows. Such was the commonly approved object of a trade union in Britain yesterday; but there are many in Britain today, even within the trade union leadership, who would see this object immediately changed to one of organized restraint, in a joint effort by labour and capital to increase productivity and improve Britain's trading position abroad. Trade unionists in colonial Africa regarded the expulsion of foreign power as their primary purpose, and now that this has been accomplished, are engaged in establishing a new relationship to government. For African governments today are not only the most important employers of labour and so the proper object of trade union assault, but generally also the self-proclaimed agents of popular revolution and so the proper object of trade union support.

A study of African trade unionism, therefore, is much more than a survey of industrial organization. It is a study of African societies, the course of their different struggles against imperial rule and the consequences for the pattern of political no less than economic power. In some states the trade unions constitute a major element of established authority, gathering the energies and loyalties of labour for the promotion of government policies; in others, they compose the command of resistance, exciting, representing and directing opposition in the absence of any other effective political force but the party in power; in still others, they concern themselves overwhelmingly with promoting the interests of their members, on the pattern of collective bar-

Editorial Foreword

gaining under liberal capitalism. They appear sometimes as a force for fundamental change; sometimes, as a force against it; sometimes, as cut off from the main flow of social effort, a tributary trickling away into the ground.

The claim of the trade unions to speak significantly for labour must itself be examined. In most African states, industrial labour constitutes a tiny minority of the work force, and the peasants are organized, if at all, by the political parties. Industrial labour, indeed, is a privileged sector, whose power to influence authority by strike action is out of all proportion to its numerical importance and whose wresting of yet higher wages may imperil the proper economic development of the whole society. What is the proper function of a trade union when it represents the interests of an economic *élite* and when popular demand is for equality of condition in the struggle for general betterment? If a few thousand dockers, by merely exercising their decent right to withold their own labour, can hold to ransom a population of millions, should the government, as representing in the main the far harder pressed peasantry, acknowledge and allow the exercise of that right?

But if the right of an industrial worker to strike is to be denied, in the cause of promoting the advantage of the society as a whole, what other rights may not be denied in the name of the same cause? To consider the trade union movement in Africa is to consider, too, the character of the new African governments, the direction of their development, their problems and objectives, the degree to which they reflect and provoke popular participation. The issue of whether poor African societies can afford organized trade unionism, and on what terms, becomes an issue of whether they can – or should – afford a host of individual freedoms presumed to be inseparable from the practice of democracy in parts of the West. And since, in denying or abridging certain individual freedoms elsewhere regarded as crucial, clearly popular governments in Africa claim to be serving the cause of individual freedom and democracy, the nature of these qualities themselves becomes the ultimate issue.

There are not, and cannot be, pat answers. The demand that trade unions should, under all circumstances, operate with as

Editorial Foreword

much – or as little – liberty and scope as they enjoy in the rich and sophisticated industrial economies of the West is silly and dangerous. But silly and dangerous too is the demand that trade unions should not exist at all, since they have no purpose that popular government cannot serve more efficiently instead. Between the unrestrained appetite of the privileged industrial worker and the unrestrained appetite of the privileged political leader, African trade unionism must set up shop. The site it chooses and the business it does must have significance for the content of democracy and freedom not in Africa alone, but wherever men, having at last escaped from formal foreign rule, seek now to escape from the numberless imprisonments of poverty.

RONALD SEGAL

Introduction

Trade unionism in Africa is comparatively recent in origin. In most countries there have been unions for less than thirty years, in some less than ten years, though in South Africa and French-speaking North Africa organizations of white workers have a longer history. Yet under conditions of rapid economic and political growth, the unions have become one of the major foci of political power. Even since work on this book commenced, unions have been involved in several major political crises. In Sudan a general strike precipitated the downfall of the Abboud régime; in Nigeria another general strike provided the occasion for a major trial of strength between the state and workers; in Dahomey, Congo (Brazzaville), Upper Volta, the Central African Republic, Ivory Coast, Guinea and Tanganyika trade unions have been identified with attempts to overthrow governments; in Algeria they became a battleground for both the Ben Bella and Boumedienne régimes. The catalogue is unending. In a continent where ruling *élites* have difficulty in legitimizing their power, the unions become an important vehicle for control or alternatively a threat to survival. In spite of the small percentage engaged in wage-labour, the workers hold a strategic place in the economies of the new nations. Because they are concentrated in precisely those industries and services on which economic development depends, they have the potential directly to influence and even control the political machine. Yet nowhere in Africa – with the possible exceptions of Congo (Brazzaville) and Mali – is a trade union-sponsored government in power. The failure is at the heart of their political dilemma.

Whether in single or multi-party states or under military dictatorships the unions are faced with a struggle to establish their identity in societies where the idea of a wage-earning class is barely accepted as a fact of life. Consequently at every turn

Introduction

African unions find themselves deeply involved in politics – a fact as true today as it was under the imperial administrations. In spite of the efforts of the imperial powers and many modern governments to insulate unions from politics, the strategic political role remains. From Pretoria to Abidjan the unions can act both as props of governments and uncomfortable critics. Where ruling *élites* are precariously maintained in power, the unions may precipitate a showdown by staging a successful strike, as recently ocurred in Upper Volta and Dahomey, only to find that their efforts have removed a civilian government and paved the way for a military dictatorship. But where a nationalist government is well entrenched, union action may result not in the overthrow of politicians but in the absorbtion of unions into the party machine. Ghana, Guinea, Tanganyika, Tunisia, Egypt, Algeria, Ivory Coast, Mali, Senegal and several smaller states all have one federation in close relationship with the ruling party. Since the main part of this book was completed the Kenya government has introduced legislation dissolving the major trade union federations and establishing one national centre under the control of the governing party, KANU.

If the severe actions of governments look simply like the ruthless behaviour of régimes attempting to consolidate their power, the causes of strikes and anti-government activity show that they often have a strong case. Many unions have gone on strike for higher wages though the wages paid were already much higher than the earnings of peasants and cultivators. (In Upper Volta the civil service unions were resisting a one-fifth cut in salary – but the salaries were originally tied to French levels; in Tanganyika in 1963 the unions were demanding increases that would have absorbed almost all the aid granted by Britain at independence). In this they ignore the sombre warning of the late Frantz Fanon:

The workers are in fact the most favoured section of the population, and represent the most comfortably off fraction of the people. Any movement starting off to fight for the bettering of living conditions for the dockers and workmen would not only be very unpopular, but would also run the risk of provoking the hostility of the disinherited rural population.

Introduction

Even so the predicament for wage-earners and governments is acute. In the face of the need to accumulate capital and a widening gap between wage-earners and peasants, governments may feel compelled to act drastically. But in doing so they may find the depressed wages of workers both a deterrent to economic growth and a potential source of acute discontent.

Inevitably the unions have been projected into international political alignments through the efforts of the union federations of the former metropolitan countries and the diplomacy of the international trade union organizations. The methods adopted by the interested outside bodies and the reactions of the Africans display in microcosm the extent of international interference in Africa and the basic social problems on which foreign powers seek to capitalize. But attempts to free themselves from the ideological commitments of the Communist and Western pressure groups inevitably bring the African unions into even closer relationships with their own governments.

For these reasons, union-government relations form the core of this study. In view of the increasing preoccupation with national wage policies and limitations of traditional trade union activities in Britain and other Western European countries, the emphasis may be instructive. If trade unions in Britain, after one-hundred years of activity, are moving towards accommodation with governments in national economic plans, African unions have been pressed into government service almost at birth. In both cases the process looks like involving a high degree of union centralization, though in Africa this is reinforced by the scarcity of top-level union manpower. The British unions, whose experience of cooperation with governments is slight, may have a lot to learn from the agreements currently being worked out in African countries. The subject certainly involves a re-examination of the fundamental concepts of trade unionism – whether Communist or Western – and the idea of a trade unionism emanating from the policies of ruling *élites* suggests a variation of 'guided democracy' and 'scientific management' theories found elsewhere. What is certain, in view of the ham-fisted tactics adopted in Africa by British, French, Belgian, American and Eastern European centres, the African

Introduction

experiments are at least as important as anything found anywhere else. As Daniel Guérin has noted; 'Our continent has not yet any certain and definitive prototype to offer in this field. We must therefore consider with modesty the plight of the African nations suddenly confronted with this problem which we ourselves find so hard to solve.'

Unfortunately when the subject is looked at from the vantage-point of government policies, official union attitudes and the complex manoeuvres of political and union *élites*, much is lost of the texture of life of African workers and *their* responses to institutions and movements. I have tried to cover some of this ground by a short sketch of the evolution of an African working class: inevitably it is only a sketch and the dynamics of a social history are probably absent. If therefore I have an apology it must be to the workers of all countries in Africa who may appear in this book as a vast undifferentiated mass being acted on by small *élites*. Documentation of the growing African working class has barely begun, and I only hope that this book provides a modest contribution to the enlargement of knowledge of an important theme.

There remains to mention briefly the method adopted in the presentation of material. In general I have avoided a country-by-country survey in the interests of presenting a pattern of the major tendencies throughout the continent. In doing so I may have been less than fair to some countries while others have been given generous coverage. This has not been done out of any partisan bias for certain countries or union movements but generally because I have thought it more instructive to explore themes than to present a collection of loosely-collected narrative accounts. The reader may find that I have been overtaken by events, that countries given short measure in this book have become overnight important centres of union activity. To some extent this is inevitable in the present fluid state of development in Africa, and it would be a rash person who could confidently predict anything for ten or even five years ahead.

In spite of such caution, it seems to me that certain patterns are already being outlined and I have selected those areas where material is more readily available. What courses African unions

Introduction

take in the future will of course depend to a large extent on the degree of industrialization. It is here that South Africa may present one of the most important examples, with a much bigger industrial sector and a more comprehensive breakdown of the traditional economies. I have accordingly given South Africa a chapter to itself and used some comparative material in Chapter 6. Beyond that I could not go. The debate on whether it represents a model of what an African industrial society will be or whether it is merely a crude abberation cannot be pursued here. But the challenge to the communitarian aims of the new states found in South Africa's social structure and in other industrial countries remains one of the underlying themes of this book.

*

Many people and institutions have given generous assistance in the compilation of material. A large number directly involved in the African trade union movement pleaded anonymity which I must respect. Among others I should mention are the library of the British TUC, the information department of the ICFTU, the Bureau of Labor Statistics of the US Department of Labor, the London offices of the WFTU, the Overseas' Employers' Confederation, and the Scientific, Technical and Research Committee of the OAU. Georges Fischer, Robert Cornevin, W. H. Friedland, George Lichtblau, Roger Scott, Hugh Clegg, V. L. Allen, Serge Thion, John Tettegah, George Foggon, Thomas Hodgkin, Thomas Kanza, Clive Jenkins and the late Arthur Creech-Jones gave me valuable help at different stages of the project. Ronald Segal was a patient and long-suffering editor – without his skill and encouragement none of this would have appeared in coherent form. Needless to say, the responsibility for the final effort is mine: indeed it would be impossible to produce a book which accorded with the views of so many different people and organizations.

IOAN DAVIES
January 1966

1 Economic Development and the Changing Social Structure

The commercialization of African economies and the development of semi-industrial societies are complex processes, because most of the impetus for industrial activity came from outside Africa. There are two processes – industrialization and imperialism – which were never so closely linked in the history of the developed countries but which are inseparably basic to the growth of modern African society. Isolating the positive consequences of external intervention from the purely destructive is not easy to do. In discussing the effects of British rule in India, Marx noted that Britain 'in causing a social revolution in Hindostan, was actuated only by the vilest interests and was stupid in her manner of executing them'; but she was at the same time 'the unconscious tool of history' in bringing about a fundamental change in the social organization of the country.[1] Because the imperialist was alien, the local nationals rebelled; but in rebelling they generally used institutions or organizations that directly derived from the economic and political intervention of the imperialists.

This dichotomy is nowhere so clearly seen as in the growth of trade unions under colonial rule, and the problem of actually defining their function and organization is correspondingly difficult. The unions came into being as vehicles of protest against working conditions, and in this they were no different from unions in any other part of the world. The employers involved, however, were foreign, and the working conditions were attributable not only to the disorder and uncertainty caused by the growth of money economies and commercial production but equally to outside intervention. The history of African trade unions to date is accordingly as much one of the reaction to imperial rule as to working conditions, and any study has to trace the major social changes introduced by European activity before discussing the role played in these by the unions themselves.

The changes can be studied by using different types of measurement – the growth of investment, the development of a wage-earning labour force, the rise of foreign trade, or the concentration on certain commodities – and throughout this book all of these will be given an important place. But the study of trade unions is a study of worker organizations, and from this point of view the changing pattern of work and living can most dramatically be seen in the reorganization of land relationships, and its effect on working habits.

The Europeans found most African land held either communally or on behalf of the whole community through its chiefs. The ethnic unit was the main vehicle of ownership – over much of Africa, though within it there were countless varieties of land-holding, the details of which can hardly occupy us here. The colonizers disrupted these patterns in three main ways: by directly acquiring land for their own use; by fostering development schemes; and by encouraging the development of cash-crop production. Land was acquired for agricultural use, for mineral exploitation or for the construction of transport routes – by treaty (as in most parts of West Africa and sometimes in Southern Africa); by military conquest (in Kenya, Tanganyika and most of Southern and Central Africa); or by government edict (as in the Belgian Congo and French Equatorial Africa, where all land 'without an owner' was declared the property of the state). In Southern Africa the effect of these measures was to reserve the lands of richest agricultural or raw material potential for European use and ownership. By 1956, some 89 per cent of all land in South Africa was white-owned; 49 per cent in Swaziland and Southern Rhodesia; 9 per cent in the Congo; 7 per cent in Kenya; 6 per cent in Bechuanaland; and 5 per cent in Nyasaland.[2] In Angola only 401,180 acres out of more than thirty million were in African hands. In other territories the percentage of land alienated to European use tended to be much lower: in West Africa the proportion was usually under 5 per cent, and in most countries less than 1 per cent. (In the Gold

Economic Development and the Changing Social Structure

Coast 5 per cent was alienated, mainly for mining concessions, but ownership was vested in central and local government.)

Though these figures reflect the extent of the European stake in Africa, they only begin to show the economic control. In most territories of Southern and British East Africa, because the land was taken for its agricultural or mineral value, the resulting distribution worked strongly against effective African agricultural development. Although Europeans in Kenya occupied only 7 per cent of the total land area, this has been estimated to include about 'half the land that is worth cultivating'.[3] In Northern Rhodesia, Europeans occupied 3 per cent of the total area, but Africans were left with the poor soils, bad irrigation facilities and areas that had 'a wide distribution of the tse-tse fly, which effectively rules out cattle-raising over five-eighths of the country, and affects human beings themselves with the deadly sleeping sickness.'[4] In Southern Rhodesia the distribution was even more rapacious; 'most of the Native Area is poor soil, usually the poorer types of granite-sand known technically as Class III land; while the European area contains nearly all the areas of fertile soil in the country.'[5] Of the native purchase areas, reserved for African farmers, most are today

'in areas of poor granite sand or even poorer fine grained sandstone soils. Others ... are in hot, malaria-infested areas, where great illness and suffering are caused among people settling there (especially as there are no hospitals or clinics within easy reach). Others ... are cursed by country so broken and rocky that agriculture is impossible over most of the area.'[6]

In such territories, production by Europeans came to dominate the whole of economic activity. What African farming existed was mainly subsistence in character, and the number of Africans dependent on wage-labour for their survival accordingly increased. Throughout Southern Africa the contrast between those working in the 'European' sector and those in the peasant agricultural one is more clearly marked than anywhere else on the continent.

Although the effects of European influence are starkest in the areas of settlement, throughout the rest of the continent the

African Trade Unions

introduction of new administrative and legal patterns and the growth of commercial enterprise had a powerful effect on altering the structure of land relationships. One form of land use which had limited application was the development project such as the Gezira scheme, introduced after the First World War in the Sudan to provide irrigation for cotton growing, and the Tanganyika ground-nuts scheme attempted by the British government in the late 1940s. Along with some fifty other schemes, these were aimed with varying degrees of economic success at providing land, capital equipment and technical direction for the indigenous population, involved the comprehensive resettlement of communities, and were geared to the demands of the imperial market. In a few instances (notably in Gezira and the Cameroons) the schemes were successful in re-establishing communities round a new economic centre, but generally 'most of these "schemes" were planned and executed with little understanding of the human values in the earlier social and economic structure. As a result Africans did not strike their roots deeply in the resettlement areas, as envisaged by the planners.'[7] Altogether the schemes have had little effect, either economically or socially, and the failure of the ill-conceived Tanganyika Development Corporation probably set the enthusiasm for resettlement schemes back many years.

Such schemes are worth mentioning, for all their failures, if only to show that the development of African agriculture has not been contemplated exclusively under European settler direction or cash-crop individualism. The failures themselves underline two points that will recur throughout this book – the badly-informed attempts of Europeans to impose certain patterns of life on Africans, and the resistance of African institutions to outside pressure and to money incentives unless these can be shown to have real social and communal attractions as well.

Outside 'White' Africa, the most comprehensive influence of European commerce on land tenure and use has been in the direction of crop cultivation. Where settler influence was small, administrators and foreign companies attempted to raise the level of peasant productivity and at the same time encourage the use of single, marketable crops. This involved using money as an

Economic Development and the Changing Social Structure

incentive and affected the traditional patterns of communal land ownership by emphasizing individual rights to crops or trees planted for cash sale. In some areas this has achieved two effects; the cultivators have been transformed from workers operating under feudal rights or through communal schemes to individual farmers, and the range of crop has narrowed down from a variety of subsistence foods to one or two marketable commodities. Throughout North Africa, Northern Sudan, South Africa, Rhodesia, Zambia, Ethiopia, Kenya and Malawi there are numbers of peasants with individual land claims, and according to a report of the International Bank, world financial pressures support a spread in this form of land holding and the type of economic activity it entails. But two other tendencies work against it. In the first place there exist large holdings of land under private or state feudal landlords. In Buganda, under the British administration of Sir Harry Johnston, much of the land was divided between the Kabaka and a group of princes and Ministers. 'The chiefs' power within Buganda came to be expressed in terms of real property. Henceforward they were not merely office-holders but also landed proprietors.'[8] It has been estimated that by 1954 some 230 landowners controlled almost three-quarters of the country. On different scales, major landowners existed in Morocco, Algeria, Tunisia, Libya, Egypt, Ethiopia. Under such conditions peasants work for landlords, and the commercial production of crops is organized through centralized direction. State feudal land-ownership is a variation of this system, where the chief feudal lord is also in charge of a state or semi-autonomous area of administration. Tax is paid by the direct producer instead of rent, but peasant cultivators are subject to all the machinery of law and economic control that marks state rather than private feudalism. In Africa the clearest example of this form of feudalism is found in the emirates of Northern Nigeria and the Muslim areas of former French West Africa, where the system of indirect rule hardened and expanded the structure of state feudalism by creating semi-autonomous Native Authorities who administered the areas under their control. Under both these forms of land-ownership, the development of private peasant holdings is improbable in the short run, and even under private ownership the tendency is slowly towards the amalgamation of units into large estates.

On the other hand, throughout most of tropical Africa communal ownership continues despite the introduction of cash-crop farming. Where feudal control was minimal or non-existent, it was normally an advantage to use the community as an agent for development; coercion, where it was tried, led to hostility and suspicion from the peasants, and unless extreme measures of coercion were used (as in Portuguese Africa) the results were likely to be negligible. Moreover, the 'communal character of African society can facilitate the diffusion of new ideas. If a new method of production, or a new product, is approved by the leaders it may be adopted by all the members of the community far more rapidly than in a highly individualistic society.'[9] René Dumont, the French agronomist, has made the point even more strongly in a highly critical study of economic and social development in French-speaking West Africa. Communal development, he argues, is not only cheaper, more efficient and rational; it helps to avoid the creation of wealthy *élites* deriving substantial profits from commercial enterprise at the expense of the peasantry. Though communal agricultural production is doubtless not generally found in recognition of such arguments, it continues because the social structures of the rural areas have so far been strong enough to resist individualist encroachment. In some states communal production has also been supported by the national governments. Ghana, Guinea and Mali have all attempted to use the community as the basis of agricultural development, and Guinea has prohibited many forms of land transaction and sale in an attempt to preserve the traditional system.

The ownership and use of land are of primary importance in assessing the deployment and quality of economic activity, and show how the coming of Europeans rapidly transformed the African economy from production for internal consumption to production for world markets. In areas where settlers concentrated – Southern and British Central Africa, Kenya and the Magrheb – agricultural exports and minerals brought large-scale European investment. By 1935 it was estimated that just

Economic Development and the Changing Social Structure

under one-half of all overseas capital invested in Africa south of the Sahara went to South Africa. The effect of this, apart from disrupting traditional agricultural cultivation, was to make South Africa dominant in the pattern of economic development and the deployment of labour. Throughout the southern half of the continent, workers came to depend on the farms, mines and public services of the Union for cash earnings, and large-scale migration rapidly came to dominate the neighbouring countries. In 1959, of a labour force of 432,234 African workers recruited by the Chamber of Mines, only 182,561 came from South Africa; of all Africans employed in 1959, only one-third are estimated to have come from within South Africa.[10] Agreements were established with most colonial governments for the annual recruitment of migrants, and by the 1950s over 200 engagement stations were established throughout Southern Africa, as far north as Nyasaland, Angola and Tanganyika. The impact of migration – to South Africa, the Rhodesias and Katanga – was such that over one-third of able-bodied males were absent from home at any one time in the whole of Southern and Central Africa. Mozambique exported over a quarter of a million people between 1952 and 1954; Nyasaland, some 110,000.

Economic dominance by South Africa and the Central African Copperbelt was underlined by the transport system. The main railways were built to connect the ports, the Central African settler and industrial areas, and South Africa. (The railway density in South Africa is one mile of track for every fifty to sixty square miles; in tropical Africa, the average ratio is one track mile for every 340–50 square miles.) For Africans seeking labour it was much more convenient to travel towards these areas than anywhere else, and where communications were poor the Witwatersrand Native Labour Association provided transport either by building its own roads or arranging for air-lifts. (In Katanga, Union Minière found by the 1920s that this transport system, though connecting up with Elizabethville, worked against migration to the Congolese mines.) The close economic links among the territories produced a common pattern of labour policy throughout Southern Africa. Wage labour developed more rapidly here than elsewhere, though the conditions of employment prevented the establishment of any permanent work-force. Migrant labour was cheap and easily obtainable once the basic recruiting machinery had been created; little effort was made to train workers, and in time legal discrimination was built into industrial contracts so that scarcely any Africans could rise above semi-skilled levels.

Throughout the areas of European settlement, industry and commercial production increased, skills multiplied and average wages rose; but the populations became stratified into complex systems of racial and occupational categories. In South Africa some Africans entered the professions, but the mass were denied elementary industrial skills; Afrikaners were mainly in farming and administration, while industry and commerce were generally the preserve of the English; Indians and Coloured became petty traders, domestic workers, clerical assistants, farm hands and industrial workers; the majority of Africans still held some allegiance to the land, but a mass of proletarians (over a quarter of the total) became more-or-less permanently resident in the towns and cities, though without opportunities for advancement within an industrial society. What African agriculture existed was conducted by tenant farmers on large estates owned by whites or was confined to subsistence farming in the badly equipped and overcrowded reserves. In 1955 the Tomlinson Commission on separate development found that 'practically every able-bodied African man in the reserves goes out to work in the industrial areas' and that some 2,140,000 men 'spend their lives circulating between industrial employment and their tribal subsistence economy.'[11] The subsistence economy in South Africa is accordingly dwarfed by the money one. The Tomlinson Commission found that half of the 3,600,000 Africans living in the reserves would have to be removed from the suffocated land and found work in industry and commerce; but recent calculations suggest that such a figure was too optimistic. Under current resettlement schemes no more than one-third could be found work on the land, and in its 'Bantustan' or separate development policies, the South African government has provided funds almost entirely for agricultural purposes. The subsistence economy, far from being a haven for people of two

Economic Development and the Changing Social Structure

worlds, has become a choked and choking dormitory area, providing all its able-bodied men for labour on the white-owned farms or in white-owned industry.

The example of South Africa illustrates in extreme form the breakdown of the traditional African economies, the reorganization of a society on industrial lines, and the relegation of Africans to cogs in an economic machine. Apart from its intrinsic importance, South Africa represents to most African countries an example of the horror in their midst. The horror does not come only from racism and the perpetuation of white supremacy, but from the picture of an atomised, 'mass' society that it represents. This is the one country in the whole of Africa where commercialized production and large-scale industry have completely transformed traditional economic and social patterns. It is not only a threat because of its political structure and military strength, or an affront because of its racial policies; it is an African example of industrialized culture and therefore poses on the continent the ultimate challenge to the social ideas of the new governments. Even if the money economy and industrialization have had much slower growth in the rest of Africa, features of the South African system extend northwards, and of course migrant labour has for many years dominated economic behaviour in the whole of Southern Africa, as well as large areas of East, West and Northern Africa.

Outside of the Copperbelt complex and Kenya, the effect of commercialized production on tropical Africa has varied enormously. The extent of such activity can be seen in the impact on traditional social and economic structures of the distribution of the labour force, the percentage and allocation of land used in the money economy, and the proportion of commodities exported. In most territories either cash-crop cultivation or wage labour is the dominant form of employment, with the division due largely to the role played by European settlement and large-scale investment in mining and industry. In a few states, notably Tanganyika and the Congo, both cash-crop agriculture and wage-earning are important, in Tanganyika because of the development of plantations, and in the Congo because of a small strip of industrial land in a vast territory of common cash-crop farming. At the extremes of wage-earning and cash-cropping, 65 per cent of Zambian males are employed as wage-earners, and three-quarters of Ghanaian land is used for crop cultivation. Most territories fall in between these extremes, though in some – for example, Kenya and former French Equatorial Africa – over 70 per cent of the adult male population is still engaged in subsistence production, and in all tropical countries, except Ghana, over 50 per cent of the land area is still under subsistence crops or unfit for cultivation. The proportion of wage-earners ranges from 25 per cent in the Congo to 4 per cent in Nigeria and the former French West African territories.

European economic interest was primarily directed towards raising the output of those crops that were needed on the world market and providing the services necessary for effective transportation, distribution and power supply. The effects of such a policy are seen throughout Tropical Africa in which all but three countries depend on three products for over 50 per cent of their exports, while a few countries – Ghana, Zambia, Somalia and the Sudan – each depend on one commodity for two-thirds of their export income. Along with specialization went the concentration of export marketing or production in the hands of a few European or (in the case of Liberia) American companies. The United Africa Company (in West Africa), the British South Africa Company and Anglo-American Corporation (in Zambia), the Imperial Tobacco Company (in Rhodesia), Union Minière de Haut Katanga (in the Congo), the Firestone Rubber Company (in Liberia) and the British Cocoa and Chocolate Company (in Ghana and Nigeria) were some of the larger concerns that established near-monopoly rights in areas of Africa. The conditions of employment and the administrative attitudes towards trade unions were to a large extent framed by the policies of the operating companies. In the middle years of the colonial period (1920–50), the political importance of such concerns was paramount. Transport was provided to open up the territories for company exploitation; health services were improved to promote fitter workers; labour exchanges were established and migration encouraged in the interests of developing a few crops or mining resources. Investment rarely went into public or communal

Economic Development and the Changing Social Structure

industry, and was in the main linked directly to overseas interests. Even though public services were often organized and owned by local or central government, their establishment and expansion were largely dictated by the needs and resources of the new industries. In the British territories for most of the period up to the mid-fifties, the infra-structure was internally financed, but linked to the needs of the growing areas of production. In the French territories, the metropolitan government and private industry financed almost all the services after 1944 from external sources, but this was mainly because the colonies themselves were so poor and not because attempts were made to develop a comprehensive infra-structure. The effects of these developments is summarized in an ICFTU document:

The result is a deterioration in standards of subsistence farming and a decline in its productivity. Thus instead of development, progress and rising living standards, the whole process may lead to increased backwardness and greater poverty among the African agricultural population. It is of course true that the development of non-African enterprise has had some favourable effects on indigenous agriculture. The export of mining and other products has necessitated the development of internal transport facilities. This in turn has brought some African farming communities within reach of markets, both domestic and foreign, and has thus given an impetus to commercialization of at least part of the indigenous agriculture. However, these effects have, according to the U.N. studies, been 'largely incidental' and their importance has remained relatively small.[12]

The immediate human consequence of the development of industry in Africa was the increase in the number of people seeking work for wages, and the creation of large forces of migrant labourers who trekked up to 2,000 miles in search of employment. This is not a particularly new phenomenon in the experience of industrialization; most countries have seen large-scale migration from rural to urban areas during the early years of industrial growth, and some, notably Britain and the U.S.A., have welcomed international migration during the crucial years of development. But there are at least three notable differences in the African experience. In the first place, very few migrants settle permanently in the industrial and urban areas; most move

25

there for short periods of up to five years and then return to their rural areas, while a surprisingly large number of young men go out to work only once for wages. Secondly, little attempt has been made throughout Africa to create conditions that would make the migrants want to stay. In South Africa, Rhodesia and formerly in Zambia, contract terms and racial discrimination actively discouraged settlement, while in the rest of Africa labour has been so cheap that employers have preferred to use casual workers than provide incentives for settlement. Thirdly, the initial incentives for Africans to take wage employment at all were largely artificial. Men in the subsistence areas were reluctant to leave their families for wage labour far away, and so various devices were used to compel them to work. At the outset this meant directly-forced labour in all colonies. The Congo Free State of Leopold II, the French Equatorial territories and the Portuguese possessions were particularly marked for their policies of coercion, but British East Africa, German Tanganyika and white South Africa were almost as heavily implicated in the system. It was not until the early 1920s that the French and British governments began to review labour policy, gradually replacing direct compulsion with an indirect form. A money tax was imposed on the peasants which made them enter wage labour themselves or produce crops for the money-market; refusal or inability to pay the tax was then normally punished by forced labour. Like slavery, forced labour left its mark on the whole area of labour recruitment, on the attitudes of employers to African work capacity, and on African reactions to industrial activity. Because labour was compulsory or made necessary by the pressure of taxation, most peasants considered it an inevitable but irksome intrusion into traditional social patterns, while the employers branded African workers as idle, irresponsible and unsuited to any degree of skilled work.

The initial causes of migrant labour are not difficult to locate; what is for us more important is the persistence of short-term migration. Walter Elkan[13] has noted three main reasons for this. Because subsistence agriculture and cash-cropping have continued on a large scale, many migrants work for wages 'only long enough to provide them with money needed to equip their

Economic Development and the Changing Social Structure

farms'. Wages are a form of capital accumulation, and are spent on transport (bicycles), accommodation (waterproof roofing), agricultural tools and labour (towards the bride-price of wives). 'The fruits of their work in town come to them not in the form of an immediate increase in consumption but rather in the higher yield of better equipped farms.' Furthermore, urban living conditions and wages are barely adequate for men wishing to move permanently. In many towns there is little provision for family accommodation, and wage contracts are normally based on the living costs of single men rather than of family units. But even if conditions in the urban areas were demonstrably better, permanent migration there would not automatically follow. The systems of land tenure prevailing throughout most of tropical Africa make it impossible for compensation to be paid to men permanently leaving the land. 'Farms cannot be sold and a man who leaves his farm simply foregoes a part of his income, for his rural income is one which cannot be compounded or capitalized.' Thus permanent withdrawal involves surrendering real income and a 'potent form of insurance against the hazards of industrial life'.

Together these conditions operate against the permanency of wage labour, but the collapse of any one may lead to a substantial withdrawal from the land. In times of famine or low prices for cash crops, peasants may consider the land uneconomic, even with occasional income from wage labour. Where decent accommodation is provided for families (as in Katanga), the labourer is clearly more inclined to consider a permanent move. And where European ownership of land has led to overcrowding in subsistence areas (as in South Africa and the Kikuyu areas of Kenya), it becomes increasingly clear that everyone cannot retain a permanent foothold in the countryside. But these are exceptions to the African rule. Most African wage-earners are employed for no more than five years altogether, and in the course of this period they may have as many as twelve different jobs. Even in the more proletarianized South Africa, one survey found that out of a work-span of thirty-one years (ages sixteen to forty-seven) the average worker spent 36 per cent of his time at home and 64 per cent in employment away, during which period

African Trade Unions

he had thirty-four different jobs averaging forty-seven weeks each.[14] The Tomlinson Commission found the proportion of a worker's life spent in employment away from home to be 62 per cent. In West Africa a different pattern appears in migration from the Upper Volta to Ghana and the Ivory Coast, mainly from the crowded Mossilands. In 1956 the Gold Coast Labour Commissioner estimated that about one-half of the number of employees in the Eastern, Western and Ashanti regions came from the Northern Territories, the Upper Volta, Nigeria and Liberia. Some estimates go as high as 70 per cent. In the Ivory Coast 80 per cent of the labour force comes from the Upper Volta. This migration is almost entirely seasonal and varies greatly from year to year, so that estimates range in Ghana from 8 per cent to 70 per cent. In the three main Sudanese towns (Khartoum, Khartoum North and Omdurman) a recent census showed that 43 per cent of the population came from Darfur (one thousand miles west of Khartoum), from French-speaking Africa and Nigeria. The majority of these were unattached males, mostly Muslims who stopped for a period of wage labour on the way to Mecca. In the Sudan, the West African 'is over half of the nation's wage labour force – without him economic development, particularly in Gezira, would collapse. He is, in economic as well as social fact, the slaves' descendent.'[15]

In some large countries there is substantial internal migration rather than migration across colonial boundaries. This is certainly true of Nigeria and the Sudan, and even in the Congo, with an industrial policy that encouraged settlement and unconditional withdrawal from the countryside, it is clear that seasonal migration is important, quite apart from the spectacular growth of the urban areas in Katanga and Leopoldville. A 1955 estimate of two and a half million Africans working outside their original village areas may be accurate. Mme Bouvier[16] has calculated that in 1958 some 50 per cent of the workers in Leopoldville province and 70 per cent in Katanga came from outside their sub-district, and even in the less industrialized provinces the proportion was almost 40 per cent. For the Congo as a whole half a million (or just under 50 per cent of the wage earners) were permanently resident outside their villages, and this means

Economic Development and the Changing Social Structure

that something like two million Congolese were short-term migrants.

Throughout Africa, labour mobility was largely perpetuated by permanently depressed wages and totally inadequate provision for urban settlement. But recently a more serious obstacle to industrial growth has been created. With the development of more sophisticated technology in Europe and America, expatriate firms as well as colonial and later independent African governments, preferred to invest in new machinery than fully utilize Africa's most plentiful resource – labour. Between 1950 and 1962 although the actual numbers of workers employed in the wage-labour force held its own in most African countries, because of the rapid growth in population, the percentage working for wages decreased The implications of such tendencies in terms of industrializing policies and the growth of unemployment are already proving extremely serious for independent African governments. Not only has industry disrupted the traditional patterns of life for most Africans; it has also failed to establish an industrial alternative.

Chapter 1: Notes

1. Karl Marx, 'The British Rule in India', *New York Tribune*, 25 June 1853.
2. Lord Hailey, *An African Survey*, O.U.P., 1956, p. 687.
3. J. Woddis, *Africa – The Roots of Revolt*, Lawrence and Wishart, 1960, p. 4.
4. Rita Hinden, *Plan for Africa*, Allen and Unwin, 1941, pp. 69–70.
5. Ken Brown, *Land in Southern Rhodesia*, p. 5.
6. op. cit., p. 23.
7. M. J. Herskovits, *The Human Factor in Changing Africa*, Routledge and Kegan Paul, 1962, p. 161.
8. L. A. Fallers, (ed), *The King's Men*, O.U.P., 1963, p. 31.
9. M. J. Herskovits, op. cit., p. 169.
10. Ruth First, 'The Gold of Migrant Labour', *Africa South in Exile*, Vol. 5, No. 3, pp. 7–31.
11. D. H. Houghton, *The South African Economy*, O.U.P., 1964, p. 85.
12. ICFTU: *Report of 1st African Regional Conference*, Accra, 1957, p. 106.
13. W. Elkan, 'The Persistence of Migrant Labour', in *Migrant Labour in Africa South of the Sahara*, C.C.T.A., 1961, pp. 299–304.
14. D. H. Houghton, op. cit., pp. 82–4.
15. P. McLoughlin, 'Sudan's Three Towns', *Economic Development and Cultural Change*, Vol. xii, No. 1, pp. 70–83.
16. P. F. Bouvier, 'Some Aspects of Labour Migration in the Belgian Congo', *C.C.T.A. Bulletin*, 1959, No. 6, pp. 45–7.

2 The Colonial Experience (Labour Policies of Britain, France and Belgium)

The European countries that controlled most of Africa for some eighty years did not begin with any clear intention of *developing* the economic resources of the continent; colonies were acquired for a variety of reasons, including immediate economic advantage, but any idea of comprehensive economic development was in small evidence. To a large extent traders, settlers and commercial entrepreneurs were allowed to produce their own schemes. Until after the First World War little effort was made to introduce legislation defining the scope of operations, and it was not until the outbreak of the Second World War that systematic legislation was drafted covering the whole field of economic activity or allowing for metropolitan governments themselves to initiate development schemes. The era of colonial rule after the 1880s therefore falls into three broad categories for the three powers considered here. From the introduction of formal rule to the First World War, political policy was mainly confined to 'pacification' and the introduction of rudimentary administration, with a general tolerance towards all forms of economic activity. Between 1919 and 1945, some legislation was introduced covering most forms of economic behaviour, including labour conditions, while at the same time programmes were initiated for some economic assistance and development. But although legislation was introduced in the imperial parliaments, in most instances it was barely implemented and in several openly ignored by the colonial administrations. After the war most of these programmes were taken further and more serious attempts made to apply legislation on working conditions; additional measures were introduced, and administration became more effective.

The three imperial powers had significantly different approaches to labour policy, though ultimately the effects were remarkably similar. Until the Second World War, the lack of any comprehensive labour legislation or effective implementation of International Labour Conventions allowed for the regular disruption of subsistence economies and the use of forced labour throughout the continent. In the Belgian Congo a collaboration between the state and private companies established from the 1890s a unique system of forced labour, 'by which private companies were granted unfettered access to a specified portion of the Free State while the rest was reserved for exploitation by the state or its concessionaires.'[1] Most of the wealth was in rubber and ivory, and the labour was recruited through bands of commercial agents employed by King Leopold's Congo International Association. Among their instructions was an order 'to furnish four thousand kilos of rubber every month. To this effect I give you *carte blanche*. You have therefore two months in which to work your people. Employ gentleness first, and if they persist in not accepting the imposition of the state, employ force of arms.' Leopold himself said, 'Placed in front of primitive savagery ... it is necessary for them (the Associations' agents) to subject the population to new laws, of which the most imperious and the most salutary is assuredly that of labour.'[2] The effects of this policy have been well documented. In North-Eastern Congo, Leopold entered into association with Tippoo Tip, the leader of the Arab slave traders, who was appointed a governor of the Association. By 1908 Leopold's private estate was valued at sixty million francs, and Morel estimated that twenty-three years of the king's personal rule had reduced the population of the Congo by 1,500,000. Casement, in his consular report of 1903, put the figure at three million.

Forced labour became such an integral part of the Belgian colonial system that it was not until 1954 that the last administrative forms were abolished. But Basil Davidson noted in 1955 that 'negligent workers in the Congo are still being sentenced in their thousands every year to prison with hard labour'[3]. The years between 1908 and 1960 were marked by decreasing use of compulsion, but the pace was slow. Drawing on the Belgian government's Commission Permanente pour la Protection des

The Colonial Experience

Indigène, Davidson traces the painful process of labour policy. In 1923 the Commission, though accepting as necessary a maximum limit of sixty days' forced labour for every male adult, complained of cases where Africans 'had to work for ninety or even 104 days'. In 1928 and again in 1947 the Commission recommended the absolute prohibition of the use of women, old people and children in the construction and maintenance of roads. In 1938 it complained that 'certain villages are being emptied of practically their entire male population, which goes to the towns in search of a better life. There remain in the village only the old people, women and children: sometimes only the old people.'

Although the Congo remains the classic example in Africa of the deliberate and persistent use of forced labour, in the early years of colonial rule all the imperial powers depended on it for plantations, public services (especially roads and railways) and porterage. In many ways the French equatorial territories carefully reproduced the system operating in the Congo. By 1900 all of French Equatorial Africa had been divided up among some forty concessionaires, under a French decree declaring that 'All the products of conceded territory, whatever they may be, are the property of the concession company.' The companies in the French colonies claimed that all rubber belonged to them and not to the African cultivators, with the result that the law, local administration and the French government connived at the violation of African rights. 'The whole of the Congo was handed over to large companies with a registered capital of $59\frac{1}{4}$ million francs. The government in France abdicated its functions and limited itself to imposition of taxes and collection of quit rents.'[4] The consequence of this policy was the introduction of a labour tax (*prestation*) as a legal method of acquiring compulsory labour. This gave to the Administration the power to compel all adult males to work for certain days each year on 'public works', but 'the definition of "public works" was very elastic, so requisitions were frequently used to help out private employers who were short of labour'.[5] *Prestation* operated throughout French Africa long after the concession companies had lost their charters, indeed, and was not removed by law until 1946. It has been estimated that for one year – 1935 – alone, 3,300,000 people were subjected to twenty-eight million days of compulsory labour, some seven million days redeemed only by cash payments.[6] Another form of forced labour – that in lieu of military service – provided 1,500,000 workers a year. Between 1927 and 1936 thousands of men were recruited under this system to build the Dakar–Niger Railway and to improve the navigation of the Niger river. Conscription involved three years' service, hard work and low pay. And when these methods failed to provide adequate numbers of workers, the French government established labour exchanges based on the use of force and controlled by administrators who were empowered to authorize employers to recruit. The labour officers generally compelled chiefs to provide the workers, and between 1920 and 1930 some 189,000 workers were 'recruited' in this way for railway construction, timber cutting, public works and commercial building. Although the Popular Front government attempted to end forced labour in 1936, the European planters and timbermen refused to comply with its orders, and, in the Ivory Coast even succeeded in getting the Lieutenant-Governor dismissed because he attempted to enforce the new measures.

What the Belgians and the French pursued with gusto, the British allowed to develop piecemeal. According to the scale of economic activities, various forms of compulsion were introduced in the colonies. Where there was a strong base of European settlers – as in Kenya and the Rhodesias – compulsory labour was introduced in agriculture and the public services. There were normally few scruples entertained over such policies, and throughout East and Central Africa the development of commerce was accompanied by a high degree of forced labour. The employers, as in the Belgian and French colonies, set the pace, with the Administration complying. In other territories, notably West Africa, forced labour was introduced by the Administration itself. In Nigeria, for example, after various unsuccessful attempts to recruit labour for new schemes in crop cultivation and the public services, Sir Frederick Lugard decided to use force, on the grounds that 'among primitive tribes, a measure of compulsion through their tribal chiefs, in order to obtain labour

The Colonial Experience

for railway construction and other important works, is justifiable as an educative process to remove fear and suspicion'.[7] After this had proved of limited effect, extensive use of compulsion was discontinued through the 1933 Forced Labour Ordinance, but chiefs and administrators were permitted to recruit workers for specific tasks up to 1956. Exceptions permitted under the International Forced Labour Convention (and originally inserted because of pressure from colonial powers) were extensive throughout British Africa. The ILO estimated as late as 1958 that in Nigeria, Uganda and Tanganyika rights to porterage still existed; compulsory agricultural work was still recognized in Gambia, Bechuanaland, Kenya, Uganda and Tanganyika; and forced labour for public purposes existed in Bechuanaland, Kenya, Uganda and Tanganyika. Hailey estimated that in 1951–2 some 19,000 men did 210,000 man-days in Tanganyika alone. After the passing of Ordinances conforming to the Forced Labour Convention, forced labour for private employers was generally discontinued, but for public services or in times of emergency the practice was widespread in a number of forms up to the date of independence.

Where directly forced labour failed, the poll or hut tax succeeded, reflecting a general doctrine of work and labour relations that was to mark administrative policy for many years. As early as 1896 Sir Harry Johnston laid down the principles of the poll tax in Nyasaland:

Given abundance of cheap native labour, the financial security of the Protectorate is established ... All that needs to be done is for the Administration to act as friends of both sides, and to introduce the Native labourer to the European capitalist. A gentle insistence that the Native should contribute his fair share to the revenue of the country by paying his tax is all that is necessary on our part to ensure his taking a share in life's labour which no human being should avoid.[8]

Whether he liked it or not, the 'native' was part of a European capitalist system, and by gentle persuasion he was to be convinced that this obliged him to work for the good of himself and the whole system. His values henceforth were to be, by a slow, very slow, process of evolution, those of his Western masters. In enunciating such a policy the administrators were not slow to

African Trade Unions

match the expediencies of economic gain with a careful fostering of the belief that what they were doing was in keeping with the interests – and indeed the traditions – of the Africans. On the one hand Sir Percy Giraud would openly defend the destruction of African agriculture and the low wages paid to labourers: 'To raise the rate of wages would not increase but would diminish the supply of labour. A rise in the rate of wages would enable the hut or poll tax of a family, sub-tribe or tribe to be earned by fewer external workers.'[9] On the other hand Lord Lugard could justify forced labour on the grounds that it was an age-old African tradition that men did a quota of work for their chiefs.[10] (In this he ignored the fact that this was normally communal work, executed by men as part of their responsibility to the local polity, not imposed wage-labour which was performed for alien governments and whose benefits were anything but clear.)

The policy that Africans had to be induced to work by coercive or implicitly coercive measures was, in the British territories, inevitably accompanied by the belief that Africans were genetically unsuited for either industrial production or wage labour. During the 1920s three separate attitudes could be clearly noted throughout British Africa. In the first place was the employer, who was characterized by 'a tendency to rely on quantity rather than quality, and a frequent failure to realize that the object to strive for is the increased efficiency of the worker, rather than the abstract reduction of the wage bill.'[11] He was gradually encouraged by the local District Officer and, later, the Labour Commissioner, to adopt a more rational attitude to labour problems. But in many areas, notably East and Central Africa, the labour officers were almost as reluctant as the employers to introduce new ideas and abandon the *laissez-faire* attitude engendered alongside early commercial activity. As late as 1944 the Tanganyika Labour Department complained of the 'growing inefficiency, lack of discipline and disinclination to regular work of the African average labourer', but it seemed to have little guidance to offer apart from greater control by officials and employers. In 1948 the Kenya Labour Department report declared that 'the majority of Africans available for employment are bent on obtaining the highest possible wage for the minimum amount of work.' The same report had discovered people who, rather than accept 'reasonable wages', 'are quite prepared to stay at home and lounge in the local market spending the money which they have either obtained from their families or procured by their wits.' The common assumption that Africans were indolent and lazy was noted by R. H. Tawney as long ago as 1922:

The denunciations of the 'luxury, pride and sloth' of the English wage-earners of the seventeenth and eighteenth centuries are, indeed, almost identical with those directed against African natives today. It is complained that, compared with the Dutch, they are self-indulgent and idle; that they want no more than a bare subsistence, and will cease the moment they obtain it; that the higher their wages, the more – 'so licentious are they' – they spend on drink.[12]

But in spite of this Puritan influence and the reluctance of the Labour Departments to dismantle the *laissez-faire* framework, a third influence – that of the Colonial Office – increasingly had its effect.

The British Colonial Office, like the various local administrations, possessed no clearly conceived labour policy prior to the First World War. In many ways this is not surprising: even in Britain a proper labour policy had scarcely begun to evolve, and it was only with the Asquith Government and the legal decisions of 1901 and 1909 that any pattern of official interest could be clearly seen. The introduction of legislation outlining minimum conditions of work, establishing labour exchanges and recognizing the unions dated only from the late nineteenth and early twentieth century, and the conflicts of interest were so great within Britain that it would have been remarkable if Colonial administrators had accepted a policy of labour relations in advance of domestic departments. Moreover, the Colonial Office's general policy of delegating most of its power to local administrators was unlikely to produce any radical investigation of labour conditions. The main impetus for developing a labour policy came during the First World War, with an increased demand for raw materials and men in Africa, and the creation of the International Labour Office in 1919. On the one hand economic stresses led the Colonial Office to examine methods

African Trade Unions

that increased or retarded productivity, and on the other the growing international scrutiny of labour standards compelled all the imperial powers to review conditions in their colonies. To underline the need for fresh examination, several parliamentary debates on labour in various parts of the Empire – notably East Africa, India and the West Indies – stressed the primitive conditions prevailing and goaded Colonial Secretaries into action. The Labour governments of 1924 and 1929 paid some attention to colonial labour conditions, and in 1925 the TUC and the Labour Party initiated a series of British Commonwealth Labour Conferences attended by trade unionists and politicians from several Dominions and colonies (though initially not from colonial Africa). In 1930 the Labour government appointed a Colonial Office Labour Committee, drawn from officials of the Colonial Office and the Ministry of Labour to consider 'the basic formulation of Colonial Office labour policy, the drafting of model laws and the effects on dependencies of some of the international labour conventions of the period'.[13] A conference of colonial administrators and governors was also held in the same year, and this paid some attention to labour questions. To back the exhortations of the conference and the work of the Labour Committee, the Secretary of State, Sydney Webb, circulated a Dispatch in September 1930 to all colonial governors, urging the passage of legislation to give trade unions formal legal rights.

The immediate effects of this burst of activity were slight. Three Departments of Labour had existed in East Africa since 1924–5, and no further ones were added as a result of the 1930 Dispatch. In fact, the reverse occurred. In 1931, following the cut in administrative expenditure with the formation of an austerity National Government, all three existing departments were either reduced in size or abandoned altogether. None of the colonial governments was prepared to establish the necessary machinery for supervising labour conditions, and there is little evidence that they exerted much pressure on employers to reorganize their employment contracts, wage scales or basic industrial conditions.

Just before the Second World War, interest in labour problems increased again, mainly due to outbreaks of labour unrest in India, Northern Rhodesia and the West Indies. Further Dispatches were sent by Colonial Secretaries in 1935, 1937, 1938 and 1939, and in 1938 the Colonial Secretary appointed his first permanent labour adviser, Granville St John Orde-Browne, a former Provincial Commissioner in Tanganyika and author of one of the first surveys of African labour conditions. From 1938 the Colonial Office showed itself at last prepared to insist on the introduction of labour legislation, the creation of labour departments, the appointment of inspectors and the establishment of industrial disputes machinery. Within four years labour departments had been set up in most of the African colonies, and legislation on working conditions and industrial relations had been introduced. The outbreak of the war further stimulated activity, and a Colonial Development and Welfare Act was passed at Westminster in 1940 providing for economic assistance to colonies but stipulating that:

no territory might receive aid under its provisions unless it had in force legislation protecting the rights of trade unions, and unless the works for which the aid was to be used were carried out under a contract which embodied a fair wages clause, and which forbade the employment of children under the age of 14.

Finally in 1942 the old departmental Labour Committee was replaced by a Colonial Labour Advisory Committee, a unique administrative body which included members of the British TUC and employers' organizations as well as academic advisers and civil servants.

There were thus some important differences between British and French or Belgian policy. In the first place British groups with major interests in African and other colonial labour questions were provided with institutions through which they could press their case and were granted facilities for investigation that directly affected the course of events. (This contrasted with French policy, where the trade unions and commercial interests had to use the metropolitan machinery or struggle on as best they could, and Belgian, where only the commercial interests were given consultative status.) British trade unionists became active participants in the development of colonial policy; apart

39

African Trade Unions

from being represented on the Advisory Committee, they were frequently included in Royal Commissions and other advisory bodies, as well as providing from their own ranks trade union advisers who were seconded to colonial administrations for assistance in the development of local trade unions. Equally significant were the implications of this institutionalization.

The Labour Party's intellectuals and the TUC representatives wished to see the development of an institution which they considered an integral part of a democratic society. On the other hand the Colonial Office and local administrations feared that unions might 'without supervision and guidance ... fall under the domination of disaffected persons, by whom their activities may be diverted to improper and mischievous ends.[14]' The effect of this alliance – between metropolitan labour and colonial administration – was to devise a system that allowed for both the tolerance of 'liberal' institutions and for ensuring that they were controlled in the interests of the administration. Although the British TUC repeatedly emphasized that it was not aiming to introduce alien institutions and ideologies but rather to encourage 'the strengthening of individual trade unions', the TUC's policies and the practice of the individual trade unionists seconded for colonial service reproduced the form of industrial relations existing in Britain. In fact they went further than this. One of the areas of compromise reached with colonial administrations was TUC insistence that trade unionism in the colonies should be 'non-political', hardly itself a marked feature of British trade union affairs. In a perceptive study of British trade union influence in Africa, a French critic[15] has shown how remarkably inconsistent this policy was:

One cannot but be struck by the contradiction inherent in the attitude of Metropolitan unionists. On the one hand, they advocate democracy and, on the other, try to impose it from the outside. The overlap between trade-union and government duties is accepted (labour advisers being British unionists entrusted with official duties) and no objection is raised to the fact that, in the colonies and in the trade union sphere, the government practices an enlightened paternalism, unthinkable at any moment of Britain's social history.

So labour policy developed, or 'matured' according to a

The Colonial Experience

British professor. Slowly the systems of factory and location inspection were improved, and schemes for training labour officers initiated. In spite of some recognition that conditions in developing countries were unlike those in Britain, almost all of the legislation introduced was based on the existing British Acts, and by 1950 most of the measures envisaged in the earlier circulars and the 1940 Development and Welfare Act had been introduced. Different factors, however, limited the effectiveness of such action. The Labour Department staff were drawn from three sources – the local provincial administration, the U.K. Ministry of Labour, the trade union advisers – and in most instances the relationship between these categories was uncertain and even unhappy. The rate of turnover in most departments was high, and few were easily able to accommodate the trade unionists. Some labour commissioners, indeed, were either apathetic or hostile to the idea of effective trade union development, so that the British trade unionists often found themselves operating within an organization that suspected their motives. Tom Mboya quotes the ambiguous role of the Kenya trade union adviser, James Patrick, who, soon after his arrival, was told by Europeans and the Labour Commissioner himself that 'the time had not yet arrived for the establishment of trade unionism in Kenya; he should come back in twenty years or so.'[16] In Uganda J. S. Brandie was dismissed because he 'acted in conflict with official policy' by advising unions on negotiation tactics.[17] Only in Sierra Leone does a British trade unionist seem to have achieved any measure of success – by becoming Labour Commissioner himself and introducing a system of industrial relations that approximated to the Colonial Office model. (But even here activity was confined to the Creole minority and centred on Freetown; the mass of workers were untouched and, after fifteen years, political unionism became a marked feature of Sierra Leone trade unions.)

This emphasizes the second point of failure. The British model – derived partly from existing patterns and partly from theoretical ideas of a political unionism – failed to take account of the inevitable relationship between the growth of unions and political opposition to British rule. In many respects indeed, this

African Trade Unions

corresponded to Belgian paternalism in the Congo. African workers were to be encouraged to participate in colonial institutions (because these were 'good' for them), but on no condition were they allowed to use these institutions for their own ends. The conflict of interests was present from the beginning. It only required the rise of strong nationalist movements for the whole paternalist structure to crumble, and for trade unions to remould their organizations and objectives on lines that owed little to the British. Their effort to mould trade unions was not, as the British supposed, simply an exercise in industrial relations; it was an attempt to order a whole political movement.

Finally, the British administration seemed unaware where the logic of its own position led. Trade unions throughout Africa were registered and closely supervised by the labour departments: accounts were scrutinized, political affiliation was discouraged, union offices were closed, and, in practice, the right to strike was severely circumscribed by the 'emergency' actions of Governors or by the introduction of long lists of 'essential services' in which strikes were illegal. During the 1950s the Tanganyika government listed fifteen such essential services; Kenya, thirteen; and Nyasaland, ten. The effect of this policy was to give labour departments a real or potential power rare in Britain's own industrial experience. At independence this power was used by most of the new governments to establish a structure of industrial relations that was very different to that advocated by Britain. The policy of close administrative control prepared the way for the integration of party, bureaucracy and trade unions that is a marked feature of several African countries today. In other states (e.g. Nigeria), where integration of unions and parties was not achieved, the administration has continued to operate in much the same way as under British rule, attempting to influence – but always paying lip-service to the idea of – voluntarism.

In his study of the Cameroons Development Corporation Union, W. A. Warmington noted:

The department has had some influence on almost every aspect of union development and on the whole course of industrial relations in the plantations. It was consulted in the first stages when the members

The Colonial Experience

of the employees' committee were discussing the possibility of forming a union; it had considerable influence on the form of the original constitution of the union; and its advice was sought, and given, in the earlier years on many organizational matters. Labour officers have always been ready to give advice on administration and organization when they were approached, and it was to the Labour Department that the officials applied for support against an unpalatable decision made by the Registrar of Trade Unions in 1953. The pressure which the Department put on the union in 1956 to reorganize itself was quite strong, and its participation in the large-scale elections of that year was crucial.[18]

The conflict between democracy and 'guided democracy' was one that was never consciously examined, and ultimately this confusion, together with the rooted objection of many employers to even the Colonial Office's idea of industrial relations, produced a system that was unlikely to survive political independence.

In the French African territories the role of the administration was less ambiguous. The stages in the development of labour and trade union legislation were more deliberate than in British Africa; and, because of France's tendency to develop a common policy throughout its colonies, there was less marked a difference in the implementation of legislation in the various territories. If in the British colonies the effectiveness of labour policy depended more on the enthusiasm of the local administration and the co-operation of employers, in the French it relied on the power of popular movements to urge the implementation of the extensive labour laws. In Algeria and Tunisia the right to organize trade unions was granted in 1932, and in West Africa legal rights were granted by a decree of the Popular Front government in 1937, but membership was restricted to those who were literate in French and possessed an elementary school diploma. In 1944 a further decree abolished literacy requirements and thus opened the way for large-scale organization of the wage-earners. (In Morocco the situation was rather different. Non-Moroccans, mainly Frenchmen, were allowed to form unions in 1936; but although Moroccans secretly organized, it was not until after the war that legal rights were granted.) General labour conditions were regulated by the Lamine-Guèye Law of 1950, which laid down working conditions in the Civil Service, and the Overseas 'Territories' Labour Code of 1952, which applied the Lamine-Guèye provisions to all colonies and occupations. These laws established the machinery for wage negotiations and works inspection, and stipulated that equal pay for equal work, regardless of race or origin, should apply throughout the colonies.

Though it was not until the end of the Second World War that any systematic labour policy began to be implemented, the eventual introduction of the Code and its egalitarian philosophy provided a base from which action could develop. Employers and administrators were no more willing to negotiate with Africans in French colonies than they were in the British ones – if anything, there existed a more totalitarian attitude in the French empire – but the policy of assimilation provided a lever of which the Africans made successful use. Because there were Africans represented in the French Parliament, the campaign to improve working conditions increasingly switched after the mid-1940s from the colonies to Paris. African deputies played an important part in drafting the Overseas' Territories' Labour Code (indeed, the Lamine-Guèye Law was named after the senior deputy for Senegal), and, after its introduction, they worked together with the trade unions in Africa to implement it. Throughout the 1950s regular debates in the French Parliament and in the local African assemblies took place on points arising out of the ineffective application of the Code.

This use of French laws to outwit the French government was complicated by a second feature of French colonial labour experience. Unlike the British, who possessed only one trade union centre working closely with the Colonial Office, the French had three, none of which had any close relationship with the government. Instead of collaborating with authority on the main features of labour legislation and trade union policy, therefore, the French unions developed their own policies and, because the French colonies were considered to be simply 'France Overseas', their own African affiliates. Up to 1955 the pro-Communist Confédération Générale du Travail (CGT) claimed half of all African trade union members; the Catholic Confédération Française des Travailleurs Chrétiens (CFTC), 18 per cent; and

The Colonial Experience

the Socialist Confédération Générale du Travail – Force Ouvrière (CGT–FO), 10 per cent; the rest belonging to autonomous unions. This relationship was strongly reflected in most features of African trade union growth. The structure of unions was largely dictated by French models: there was a basic unit of the *syndicat professionnel* (a local union of workers in one trade or industry), followed by a regional or city grouping – the *union locale* – which in turn was centralized into a territorial federation and ultimately within Africa into a federation for the whole of the colonial area (the *union federale*). At the French level the African unions were represented in the metropolitan union, and, through it, in the appropriate international body (ICFTU, WFTU and IFCTU – see Chapter nine). In practice this structure was significantly modified, but the introduction into Africa of French union patterns remained the main feature of colonial trade union practice.

This structural influence was further marked by the adoption of tactics. Much of the emphasis on legislative action rather than on direct conflicts with employers came from French experience, particularly that of the CGT,[18] and the early effect of this was to keep African trade union development closely tied to the political and ideological policies of the metropolitan unions. In 1954 the Algerian National Movement, on taking over control of the unions, accused the CGT and the Communist Party of 'making their attitude towards the Algerian movement dependent on the exigencies of French internal politics'.[19] In West Africa the 1956 split between the CGT and the African unions led by Sekou Touré was stimulated by very similar attitudes.

The hold on African unions by the metropolitan bodies continued into the mid-1950s. Frenchmen justified it on two counts. The French unions themselves believed that their organizations were the obvious and normal agencies for the development of working-class unity. In 1946 the French Secretary-General of the WFTU, Louis Saillant, rejected the application of the newly-formed General Union of Tunisian Workers, which had links with Bourguiba's Neo-Destour party, because 'unity must be achieved around the traditional organization already integrated in the WFTU'.[20] There was a second, more sophisticated, reason.

African Trade Unions

The 1952 congress of the CGT-FO adopted a resolution affirming 'that the mission of the trade unions is to emancipate workers of all countries, its action being in the field of class struggle and not within the narrower and dangerous field of nationalism.'[21] It is curious that in the name of international class solidarity the French unions continued to insist on their role as imperial guardians. In this their position was remarkably close to that of British trade unionists, in particular the General Council of the TUC which in 1957 attacked the Ghana Industrial Relations Act as 'a departure from the conception of independent trade unionism held in this country'. Indeed the TUC went quite as far as the CGT and the CGT-FO, and regularly recorded its belief that the anti-imperialist struggle had little or nothing to do with the development of 'genuine trade union activity'.

In spite of the tendency for union and labour policies to be formulated in Paris, however, and the consequent development of an overall French system, the role of the local administration was central to French labour policy. Some 30 per cent of all wage-earners in French West Africa, 25 per cent in the Cameroons and Togoland, and 10 per cent in French Equatorial Africa were, by 1955, employed directly by the government, and an even larger percentage were employed in services (like the railways and building construction) where the government possessed part ownership. This made the administration much the most important employer and directly involved it in battle with unions because of its industrial role. Furthermore, by the powers granted to it in the Overseas Labour Code, the administration fixed minimum wage rates for unskilled labour, so directly influencing the structure of all wages throughout the area. Thus, because it employed a large proportion of wage-earners and was responsible for setting wage-rates, the administration was at the centre of all industrial relations disputes. Its industrial power was even further extended by the latitude it enjoyed in interpreting the Labour Code, for though the Code itself was far-sighted in its egalitarian principles and, to some extent, in its provisions, the actual details were vague, so that the administration, and in some cases individual officials, had the power to decide the mode of application. The effect of this was further to accentuate the

The Colonial Experience

political nature of trade union activity. If the most important focus of industrial action was the administration, it followed that effective results could hardly be achieved through negotiation with private industry. In spite of the ideological divisions of the trade union movement, French rule itself centralized the industrial relations machinery.

Belgian labour and labour relations policy in the Congo and Ruanda-Urundi was at once more stringent and more complex than that operating in French and British colonies. Conditions of recruitment, welfare, and wages were first legislatively laid down in the 1920s, and for the last forty years of their rule the Belgians continued to pay particular attention to questions of labour welfare. But from the start they carefully divided the main legislation into European and African categories. Four main laws controlled employment in government service and in private enterprise: one for higher government administrators (all European), one for lower government employees (all African), one for Africans and one for non-Africans in private employment. Although it was theoretically possible for Africans to fall under 'European' laws, by independence only five of them had been so classified. Conditions under the different laws varied enormously, though in the last few years of Belgian rule some attempts were made to bring them into closer harmony. The economic pressure for skilled African workers also tended to raise the treatment of these far above that stipulated in the Labour Contract Law. But the basic differences were startling. Wages for Africans were lower, employment contracts less secure, and hours of work longer. Social security was similarly categorized and for Africans was only introduced in the 1950s.

Despite the detailed legislation on both employment conditions and social welfare, moreover, conditions differed considerably from one part of the Congo to another. Katanga was undoubtedly better served than the rest of the Congo. In part this was due to the importance of mining (though, as the histories of Northern Rhodesia and South Africa indicate, this alone is not a sufficient reason), and in part to the policy forced on Union Minière de Haut Katanga (the major mining company) in the 1920s, when the cost of recruiting casual labour threatened to destroy the prospects of economic development. Because of the scarcity of labour in Katanga – due to the relatively sparse population there and the vast distances that workers had to travel to reach the mines – Union Minière decided in 1927 to encourage its workers to bring their families and settle near the mines. This involved providing housing, effective living conditions, wage inducements and social welfare. From the early 1930s, therefore, Union Minière became the pace-setter in Belgian welfare paternalism and always managed, because of its large capital resources, to command the market and appear several stages ahead of the rest of Congo in labour conditions. But even in Katanga conditions were hardly uniform. In 1956 casual workers earned up to 2/– a day; semi-skilled workers, 4/3; and skilled workers, 19/–.

If it made some attempts to impose standard – but segregated – patterns on work and welfare conditions, in industrial relations the Belgian government was autocratic and ruthless. European unions were authorized by decree in 1921, but these, like unions in Southern Africa, strongly resisted African unionism. Africans were not allowed to organize until 1946, and even then they were subjected to severe restrictions. Only those who had been employed in the same profession for three years were allowed to organize at all; the unions themselves were confined to local crafts or industries and forbidden to federate even on a provincial level; the local government authority was given power to inspect all union records, files and accounts, could attend any union meeting, and could insist that the union exclude any person from its proceedings. There was very little scope for unions to negotiate with employers on anything significant, and none of the labour laws included collective bargaining clauses. It is therefore not surprising that, in spite of having one of the largest wage-earning proportions in any African labour force, the Congo was slow to develop effective trade unions. Such organization as there was came under the control of the Belgian trade union centres. In particular the Catholic Confédération des Syndicats Chrétiens (CSC) organized union affiliates, but it was not until 1957, when unions were at last allowed by law to federate, that trade unionism in the Congo began to develop.

The Colonial Experience

One substantial all-African union, the Association du Personnel Indigène de la Colonie (a government employees' union), was formed in 1947, to act as a semi-official federation and political pressure group. The Belgian unions themselves assumed the representation of the Congolese in international bodies, and no African was delegated to attend the ILO, ICFTU, or IFCTU until 1959.

In every possible way the Belgians maintained absolute control over the Congolese workers. Wages and conditions were determined by central laws; labour and local authorities had absolute power of intervention; and unions had very little freedom of action. Even the two decrees of 1957 did not remove all important restrictions on organization. To be members of unions, workers had to have at least six years of schooling, to be eighteen years of age, and to have worked for at least three years. Political activity by unions was banned, and every union had to obtain government authority to operate. The procedure for negotiation and wage settlement was elaborate; but, contrary to earlier decrees, strikes in private industry were permitted after negotiations had been exhausted. Government employees themselves were still forbidden to strike. Moreover, wage policy was still strictly controlled by the government. It was not until a Leopoldville meeting in 1959 between Belgian trade unionists and the major business interests that private industry so much as recognized the rights of unions to organize and represent workers, and this in an ambiguous protocol that no Africans signed. To the end the Belgians attempted to retain the paternalist structure that had marked the previous forty years of Congolese history.

In both the British and French systems – despite differences in emphasis over the structure of trade unionism (the British in theory advocated and in practice encouraged 'grass roots' unions, while the French tended to promote centralized federations) – the administrative results were similar. Throughout West, Central and East Africa the governments became the centre of industrial dispute, and, with very few exceptions (Nigeria and Senegal are the most significant), the development of effective trade unions necessitated a united front with a large

African Trade Unions

measure of central control by the federal bodies. It would be facile to argue that this was the only factor behind centralization, but it clearly played a leading role. The Belgian system, with even greater administrative control and tighter restrictions, defeated itself: there was no African *élite* ready to assume responsibility, and no effective trade union federation on which a national labour policy might be built (at independence there were no fewer than five federations). In all cases, if the failure to introduce European-type trade unions was marked, the causes of that failure lay as much in the intentions and the practice of European administrations as in any suitability of the European pattern for an African context.

Chapter 2: Notes

1. E. Bustin, 'The Congo', in G. Carter (ed), *Five African States*, Pall Mall, 1964, p. 26.
2. Quoted in C. Legum, *Congo Disaster*, Penguin, 1962, p. 30.
3. B. Davidson, *The African Awakening*, Cape, 1956, p. 75.
4. Stephen H. Roberts, *The History of French Colonial Policy*, Cass, 1963, p. 350.
5. Elliot J. Berg, 'French West Africa', in W. Galenson (ed), *Labour and Economic Development*, John Wiley, 1959, p. 194.
6. Elliot J. Berg, *Recruitment of a Labour Force in Sub-Saharan Africa*, Unpublished Ph.D. thesis, Harvard University, Cambridge, Mass., 1960, pp. 139–40.
7. Quoted in T. M. Yesufu, *An Introduction to Industrial Relations in Nigeria*, O.U.P., 1962, p. 8.
8. Quoted in J. Woddis, *Africa – the Roots of Revolt*, Lawrence and Wishart, 1960, p. 50.
9. Quoted in Norman Leys, *Kenya*, London, 1925, p. 186. The importance of the myth of the backward sloping supply curve of labour is discussed by Elliot J. Berg in 'Backward Sloping Labour Supply Functions in Dual Economies – The African Case', *Quarterly Journal of Economics*, Vol. 75, pp. 468–92.
10. Lord Lugard, *Political Memoranda*, H.M.S.O., 1918, p. 243.
11. *Tanganyika Labour Department Report*, 1928, Dar-es-Salaam, para 7.
12. R. H. Tawney, *Religion and the Rise of Capitalism*, (Holland Memorial Lectures 1922), Penguin, 1938, p. 267.
13. Quoted in B. C. Roberts, *Labour in the Tropical Territories of the Commonwealth*, London School of Economics, 1964, p. 176.
14. The 'Passfield Memorandum', quoted in W. Bowen, *Colonial Trade Unions*, Fabian Society, 1954, p. 4.
15. Georges Fischer, 'Trade Unions and Decolonisation', *Présence Africaine*, Nos. 34–5, p. 153.
16. T. Mboya, *Freedom and After*, Deutsch, 1963, p. 31.
17. W. Elkan, *Migrants and Proletarians*, O.U.P., 1961, p. 61.

18. W. A. Warmington, *An African Trade Union*, London, 1960, p. 126.
19. Quoted in Fischer, op. cit., p. 136.
20. Quoted ibid., p. 139.
21. Quoted ibid., p. 137.

3 Industrialization and Race in South Africa

In contrast to the history of labour policies in the rest of Africa – which demonstrates the growing power of African politicians over labour legislation as well as over the whole administrative apparatus – the history of South Africa reveals the reverse, the development from a limited African political participation to his total exclusion. But it is much more than that. For it also registers the growth of the only major industrial nation in Africa and consequently offers some of the most important lessons in the continent's labour evolution.

This history falls into two convenient parts – the early industrializing era when South Africa was still a 'developing country', and later when she emerged as one of the few countries in the world with a net *per capita* income of over $300 a year, almost double that of Ghana, her nearest African competitor. During the 'transitional' period of economic growth, an unplanned capitalist economy with minimum government interference in the market mechanism was the main characteristic of policy, as it was in nearly all countries at the time. Though the first quarter of the twentieth century did see an increasing number of discriminatory laws to restrict these *laissez-faire* tendencies, on the whole the market was supreme and allowed the growth of a large African labour force (alongside a mass of 'poor whites') assigned – like the developing working class in Europe and the United States – the unskilled jobs and given little chance of promotion or responsibility. The emergence of a small African middle class did little to correct the basic racial imbalance; most of the middle class jobs were outside the main 'European' sector and were created by Africans to provide services and local commerce for themselves. Inexorably the growth of an urban proletariat continued, despite increasing

African Trade Unions

discrimination in the second quarter of the century. Even after the Labour-Nationalist Pact Government had introduced its 'civilized' labour policy in 1924, in part to deal with the 'poor white' problem, the rapid growth of the economy, especially after 1933, demanded an ever greater extension of the labour force. With insufficient whites available to take all the new jobs, the industrial prosperity brought by the Second World War mopped up the remaining 'poor white' surplus – African recruitment continued, and until the triumph of militant Afrikanerdom in 1948, most of the discriminatory laws were at some stage or other disregarded by employers eager to improve the efficiency of their enterprises. But after 1948 the situation changed dramatically. Using the foundations laid by the labour laws of the Pact and subsequent administrations, the Nationalists introduced measures that subjected the workers to increasing restrictions. The era of the large private mining corporations – who up to 1948 largely shaped the operation (if not the legislation) of labour policy – was replaced by state capitalism and the subjugation of all labour policy to the rigid doctrine of white supremacy.

Against this background the trade unions in South Africa have played out one of the most tragic periods in world labour history. The early years were marked by increasing white organization, modelled on British experience and in some instances (notably the Amalgamated Engineering Union and the Amalgamated Society of Woodworkers) started by British immigrants and affiliated to British unions. At the same time there was little activity among African workers until the emergence in the 1920s of the Industrial and Commercial Workers Union of Africa (ICU) which became, in the manner of other early unions in Africa or indeed Robert Owen's Grand National Consolidated in Britain, an omnibus political-social-industrial union, with a spectacular rise and a no less spectacular fall. The failure of the ICU and the election of a Labour-Nationalist coalition government, both in the 1920s, are probably the most important events in South African trade union history, because after 1930, although the white unions increased in numbers and effectiveness, they were unable to create a united central organization, and although several of them included Africans, Coloured and

Industrialization and Race in South Africa

Indians in their membership, there was also a powerful parallel movement to create separate segregated unions for non-whites. The efforts by Africans and some of the whites to find progressive solutions were submerged in measures introduced by the Nationalist government after 1948 to prevent white-African collaboration and make African union organization virtually impossible. For eighteen years a constantly deepening terror has worked the almost complete destruction of serious industrial relations.

Against the background of industrialization and the ever-present, hardening realities of race relations, it is necessary to pick out the significant features of trade union history: the search for a system of industrial relations in a developing country, an African attempt to come to terms with industry and evolve representative institutions, a white search for political, industrial and racial identity, and the future of capitalism in a plural society. In the years before 1948 there were many occasions when flexible solutions seemed possible and industrial relations by the dictate of a racial caste at least not inevitable. The ultimate decision was made by the overwhelmingly white South African electorate when, on a minority vote in 1948, it chose a government dedicated to racial dictatorship. But in the history of the South African labour movement there were times when that decision was brought a little nearer, when the movement itself made fatal choices, adopting wilfully a course that would lead to its own destruction. In these choices there were many external influences – the Nationalist Party and its controlling secret society, the Broederbond; the Communist Party of the Soviet Union; the British TUC; the hypocrisies of the United Party government under Smuts; the well-meaning activities of liberals and clerics – but the dramatic failures of the labour movement itself, the economic and social factors behind decisions and indecisions, were crucial.

The origins of trade unionism in South Africa were in many ways not unlike those in the French North African territories. As the French, so the British settlers established local branches of metropolitan unions in the late nineteenth century and retained close contact with the parent bodies. The pattern of

African Trade Unions

union organization in South Africa accordingly resembled the British very closely. Even when unions were established without British connexions, their constitutions and objectives were very closely linked to British models, and regular contact was maintained with individual British unions and the TUC.

From the outset there was an uphill struggle for recognition, and as the mines began to employ large numbers of Africans – and, for a short time in the first decade of the century, Chinese – this struggle became increasingly related to job security for the growing numbers of European immigrants. The racial issue therefore assumed an importance within the industrial conflict at an early date. The formation of the white Transvaal Mine Workers Union (later the South African MWU) in 1902 set off the first in a series of very bitter campaigns against the mining companies that marked industrial relations up to the passing of the Industrial Conciliation Act in 1924. A major strike of Witwatersrand miners in 1907 was followed by the repressive Transvaal Industrial Disputes Prevention Act of 1909, which tried to outlaw strikes. But in 1913 one of the most serious disputes in South African history – on trade union recognition – produced strikes over the whole region of the Reef and led to a judicial commission which recommended recognition of the SAMNU by both the Chamber of Mines and the government, as well as establishing a procedure for dealing with future industrial disputes. Over the next few months further major disputes resulted in the calling of a general strike in 1914 which seriously affected the miners and the railways, and parliament replied by passing an Act of Indemnity and a Riotous Assemblies Act which were designed to prohibit strikes in the public services and make peaceful picketing illegal. In spite of these measures, however, the rapid development of industry during the First World War put the unions in a powerful position and resulted in greater recognition. The Chamber of Mines as well as several municipal authorities and private companies accepted the 'closed shop' principle, and wages rose dramatically. Between 1915 and 1918 the unions increased their membership from 10,538 to 77,819.

But the end of the war brought with it even greater unrest

Industrialization and Race in South Africa

than before, this time involving non-white workers as well. A rapid rise in the cost of living swallowed the war-time wage gains, and the gap between job-secure workers and the rest dangerously widened. Unemployment and the sudden growth in the numbers of 'poor whites' led to wide-scale depression. African workers, without effective unions or organization, went on strike in several places, and discontent mounted till 40,000 African miners came out in February 1920. Various attempts to organize Africans, including the Industrial Workers of Africa started by S. P. Bunting and Ivon Jones on the lines of the American International Workers of the World, came to nothing; but in 1919 Clemens Kadalie, a worker from Nyasaland, formed the Industrial and Commercial Workers Union of Africa, which became the centre of African political and industrial struggle for the next decade. Then, before the full impact of the ICU's organization began to be felt, the white workers were swept into one of the most dramatic events in South African history.

Although the trade unions had succeeded in gaining recognition during the war, the earlier efforts of Smuts and Botha to kill the unions had led to a widespread militancy among white workers which the depressed economic conditions of the peace further excited. The Chamber of Mines decided to employ larger numbers of badly paid African workers and in 1922 announced that it proposed to repudiate the earlier agreement of 1915 with the white mineworkers, redefine the ratio of white to black workers, and reduce the wages of white miners. The result was an immediate strike in the Transvaal collieries, spreading to the gold mines and the Victoria Falls power station. Within nine days a general strike broke out on the Witwatersrand, lasting for eight weeks and followed by a fortnight of armed revolt. Led by a group of Afrikaner nationalist 'commandos', who created a paramilitary organization, and a 'Council of Action' made up of dissident unionists expelled from the Mineworkers Union and some members of the Communist Party, the strikers sang the 'Red Flag' in English to the tune of the old Transvaal Republic's anthem '*Die Volkslied*' and marched under a banner which proclaimed 'Workers of the World Unite and Fight for a White South Africa'. Despite attempts by the Council of Action to prevent the strike from becoming a crude racist campaign, striker commandos began attacking Africans and Indians indiscriminately, and serious clashes occurred in February and March. The few trade unionists and left-wing politicians who wanted the strike to be a struggle of all workers (white and black) against the Chamber of Mines were trampled in the stampede of poor whites who were claiming their racial rights. Nationalist politicians appeared on the strike platforms alongside Communists, and at a mass rally in Johannesburg on February five strikers overwhelmingly passed a resolution calling for a Nationalist-Labour *coup d'état* and the proclamation of a South African Republic. The Nationalist leadership, prepared to jump on any racist band-waggon but not ready for revolution, rejected the proposal and abandoned the workers to their fate. In mid-March Smuts called out aircraft and artillery to smash the strike, killing 230 workers and injuring hundreds more. The white worker rebellion was crushed, and the Nationalists scuttled back to constitutional politics.

In 1923 the Nationalist leadership formed a pact with the Labour Party, and at the 1924 election a Labour-Nationalist Coalition was swept to power, pledged to oppose 'capitalist and monopolistic domination' and to introduce a 'civilized labour policy'. Thus a Nationalist 'Socialism', formed by a merger of Afrikaner white supremacy dogmas with English-derived socialism, came into being, the white workers, mesmerized by slogans, preferring to promote racialism than make any radical attack on the fundamentals of the society. In 1925 the Mines and Works (Colour Bar) Act was passed, making the 'right' to do skilled work dependent on race and colour; wage-fixing legislation followed; and, even though the late 1920s saw unprecedented economic growth, thousands of Africans were thrown out of work or had their wages reduced.

Due to the rapid growth of the South African economy, however, and a series of tactical blunders by the Nationalist government, the restrictive measures had only a partial effect. Africans were promoted to responsible jobs, and some schemes for industrial training were started. More important still, at the same time that Hertzog and Creswell (leader of the Labour Party)

Industrialization and Race in South Africa

were planning their remarkable alliance, the ICU was gathering support, and it looked as if the balance of forces in South Africa would be more evenly matched than the growing strength of the white racists might suggest. As early as 1921, Hertzog, an inveterate opportunist, had donated funds to the ICU, apparently out of respect for its potential strength. But the Rand Rebellion and the 1924 election changed all that, and by 1928 Hertzog was resigning from office as Prime Minister to rid himself of a Cabinet colleague who had dared to negotiate with the ICU. Such was the uncertain reception given to the first major African workers' movement to appear in South Africa. The ICU grew rapidly in strength, partly as a messianic movement under the absolute control of Clemens Kadalie, moving from province to province in the first half of the decade and gaining the rooted attention of all – with the careful approval of some – white politicians and newspapers. By 1927 it was riding high. Kadalie himself was being fêted by the British TUC as the representative of over 100,000 workers, and the ICU was applying for affiliation to the (white) South African Trade Union Congress. But by 1930 the whole organization, with its mass enthusiasm and support, was in fragments, with distrust, disillusionment and apathy its results! Why did it fail? The reasons go far towards explaining the plight of African workers today.

The beginnings of the ICU, at a time when industry was expanding and political militancy a marked feature of white as well as African workers, were as auspicious as could reasonably be expected. In spite of the spreading racialism among white workers under Nationalist influence, the lines of battle were by no means clearly drawn, and many whites still thought of industrial conflict mainly in terms of workers and employers. African workers, too, had not yet been involved in much organization, and their struggle with whites was generally local. Out of the huge mass of African workers strong leadership was needed to create a powerful organization that would lay the basis for a transformation of the African place in industry and hence the whole political system. But the ICU foundered, mainly because it could not decide whether to pursue a militant or a 'moderate' role – a problem that affected unions in other areas of white

African Trade Unions

settlement at one time or another until 'solved' by the outbreak of direct (sometimes military) confrontation as in Algeria, Kenya and Morocco. Kadalie promoted his organization by promising to raise the dignity of the African and his standard of living, and as a result attracted not only thousands of workers but even Africans in the professions. Some 250,000 joined during the 1920s, and like Marcus Garvey's Negro Improvement Association in the U.S.A., a large amount of money was subscribed and great expectations were raised. But by 1927 the results were meagre, the money had been misspent, membership was dropping off, and Kadalie was being urged from two sides to review his policy. The left – backed by the Communists, including five out of the ICU's National Council of eleven – wanted more positive action and a thorough overhauling of the ICU machinery. The right – supported by many liberals who wanted a 'respectable' organization, and the government which aimed to smash the ICU's effectiveness – urged caution and the expulsion of the Communists. In December 1926 Communists were banned from the ICU altogether, on a majority vote of one in the National Council, and though some members resigned their Communist party membership rather than leave the ICU, the purge marked the beginning of the end. Left-wing efforts to get the ICU to adopt a more militant policy were frustrated by demagogy from Kadalie, and by the end of 1927 various leaders were making a bid for the autonomy of their provincial sections. In early 1928 the large Natal section disaffiliated from the central ICU, to be followed by a series of splits and secessions across the country. The arrival of a British adviser, W. G. Ballinger, in July 1928 hardly made things better. Within a short time Kadalie himself had left the ICU along with most of the remaining members to form an Independent ICU, leaving Ballinger with the creaking old organization, an abundance of debts and the ICU journal. Ballinger's policy had been even more moderate than Kadalie's, with the result that Kadalie now moved once again to the left and sought support from the Communists. But it was too late. The failings of Kadalie as a union or political leader were now too obvious, and the Communists turned their attention to creating unions outside the ICU.

Industrialization and Race in South Africa

From 1926 the Communist Party, excluded from the ICU and measuring the frustrations caused by Kadalie's efforts, initiated an intensive campaign to organize African workers. Repelled in the mining industries, it helped to start unions in the laundry, baking, clothing and furniture industries, and in 1928 a Non-European Trade Union Federation was established. At the same time the S.A. TUC, which was composed almost entirely of white workers, began to review its policies towards Africans and recommended to its affiliated unions in 1929 'the enrolment of all employees in their respective unions, irrespective of race or colour ... or, alternatively, that a policy of parallel branches in the unions be adopted'.[1] Reconstituted a few years later as the Trades and Labour Council, it urged the government in 1939 to recognize non-white trade unions on the same basis as other workers' organizations.

By the outbreak of the Second World War, despite the failure of the ICU and the confusion caused in South Africa by the 'hard line' policy of the Russian Communists (which effectively killed new attempts to create a 'popular front' movement based on Africans and the white left) the prospects of African trade unionism looked distinctly good. In 1939 the government made its first offer of 'administrative recognition' for non-white unions, and renewed it in 1941, while in 1942 the Minister of Labour in Smuts's wartime Cabinet, Walter Madeley, leader of the Labour Party, opened the first annual conference of the new Council of Non-European Trade Unions. With twenty-five unions and 37,000 workers represented there, the government clearly considered that African labour had reached a new stage of organization and consequently made efforts to win its support. But the offer of 'administrative recognition' was rejected; African unions wanted full, statutory recognition on the same basis as the white unions. Since many employers were already negotiating with the non-white unions, there seemed little point in accepting a government measure which was at best timid, and at worst an attempt to convert African unions into an arm of the state with political activities subjected to administrative control. Besides, by 1942 the unions were gaining rapidly in strength and numbers. At the end of the war over 100,000 Africans belonged to trade unions – their interest stimulated by the rapid rise in the cost of living, the favourable reports of several government commissions, and the recovery of the Communist Party from its disastrous upheavals in the 1930s. Not only were unions created in the public services and distributive industries, but an African Union of Mineworkers began to have some impact on the Rand. With the coming of peace, the strong multi-racial element in the unions appeared to be winning, and the evolution of a more balanced system of industrial relations looked at least possible.

But the growth of African unionism had been accompanied by the increasing activity of militant Afrikaner Nationalists within the trade union movement. As early as 1937 Afrikaner organizations had set out to infiltrate and dominate the unions; a Dutch Reformed Church Commission on 'Communism and the Trade Unions' had warned against the activities of Communists in the unions and called for increased action by Afrikaner unionists, especially in the mining industry. Communism was a 'threat to Christian civilization because it (a) propagates a bitter class struggle, and (b) agitates strongly for equality between Black and White.'[2]

In 1939 a Nationalist conference decided to set up a labour section aimed at eliminating 'foreign influences' from the trade unions and at preventing the Afrikaans-speaking worker from constituting a separate class outside organized Afrikanerdom. This in turn spawned the White Workers' Protection Society, dedicated to job reservation, apartheid in unions, and avoidance of 'undesirable contact' between white and non-white workers. Among the leaders of the Protection Society were several men who were later to become Cabinet Ministers in the Nationalist government, including Jan de Klerk, B. J. Schoeman, and Dr N. Diedrichs. The creation of a Nasionale Raad van Trustees in 1936 had provided funds for an offensive against the Mineworkers' Union, and, led by Dr Albert Hertzog and a group known as the 'Reformers', this offensive had rapidly made inroads into the organization of the union. Nationalist nominees were able to take over strategic offices, and in 1939 Charlie Harris, Secretary of the Union, was assassinated by an Afrikaner youth. In spite of a government commission in 1941 which found that the Reformers 'constitute a subversive movement which is detrimental to the interests of the mineworkers', the Nationalist activity continued, and by the end of the war the Reformers were in a strong enough position openly to challenge the Mineworkers' Union leadership. Under the secretaryship of B. Brodrick and the presidency of Paul Visser, the white miners' union had become a top-heavy bureaucracy, having little contact with the miners. It was therefore comparatively easy for the Nationalists to displace the leadership with a campaign of militant, if spurious, slogans and promises. When, in 1947, the Reformers led a seven-week strike against the Union leadership, it was clear that the end was near. The government ordered elections to be held for officials, and candidates of the Nationalist United Mineworkers' Committee were successful. D. E. Ellis, one of the workers sponsored by the Nasionale Raad van Trustees, was elected secretary in place of Brodrick.

Alongside the campaign in the Mineworkers' Union, other attempts were made to gain control of unions where there was a majority of Afrikaner workers but where non-Afrikaners were in control. The most important of these were the Garment Workers' Union, the Food and Canning Workers' Union, and the Building Workers' Union, and similar tactics to those employed in the Mineworkers' Union were used to try and unseat the union leadership. But in these three instances, mainly because the structure of the unions was more democratic and the leadership (E. S. Sachs, Ray Alexander and Piet Huyser) more vigilant, the attempts were not successful until the Nationalist Government itself introduced legislation in the early 1950s to remove uncongenial officers from their posts. In the Garment Workers Union, various attempts were made to intimidate the members, including personal assault, violent propaganda and the use of armed gangs to disrupt meetings. In 1948 a meeting at Johannesburg was wrecked by a mob which stormed through the doors, assaulted men and women, and broke furniture. A government commission (appointed to investigate the union's affairs as well as the disturbances) attempted to discredit the union leadership and administration, but without significant effect. Sachs continued in office until he was forced to resign under the Suppression of Communism Act.

And so the growth of trade unions, already existing under difficult enough conditions and with sufficient problems of their own, was attacked by white racists, striving to control the whole structure in the interest of Afrikaner dominion. By 1947 the violence and intrigue were having their effect on the Trades and Labour Council. Although a proposal to exclude Africans from membership was defeated that year, several unions controlled by Nationalists resigned in consequence from the Council, and in 1949 the Council itself proposed the setting up of a Co-ordinating Council of African Trade Unions under its own guidance and control. This effectively separated the African unions from the white ones and initiated the decline towards trade union apartheid. To make matters worse, in 1953 the British TUC, whose activities in South Africa had never been very constructive, volunteered its help. A delegation (James Crawford and Ernest Bell) visited the Union late that year and recommended that 'in the greater interest and urgent necessity of unity' the Council should

> temporize upon such basic principles and agree to the membership of the Council being restricted to registered unions, whilst at the same time leaving individual organizations in the Council to organize African workers in parallel unions if they so wished.[3]

This remarkable proposal – that in the interests of unity, apartheid should be applied to the trade union movement – was typical of the TUC's 'temporizing' attitude to unions in the whole of Africa at the time, and demonstrated a total inability to grasp the essentially political nature of the industrial struggle in Africa.

The TUC's report was made the occasion for the final reorganization of the Trades and Labour Council. The Council was killed in favour of a South Africa Trade Union Council, which excluded Africans and any union whose membership was open to Africans. Explaining that they had to accept the presence of a new political order in South Africa, the unions involved were ready to surrender their principles – or such of them as

Industrialization and Race in South Africa

they had left – in favour of a social system that promised them little or nothing in concrete terms. In fact, the white 'unity', for which so much had been sacrificed, did not materialize. The Nationalist-dominated unions refused to join the new federation and remained apart in three separate federations of their own: the Co-ordinating Council of S.A. Trade Unions, the S.A. Federation of Trade Unions, and the Federal Consultative Council of South African Railways and Harbours Staff Associations. Then, in March 1955, a new federation, the S.A. Congress of Trade Unions, was founded from African unions and unions with African members. But the chances of success for this new federation were slight, in a country where the largest white unions were prepared to sink their ideals in compromise with an increasingly fascist government. Without trade union unity, the government was able to exploit the differences in the working class and rapidly bring all unions, white or non-white, under its control. By 1965 there were four main union federations: the Trade Union Congress of South Africa, a successor to the Trade Union Council, with 177,701 members – on friendly terms with the British TUC and the United States AFL-CIO; the South African Confederation of Labour, grouping all the pro-government unions, with 155,000 members; the S.A. Congress of Trade Unions, which in 1961 claimed 53,323 members of whom 38,791 were Africans, but which lost over fifty of its leaders in 1963–4 under orders prohibiting them from doing all trade union work; and the Federation of Free African Trade Unions with 14,000 members, an ICFTU affiliate. Some of FOFATUSA's members were also affiliated to TUCSA, which formed an African Affairs group in 1962 to organize African trade unions. The total number of trade union members in South Africa is around 450,000, of whom barely 3 per cent are African, 18 per cent are Coloured, and 6 per cent are Asian. In the mining industry, where over 560,000 of the 636,000 workers are African, the mining unions represent less than 10 per cent of the miners. Such, after nearly eighteen years of Nationalist government, is the state of industrial relations in South Africa.

It only remains to outline the administrative measures introduced by the government to curb the unions and prevent

African Trade Unions

Africans from organizing. One of the first acts of the Nationalist government elected in 1948 was to appoint an Industrial Legislation Commission to investigate the working of all industrial laws and workers' organizations. Reporting in 1951 this Commission recommended that white and non-white workers should be organized in separate trade unions, and that a National Labour Board should be established to coordinate wages and other conditions of employment. But it was reluctant to recommend job reservation, the introduction of compulsory arbitration and the abolition of the closed shop. In addition it proposed a measure of recognition for African unions 'in separate legislation from that applicable to other races'. The government, unhappy about some of the more 'liberal' recommendations in the report, accepted only those that suited its objectives. Instead of either banning or legalizing African unions, it decided that African unions had no standing and would not be legally recognized. This gave it greater flexibility of action; with no rights granted to Africans and no open suppression, the authorities had the advantage of surveillance without conceding any function or security.

Efforts to frustrate African trade unionism included the prevention of African meetings by limiting the right to gather and eliminating the places where meetings could be held, by outlawing strikes, by providing that African unions (whenever the government thought it fit) could be banned as 'Communist', and by removing union leaders from office under various pretexts. In addition the government, under the Native Labour (Settlement of Disputes) Act of 1953, established an intricate system for the settlement of disputes, involving a Central Native Labour Board, with members (white only) appointed by the Minister of Labour; Regional Native Labour Committees (with a white chairman and African members appointed by the Minister); and works committees elected by workers at their work location but supervised by the Native Labour Officer for the area. The effect of this procedure is to make the Native Labour Officers supreme in handling disputes and to prevent the growth of African representative organizations. The Suppression of Communism Act, 1950, has also been used with unfailing regularity to prevent the growth of unions. Successive union leaders have been removed from office in terms of absurdly loose provisions, and the unions themselves have either been disbanded or prevented from holding meetings as suspect organizations. By using such methods the government in 1963-4 sought to destroy the only major trade union federation, SACTU, which had a high proportion of African members.

The failure of Africans to develop trade unions over the past few years is accordingly not surprising. Without any form of recognition under the Industrial Conciliation Act of 1957, and subjected to endless measures of suppression and intimidation, African workers have been reluctant to join unions and endanger their jobs, while the system of migrant labour, ruthlessly enforced by the government, has stunted the growth of stable occupational groups which union organizations would hope for their strongest support. Because of the great pressure for work from the rural reserves, employers are able to keep wages low and maintain a rapid turnover of labour. To be sure of a job and so continued residence in an urban area requires docility and a safe absence from any collective action. It is therefore scarcely strange that in 1960 there were only thirty-three strikes involving 2,199 workers; and in 1961, twenty-six involving 1,427.

With such harsh control, it might be concluded that the South African government is producing exactly the kind of industrial relations that it has sought. After all, South Africa is relatively free of major industrial disputes; economic growth continues, and wages, even if enormously different from race to race, sporadically increase. Yet there are many menacing signs. The principle of job reservation, originally introduced in the mining industry, extended in 1951 to the building trades and in 1957 theoretically to all industries, is steadily being eroded by the development of the economy. It is hardly possible to acquire all the skilled workers needed for an industrialized country of seventeen million people from a privileged sector of three and a half million whites. In the expanding metal and mineral industry, employing 250,000 workers and accounting for nearly half of the country's industrial activity, orders reserving jobs for specific races have been postponed; in gold mining, an experiment allowing Africans to do certain supervisory jobs has been undertaken; in road-making Africans drive more than half of the earth-moving and other machinery. Even in government-operated services, like the railways, some Africans have taken over semi-skilled work formerly reserved for whites. In Capetown the Coloured have made remarkable advances in the past few years, annexing most jobs up to that of manager. The declining productivity of the white worker (in ratio to economic growth) is causing anxiety among employers, who have declared that industry 'will have to rely increasingly on (white) recruits of a poor type as far as mental capacity and educational standards are concerned'.[4] Over the next four years the building industry expects its labour needs to increase by 52 per cent. Such are the erosions of a rigid apartheid régime in industry that economic growth has caused and must continue to cause. With only 0.1 per cent of the economically active population educated to matriculation standards, the government is faced either with abandoning its futile education and apprentice schemes or courting economic stagnation and even disaster. Having taken so much in the regulation of industrial conditions into its own hands, the Nationalist government has to decide whether to jettison its racial policies or accept the inevitable and allow those policies to lead the country away from economic growth. It would not have been the first time that a country, capable of ensuring general prosperity, preferred to allocate privileges and high earnings to an *élite* which had ceased to provide the drive necessary for expansion, and so instead declined into industrial mediocrity. Argentina and Chile are warnings from this century.

Meanwhile, industrial peace is preserved at a price. While the economy continues to grow without serious crisis, it may be possible for the government to dispense with unions. To do this it is encouraging employers to use the most modern personnel management techniques with their African workers – but as a way of preventing the growth of trade unionism, instead of as a complement to dynamic trade union activity. Higher wages are also being advocated as an incentive to increased African productivity and as a method of reducing the area of discontent. From all the evidence, however, Africans do not see their pre-

Industrialization and Race in South Africa

dicament as economic alone – though the wages are shrunken enough – but as social and political too. The periodic outbursts of protest – as in the events accompanying the Sharpeville shootings – demonstrate that wider social questions are at present more important than the size of the wage packet. This the government clearly recognizes; in the many statements made by Nationalist politicians on the reasons for not giving Africans trade union rights, fear of the political consequences looms largest. Most of the policies for containing industrial unrest are therefore desperate efforts to find an alternative that will maintain the Nationalist government in power. In making the effort a government which dedicates itself to anti-communism is building up an absolute state control that is beginning to rival Stalinism in its heyday. But it is unlikely that Stalin would have committed economic suicide in the interests of political principle; indeed, his overall policies demonstrated the reverse.

*

The history of labour in South Africa is important not only for its past effects both inside the country and outside – white unions in the Protectorates and Central Africa were all strongly influenced by the example of the South African unions, while the rise and fall of the ICU provided an important lesson for trade union and political movements elsewhere in Africa – but today the South African state demonstrates in an extreme form the problems of trade unions in a developing country. Many African states have chosen to bring the unions under government or party control, and some show almost as much hostility to the idea of trade unionism as does South Africa. The major lesson from South Africa is that if unions are to be subjected to party discipline, they must also be given an important say in the whole direction of the economy, while their structures must be democratic and be seen to operate democratically. If the government insists on controlling the unions without giving them a real place in the development of the country, the unions will cease to command the respect of the workers (even the white unions in South Africa now experience massive apathy from their members), and a discontented working class will attempt to improve its conditions by other methods. The government will either capitulate or be forced to take extreme repressive measures. In many respects the treatment of the unions is at the heart of the economic and political development of an industrializing country, and, for all its important idiosyncrasies, South Africa provides essential material for examination by other African countries faced with a growing working class.

Chapter 3: Notes

1. Quoted A. Hepple, *The African Worker in South Africa*, Africa Bureau, 1956, p. 7.
2. B. Bunting, *The Rise of the South African Reich*, Penguin, 1964, p. 254.
3. *Trade Unions in South Africa* – Report of TUC Delegation to South Africa, TUC Publications, 1954.
4. See: 'White Man's Country, A Survey of Southern Africa', *The Economist*, 7 August 1965, especially pp. xxv–xxvi.

4 The Rise of Trade Unionism in Africa

Trade unions developed in Africa as a response to five main stimulants: tribal associations, industrial conflicts, political campaigns, foreign labour movements, and labour administrations. In many instances the sources overlapped, but the distinctions are useful enough to indicate the problems of growth and, to some extent, the present organization of African unions.

The growth of tribal unions was closely related to the tribal 'improvement associations', and the tribal unions themselves were the first forms of organization to represent African workers. It appears from reports of British colonial labour advisers that some early trade unions were actually based on tribal units and included among their aims the provision of social services for people in a particular area, irrespective of whether they were wage-earners. They were also frequently confused with craft guilds, often operating within a tribal structure but providing services, regulating wages, making laws on apprentice schemes and guarding against unfair competition. These 'unions' as often as not were a spontaneous development within the indigenous African economy, possessing little relation to the payment of money. Their survival, as well as the existence of 'improvement' associations, subsequently provided difficulties for trade unions organizing on a national basis. Because they provided tangible benefits (even though they often charged higher dues than the unions did), it became difficult for workers to see the advantage of joining an organization that seemed to offer less. Further, as T. M. Yesufu has pointed out,

In the tribal union, for example, the worker can speak and be spoken to in a language he understands well, against a background of customs and traditions which he comprehends.... The worker feels that in the gathering of his tribal association he truly 'belongs'. In the trade union meeting on the other hand, matters are often discussed against an industrial and economic background which the worker hardly understands; the secretary of the trade union may be of a different tribe.[1]

If the 'improvement' association acted as a substitute union in the villages, in the towns a variation of tribal representation came into existence to meet the demands of industrialization. The clearest example of this was found in Northern Rhodesia, where elders were appointed by tribal chiefs to watch over the interests of tribesmen in the mines. The chiefs were themselves responsible for recruitment to the mines, and for some time they had absolute control over the selection of elders. But after 1940, partly due to Labour Department pressure, the elders were elected by the workers, though still on a tribal basis, and as such they continued to play some part in industrial disputes for several years. Their functions extended beyond industrial mediation, and they frequently acted as magistrates in personal disputes between tribesmen. Their position in the towns was, however, rapidly undermined by the growth of industrial attitudes among the miners. Boss Boys' Committees were formed in 1942, chosen across tribal groupings, and immediately began to express an independent workers' viewpoint. (Boss Boys were sub-foremen, each responsible for five or six workers.) Their brief existence – until about 1950 – acted as a transition stage to trade unionism, though it seems likely that unions would have emerged earlier but for the authoritarian attitudes of the management and government. As late as 1940 the Foster Commission considered that

The African worker in Northern Rhodesia is clearly not ready yet for trade unionism. His introduction to industrialism and industrial conditions is of a very recent date, too recent to admit of his intelligent participation in the more elaborate trades union system existing in Great Britain.

One of the reasons for the failure of the elder system was that it was too obviously an administrative convenience for management, reproducing many disadvantages of the tribal system without providing the advantages of close association and contact. Ethnic groups in towns survive as long as the tribal unit

African Trade Unions

appears to have greater meaning than urban and industrial life. As Georges Balandier noted in his study of Brazzaville,[2] most Congolese preferred not to join trade unions because these tended to be run by *élite* groups and were controlled by the administration. The same would seem to be true of quasi-ethnic associations subject to management or administrative supervision. The argument advanced by Balandier, that trade unions were also unpopular because they charged dues, does not seem to stand up to evidence in other areas. Both Yesufu in Nigeria and Comhaire-Sylvain in Leopoldville[3] noted that improvement associations required membership subscriptions, often higher than those demanded by unions. The distinction that Africans made between the two demands for money was almost certainly due to their appraisal of the relevance that the different kinds of union had to the day-to-day problems of workers. As industrialization developed and conflict with employers demanded more effective organization to deal with disputes, the need for trade unions became obvious, particularly to workers on long-term engagements. Some of the tribal associations accordingly transformed themselves into trade unions open to people from other tribes, and in some cases (for example, the Kenya Africa Drivers' Union) trade unions still active today have developed directly from tribally-based associations. In addition some craft guilds, particularly those catering for semi-skilled workers, often became the basis for a trade union or were absorbed by one which came to represent artisans.

But although tribal organizations contributed in some measure to trade union development they could hardly themselves form an important segment of trade unions because of the very nature of wage employment. Most labour locations recruited their workers from a variety of tribes and thus the prospects for tribal unionism were remote. Moreover, in the tensions that inevitably occurred between workers and employers, tribal organizations were powerless to act since they had little authority to negotiate with management. Most types of trade union, therefore, came into being out of a direct confrontation of workers and employers or else out of collusion between workers and politicians. In ways not dissimilar to the development of

The Rise of Trade Unionism in Africa

industrialization in Britain or France, the early protest organizations in Africa were spontaneous in their appearance. While there were no trade unions, sudden outbreaks of violence or strikes were characteristic demonstrations of discontent. As early as 1874 a strike took place in Freetown harbour; in 1919–20 South Africa saw a whole series that brought the docks and railways to a halt. Across West Africa in the inter-war years railway strikes occurred in Sierra Leone (1919 and 1926), Nigeria (1921), and among the Thiés-Niger railway workers in 1925. In 1930 serious strikes and disturbances occurred among the mineworkers in the Gold Coast and among dockers at Bathurst. In Kenya a general strike organized by the Young Kikuyu Association led to the massacre of some 150 people by the King's African Rifles. In Northern Rhodesia major strikes on the Copperbelt in 1935 and 1940 provoked a commission of inquiry and a report on labour conditions by the Colonial Secretary's Labour Adviser. All of these strikes, and many lesser ones throughout Africa, were organized by groups of workers without formal unions. In some territories, notably Kenya and Northern Rhodesia, tribal associations seem to have played some part in organizing the strikers, but generally the strikes were supported by an ethnic cross-section of workers.

These strikes did not automatically lead to the creation of trade unions, mainly because of the attitude displayed by management and the administration. Industrial agitation among Africans was not only disapproved of, it was frequently identified with rebellion, even though no formal method of negotiation existed. The Governor of Sierra Leone described the 1926 railway strike as 'a revolt against the Government by its own servants'. Troops were summoned; strikers and demonstrators shot; strike leaders imprisoned, exiled or at least sacked; and any tribal association connected with the disturbances was banned or dissolved. The growth of African industrial organization in any form was outside the comprehension of most Governors, while most European employers in Africa had hardly progressed beyond early nineteenth century European attitudes. Indeed many of them seemed to be in Africa because they had failed to keep pace with changes in their native countries. Labour in

African Trade Unions

Africa was cheap and, as they hoped, docile; they wanted to keep it that way. Certainly most of them preferred to think of Africans as naturally belonging to the tribal compound; an African 'industrial man' seemed a contradiction in terms. If there were any traders or industrialists who realized that economic growth depended on the more efficient use of labour, they were soon disillusioned by administrators whose 'dominant vision of African development ... was of an agricultural society, based on the village, technically improved, wisely guided by more educated chiefs and later by democratic counsellors.'[4]

It is not surprising, therefore, that when the British and French colonial offices changed course during the late 1930s, the local employers and administrators resisted as far as they were able. In the short run – in Algeria, Tunisia, Morocco, the Ivory Coast, Kenya, Tanganyika, Northern and Southern Rhodesia – the settler *élite* was able to sabotage all efforts at permitting the growth of African trade unions and the introduction of industrial consultation. In other colonies, where embryo unions to some extent already existed when legislation permitting them was passed, the battle for recognition was less intense, though practical recognition (at the level of negotiation) took many years to achieve, and in many cases had to wait till independence.

The most important difference that trade union legislation made in many colonies was to remove the unions from the level of spontaneous, 'guerrilla' struggle to more institutionalized, if administratively suspect organizations. But because of the antagonism of administrators and employers, it was many years before unions in some colonial territories were able at last to emerge from the twilight world of semi-legality. In the British colonies, all unions had to be registered and were subject to administrative approval, and these provisions were used, particularly in East Africa, to prevent the legal recognition of some unions that had already established a following among the workers. In Kenya for twenty years after the Passfield Memorandum, the Labour Department conducted a vendetta against unions organized by Asians and Africans. Although it registered a Labour Trade Union of East Africa in 1937 and an African

The Rise of Trade Unionism in Africa

Workers' Federation in 1947, it succeeded in banning both because they subsequently helped to organize strikes in Mombasa. An East African TUC founded in 1949, after the Labour Trade Union had been de-registered and union leaders banished, was refused registration, while in the same year a Trade Union Registration Ordinance, a Compulsory Labour Act and a Deportation Ordinance were introduced to give the government stronger powers of control over unions and workers. (The Deportation Ordinance was aimed at militant Indian workers; the President of the EATUC was an Indian.) In 1950 the leaders of the AWF and the EATUC were arrested, and a general strike in Nairobi was crushed by armed police and a show of strength from the Army and R.A.F., who between them covered the city with armoured cars, trucks, bren-gun carriers and planes. Three hundred workers were arrested and some of the union leaders sentenced to 'banishment' or terms of imprisonment for declaring illegal strikes. The attitude of the Labour Department is best described in its own words.[5] After noting the 'striking progress' in industrial relations – 'In nearly every part of the colony groups of employers and employees were to be seen sitting down together every month for the purpose of attempting to understand each other' – it went on to explain the 'exception' provided by the strikes in Nairobi and Mombasa.

From the beginning of the year a prominent Communist agitator made every effort to stir up discontent and unrest among workers generally. The method he used was to form an unregistered and illegal TUC, to which attempts were made to affiliate existing trade unions: the real object was the disruption of industry.... The strike broke down due to the careful preliminary planning of those concerned with law and order; the firm action taken had the complete support of all responsible people. For some time past the whole question of the lack of industrial organization had been undergoing examination in the light of the policy that the trade union movement should be encouraged to develop slowly. With the disappearance of the TUC and its Communist leader off the scene, the field was left clear for this policy to take shape.

Since the industrial features of the 1950 strikes in Kenya were no different from those of similar strikes in Ghana and Nigeria

African Trade Unions

that year, the failure of the Kenya Labour Department to understand the necessary political involvement of trade unionism in colonies is particularly striking. As in Tanganyika, Uganda, Nyasaland, Northern and Southern Rhodesia, the Administration in Kenya persisted in trying to control the leadership, structure and politics of the unions – in this case, with disastrous results. By identifying and persecuting trade union leaders as 'Communist', it succeeded in delaying the effective organization of African workers by several years and meanwhile precipitated the popular resistance that culminated in the 'Mau Mau' rebellion of the early 1950s. It also effectively divorced African from Asian workers and set back the necessary process of inter-racial integration and cooperation for decades.

The débâcle in Kenya is important for suggesting the strength of local Administrative attitudes in shaping the whole direction of trade union growth. By curbing the activities of militants, the Administration was able for a while to reduce the political content of trade unionism, and by fostering its own probationary unions it had some influence in containing labour unrest. But however hard it tried, it could not keep pace with the economic upheaval following the Second World War. Even if strikes were 'of a political character', they had much economic substance. The Dow Commission found in 1955 that 'the extent of actual unemployment and underemployment cannot be measured, but there is general agreement that it is considerable.'[6] Wage conditions were so bad that the Kenya Government issued a Regulation of Wages and Conditions Ordinance in 1951 which established minimum wage rates on an area basis, and in 1953 a Committee on African Wages was appointed by the Governor. The Committee found that the statutory minimum wage, even when revised to take account of price changes, failed to provide adequate cover for the cost of living and 'acted like a magnet to hold down wages'. The unemployment crisis was caused partly by the demobilization of soldiers and partly by the land squeeze which made agricultural activity uneconomic for many Kikuyu. Nairobi acquired a large floating population without housing and, in most cases, without jobs.

The history of the Kenya unions stands at one extreme of the

The Rise of Trade Unionism in Africa

experience of African workers and, with the Rhodesias, South Africa and the Maghreb illustrates the power of vested settler interests to thwart the evolution of labour unions. By opposing such African unions as existed, the Kenya Administration succeeded for a time in maintaining them as illegal, politically militant bodies obliged to work against the policies of the government and employers by direct, even violent confrontation. At the other extreme lay Sierra Leone which, largely through the efforts of Edgar Parry, a British trade unionist who ultimately became Labour Commissioner, succeeded in establishing by 1946 a stream-lined union organization on industrial lines, with a Sierra Leone Council of Labour as a non-political coordinating body. It was of course, rather easier for the government to keep a check on the development of unions in Sierra Leone, based as they were on the Creoles of the Freetown area, than in the rest of West Africa. Most of the early unions in the territory were connected with government-owned enterprises – railways, mines, docks and schools – and it was not till much later that artisans and agricultural workers were organized. Because of the homogeneity of this labour force and the absence of marked racial or tribal differences within the industrial sector, a kind of group cohesion provided the connecting points for organization. Joint industrial councils were established as the bases for collective bargaining; the unions were persuaded to combine on industrial lines; and legislation was passed forbidding the registration of competing unions. No union leaders were markedly involved in politics until the late 1950s, and although it included among its aims the extension of state and municipal enterprise and workers' participation in the management of public services, the Council of Labour did not ally itself as a body to any political party. An important strike in Freetown in 1955, though led by the Secretary of the Council of Labour, was not endorsed by the Council's Executive Committee, and even when two of the most prominent labour leaders, Marcus Grant and Siaka Stevens formed political parties with trade union support in 1957 and 1961, the Council of Labour itself was not involved. The Council's attitude was clearly revealed at the time of the 1955 strike; in its evidence to the Inquiry Board, it declared that

African Trade Unions

Of all the British colonial territories, the trade union movement in Sierra Leone has always enjoyed the enviable position of having the highest reputation in the field of industrial relations and boasts of a negotiating machinery which conforms very closely to that which obtains in the United Kingdom.[7]

The Labour Department had earlier commented approvingly: 'Unions mainly negotiated wages and tried to recover arrears of wages in accordance with Wage Boards' agreements.'[8] Thus up to the 1955 strike, industrial relations in Sierra Leone were presented as something of a model with close cooperation between unions, the Labour Department and employers; the existence of wage councils, joint-industrial councils, and a National Joint Consultative Committee representing government, unions and employers, which acted as a central advisory body on labour legislation and policy; and the moderate political nature of the Council of Labour. By 1958 some 60 per cent of the wage-labour force were enrolled as union members, and a very slow increase in the size of the wage-labour force (from 4.6 per cent in 1938 to 8.5 per cent in 1958) meant that the unions were able to keep pace with developments. Furthermore, because there were very few migrant workers and the wage-earners remained largely Creole, there were few problems of organization and communication. The trade union leadership itself was remarkably stable over the period, and union finances were more secure than in many other African territories. It seemed that something like the British model had, indeed, been successfully transplanted to Africa.

Somewhere in between these extremes came most other colonies in French and British Africa. Trade unions were legalized, even encouraged; but although administrations tried to influence their direction, they were not as ham-fisted in their tactics as in Kenya nor gained such initial successes as in Sierra Leone. The varieties of union experience are most usefully suggested by examining three sufficiently different situations – Nigeria, French West Africa, and the Sudan.

In West Africa trade unions first became really active during the Second World War, due – as in Kenya – to the rapid economic and social transformation of the colonies. The war saw the

The Rise of Trade Unionism in Africa

first large-scale involvement of Africans in the affairs of the metropolitan states. Soldiers were moved thousands of miles to fight Europeans in the name of democracy, and they came increasingly into contact with soldiers from other countries, including African ones. Furthermore, air bases, docks and army camps were built across Africa itself, to provide new employment for thousands of Africans. The Wartime Emergency regulations, however, limited freedom of activity; trade unions found that they could not strike, and political parties that they could not function openly. (In the French West African territories, the Vichy government reversed assimilationist legislation, introduced discriminatory racialist edicts, and gave a free hand to fascist-minded settlers and civil servants.) Such restrictions contrasted strongly with Allied propaganda that Africans were sharing in a fight for democracy. The war also brought a steep rise in the cost of living, with no appreciable increase in the level of wages. In Ghana the prices of sugar, corned beef and flour all increased by over 50 per cent in the first twelve months of the war, and the real-wage index fell from one hundred in May 1939 to sixty-six in November 1941. In Nigeria the cost of living rose by 75 per cent between 1939 and 1942, with no marked increase in the level of wages. Similar changes occurred throughout Africa. It is not surprising, therefore, that in those colonies where wage-labour was in any way important, there was a rapid growth in discontent. In Nigeria the unions increased their membership from 4,000 in 1940 to 30,000 in 1944; in the Gold Coast, from 900 in 1942 to 6,000 in 1945. Strikes became commonplace. In Nigeria, none was recorded in 1940, but in 1942 there were eleven major ones, involving 5,300 workers. In 1942 the Gold Coast suffered ten major strikes, and Sierra Leone thirteen; but it was in Nigeria that labour unrest assumed most dramatic proportions.

The spearhead of the Nigerian trade union movement was the Railway Workers Union, under its secretary Michael Imoudou, which in 1940 launched a series of strikes that continued throughout the war. This militancy stimulated the growth of other unions and compelled the Administration to consider the wage situation. In 1942 the government granted a cost-of-living

81

African Trade Unions

allowance to its employees, and other employers followed suit. But the cost of living continued to rise. Between 1942 and 1946 prices went up by a further 52 per cent, and most public employees received no increase in either wages or allowances. In 1942 Imoudou successfully organized a Nigerian TUC which was backed by prominent politicians (Azikwe, Awolowo, Macaulay, Ikoli), and the subsequent course of union development became closely related to the nationalist campaign. This soon produced stresses, however, and though the TUC was a founder-member of the NCNC in 1944 and provided some of the leading organizers for the party, the conflict between party militants and trade union officers soon began to show itself. Most of the industrial militancy was not the work of the TUC secretariat, which was itself divided between those who wanted to work closely with the Labour Department and those who wanted direct action. Moreover, some of the TUC leaders (notably Awolowo, Macaulay and Ikoli) were not workers at all, and their preoccupations were less with agitating for workers' rights than with developing a successful political movement. There were accordingly three tendencies at work, and these revealed themselves starkly when various individual labour leaders called for a general strike in 1945 as a protest against the government's refusal of a wage and allowance increase to compensate for the rise in prices since 1942. Shortly before the deadline, the leaders of the TUC revoked the strike order, but many individual unions ignored this; the strike lasted thirty-seven days, to involve 30,000 workers and seventeen unions. The conflict between the union militants and the TUC leaders wrecked the TUC, but the strike itself had a profound impact on the industrial and political scene in Nigeria. For the first time Europeans and Nigerians saw the potential strength of efficiently-organized workers. Azikwe was able to use the strike as an important weapon in his political campaign, while the government made concessions to the strikers and set up a commission of inquiry to investigate wage rates.

Although, as it was able to demonstrate several times during the next twenty years, the Nigerian trade union movement could organize itself against the social and political structure, the 1945 strike revealed the limits of its political powers. By 1950 over 125,000 Nigerian workers belonged to trade unions, but 50,000 of these were scattered among 144 different unions, representing all forms of work location and occupation from the United Africa Company to the Church Missionary Society Bookshop in Lagos. Among the unions listed were: the Ote Tomo Native Herbalist Union, the Ijesha Goldsmiths' Union, the Lagos Cycle Repairers' Union, the Ajikengbe Canoe Transport Pullers' Union, and the Trans-Arab Workers Union. Some of these unions had fewer than ten members each, and most did not affiliate to a national centre. In 1950 the mainstays of union organization were the five leading public service unions, which had 75,000 members in all, but even this degree of organization was not maintained for long. After 1950 the political differences within Nigeria and the dispute over affiliation to international organizations split the movement further. In 1948 a second national federation had been established in opposition to the TUC, and in 1950 a third came into existence. The two new federations were supporters of the NCNC, while the original TUC had drawn close to Awolowo's Action Group.

In 1949 a serious incident at the Enugu colliery had effected a temporary reconciliation among the different factions. Some 7,500 miners at the colliery staged a 'go-slow' strike for back pay, and fearing that the strikers would gain control over some explosives stocked in the mine, the police opened fire on a crowd of demonstrators, killing twenty-one miners and wounding fifty-one. (The subsequent official inquiry found that the management had been insensitive and incompetent, the strikers provocative and 'misled', and the police foolhardy.) The effect of the shooting was electric. National political parties coordinated their efforts; the two central trade union federations attempted to merge into a Nigerian Labour Congress; and the number of strikes increased – involving 7,375 workers in 1948–9 and 50,000 in 1949–50. For ten months a daily trade union newspaper, the *Labour Champion*, was published in Lagos. But the prospect of a trade union backed political movement vanished as quickly as it had appeared. In December 1950 a badly-organized general strike ended disastrously for the unions, and the new-found unity was quickly lost. Henceforth

African Trade Unions

the Nigerian unions ceased to play a major part in politics.

The next decade was marked by several unsuccessful attempts to create a central labour organisation. The most important sources of discord were international trade union affiliations and the lasting conflict between those leaders who wished trade unionism to perform a purely protective function, as encouraged by Labour Departments, the British TUC and the ICFTU, and those who wanted to use it as a base for building a socialist party in Nigeria. Leaders like Michael Imoudou and Wahab Goodluck tried repeatedly to form labour parties, while the other wing, led by A. H. Adebola and Lawrence Borha, tried to reach some working arrangement with the government. The difficulty for both sides lay in the indifference of the main political parties (especially the Northern People's Congress) to any coherent labour policy and the inability of the Labour Department to enforce trade union rights in most prominent European enterprises. Although during the early 1950s four British trade unionists were active in the country as Labour Advisers, and after 1958 both the WFTU and the ICFTU concentrated their attention on Nigeria, the union movement remained weak. Employers were able to ignore the various trade union ordinances and either refused to countenance union activity or made great efforts to 'dictate to the union how it must organize and who are to be its officers.'[9] The years of greatest trade union activity were not related to the amount of effort put in by the British or the international organizations, but to the degree of militancy among the Nigerian workers themselves. The peak periods for membership were 1942, 1946, 1948–50, and 1955–6, and in all these years the most important spurs were strikes, the demonstrable growth and influence of nationalism, and the existence of militant unions and united trade union federations. But the British attempt to create unions free of political ties in a situation that was highly charged politically had its effect. At independence there were two competing federations, and 40 per cent of the union members preferred not to affiliate to either.

The growth of trade unions in French West Africa was even more dominated by metropolitan patterns than in Nigeria, but the presence of large numbers of Frenchmen made the unions

The Rise of Trade Unionism in Africa

much more conscious of racial inequalities than in the neighbouring British colonies. The French West African unions operated in territories where equality of opportunity and status was, after 1944, a political creed but also where all the major posts in the administration and in commerce were held by Europeans. By 1957 the 22,000 Europeans constituted 5 per cent of the total wage-labour force; but 10,000 of these held managerial or senior supervisory posts, 8,000 were clerks, and 4,000 were skilled manual workers. The growth of a 'poor white' class in the 1940s and 1950s added to the tension; most of the unskilled Frenchmen expected, and generally got, jobs in preference to Africans. Senegal, where the capital of the federated territories, Dakar, provided the centre for administration, shipping and such industrial development as there was, contained over half of the Europeans, while another third lived in Guinea and the Ivory Coast. The discrepancy between the wages, living conditions and work opportunities for Europeans and Africans provided the main stimulus for trade union development.

The early union leaders were all white-collar workers who, as the Africans closest to the privileged jobs, were the most incensed by the racially unequal conditions. When they began full-scale union organization in the late 1940s, they 'combined the qualities of an intelligentsia with those of a rising middle class'[10] to produce a militant movement that saw the unions as a major vehicle in reaching a more egalitarian society. The unions rapidly took on the character of political bodies with a strong ideological content, and were led by intellectuals whose talents had been directed to trade unionism because of the restrictions abounding in political and economic life. The links with the French trade union centres, and particularly the CGT, provided the opportunity for conducting campaigns that directly attacked the metropolitan seats of power. Initially this did not involve any demands for autonomy or independence; the whole basis of the trade union campaigns was equality. The first major industrial action organized by African unions was the prolonged railway strike involving the whole of French West Africa from October 1947 to March 1948, launched to get a unified code on working conditions for African and European. Although the railways were kept running by the introduction of imported labour from France, the remarkable solidarity of the workers provided the first real impetus to trade union organization, and by 1952 unions were becoming an increasingly important factor in political life. They began to develop a strategy for dealing with the Administration, based on a campaign for the provision of a labour code that would eliminate racial inequality at work. Between 1948 and 1953 they conducted strikes, organized demonstrations and lobbied deputies so that pressure could be put on the government in Paris. The passage of the Lamine-Guèye Law in June 1950 and of the Overseas Territories' Labour Code in December 1952 marked the success of this stage in the campaign. Just before the 1952 Code was introduced, the African unions demonstrated their strength with a general strike throughout French West Africa in successful protest against delays, and once the Code at last reached the statute book, the campaign turned towards ensuring its implementation.

Although African wages had risen between 1949 and 1952 by amounts ranging from 87 per cent to 39 per cent in the major cities, these had been largely in compensation for increases in the cost of living, and were at least 20 per cent below the effective provisions of the Labour Code (which stipulated a forty-hour working week compared to the existing practice of fifty hours). The Administration and private employers in French West Africa protested that such wage increases would be disastrous for the economy; they offered increases of less than 15 per cent. The unions claimed that the cost of living alone had gone up by more than 15 per cent since the last wage rise, and they therefore demanded more than 20 per cent. The ensuing deadlock led to a further massive campaign against the Administration and six months of intensive strike activity from July to December 1953, with Dakar, Bamako and Conakry as the centres of unrest. For the year 1953 the number of workdays lost in strikes was 692,280, compared with only 25,761 in 1950. In the consultative bodies of the French Republic, African and French labour representatives argued for a change in government policy, and in the French Parliament and the French West African territorial assemblies, deputies repeatedly raised the

The Rise of Trade Unionism in Africa

subject. Telegrams and letters swamped government officials, newspaper offices, the desks of deputies and French labour leaders, protesting against the failure to implement the code and denouncing the 'treasonable' conduct of employers. In addition the unions hinted darkly that if the Administration

> does not revise its position, we will go beyond – in demanding things which will not be of an economic nature. The African labour organizations, having behind them all social groups ... will demand the revision of the ties which bind them to the French union. For we will not tolerate that a people live in misery while in our full view a minority lives luxuriously with the most insolent superfluities.[11]

After much hesitation and warnings by several African politicians that there was a danger extremists would take over because of the government's lack of foresight, the French Overseas Minister announced that the full 20 per cent increase would be granted. For the next few years wages rose dramatically – by 29 per cent in Dakar, 80 per cent in Abidjan, 27 per cent in Conakry and 49 per cent in Bamako. In addition, prices, which were tied to French levels, fell by estimates ranging from 10 per cent to 20 per cent in the major cities, legislation covering family allowances came into operation; and the number of wage-zones was reduced, leading to a drop in wage differentials between urban and rural workers. The total gains in real income were therefore considerably greater than the wage increases suggest.

But although the campaign over the 20 per cent increase showed that unions were an important element in the nationalist movement, the degree to which the unions were themselves directly involved in the political process varied greatly from region to region. In only two territories, Sudan (later the Mali Republic) and Guinea, did the unions participate fully in the political parties, and, in both cases, this was in some measure because the parties that were ultimately to gain power, the Parti Démocratique de Guinée (PDG) and the Union Soudanaise, were for a long time in opposition to the French-sponsored parties of the chiefs. The connexions between leading personnel in the two territories was very close, and the political struggle in both was increasingly related to trade union demands. Sekou

African Trade Unions

Touré, secretary-general of the CGT-Guinée, conspicuously used the unions as a basis for political campaigning, and this had a substantial influence on the political history of Guinea. The 1953 strikes – and particularly one in Conakry that lasted for sixty-six days from September to November – became an effective instrument for political education. Throughout the strike period, Touré emphasized the unity of African workers, the irrelevance of tribalism, and the need for the cooperation of rural workers in industrial action. The impact of the campaign was profound. Union membership in Guinea rose from 4,000 in early 1953 to 20,000 in 1954 and 55,000 in 1955. The Guinea leaders acquired fame throughout West Africa as heroes of the successful campaign, and the CGT, afraid of losing control over the unions to Touré's incipient nationalism, appointed three secretaries of the AOF-CGT instead of one. In Guinea, 'the strike had most important political consequences, since trade unionists also led the PDG ... Within less than two years PDG leaders displaced in elected office the leaders of the ethnic and regional associations.'[12] The wage-earners who joined the CGT in Guinea saw the unions as part of the party and all industrial action as political. Union leaders urged that 'the trade union movement ... must integrate itself as the nationalist revolutionary and not as a reformist force within the context of other progressive forces. Its role in every instant is political.'[13] Because of their trade union base and the contact with working people that trade unionism gave them, the PDG leaders acquired a technique of protest, an ideology and a knowledge of mass organization that was deeply to influence their political campaigning. This meant that the PDG, as well as the Union Soudanaise (US) in Mali, became more revolutionary and more militant in their programmes, campaigned more vigorously than other West African politicians against the colonial system, inisted on the modernization of the whole political structure and were more vigorous in their pursuit of equality.

In Mali, the Union Générale des Travailleurs de Soudan, with only 14,000 members, acted as a base for organizing the artisans and the traders. Even though some disagreement occurred in 1955 when Touré led most of the CGT unions into a Conféderátion Générale du Travail Africain (CGTA), while Mali's Abdoulaye Diallo remained a protagonist of the CGT, the union base was not severely threatened. Diallo became Minister of Labour in 1957 and when, in 1958, he objected to the Union Soudanaise's decision to vote not for independence but for membership of the French Community, he left for Guinea. Meanwhile, without such severe upheavals as characterized their counterparts in other French West African states, the Mali unions were firmly integrated into the nationalist party structure with an influence that was exceptional – emphasizing discipline, the essential poverty of party leaders, and the importance of participation in decisions at all levels. Out of the twenty-five in the executive committee of the Union Soudanaise, eight were trade unionists.

In other territories of French West Africa the unions played a somewhat different role. In no case were they prominent within the leading political parties, while the conflict between the CGT and Rassemblement Démocratique Africain (RDA), the principal political movement, had serious effects on union loyalties. In Senegal both the Communist-led CGT and the Socialist CGT-FO were active in organizing African workers, but the majority of members belonged to the CGT. Before Senghor founded his Bloc Démocratique Sénégalaise in 1948 out of the seventeen SFIO deputies from Senegal, there existed CGT unions in Dakar and St Louis working in close sympathy with the RDA. Some of these had established a Université Populaire Africaine in Dakar to teach history and Marxist theory to workers, and during the 1948 strike had extended their influence throughout much of the urban population. Most of the CGT members rejected the decision of the RDA to loosen its Communist ties and worked actively in the Union Démocratique Sénégalaise, originally formed as a branch of the RDA but cold-shouldered when it insisted on maintaining Communist affiliation. Most other trade unionists remained affiliated to the CGT-FO, so that the unions as a whole remained outside the nationalist structure and were not in any way integrated into Senghor's party until just before independence.

In the Ivory Coast the unions and Houphouet's territorial

branch of the RDA, the PDCI, were always in conflict, although they were in theory complementary parts of the same movement; the leaders of the political party were to a large extent planters and so had interests close to those of the European employers. In the mid-1950s there were repeated conflicts between the CGT unions (later UGTAN) and the RDA. Even after Gaston Fiankan, the leader of the railway workers' union, had been made Minister of Labour, and Gris Camille, secretary of the CGT-Ivory Coast, had been elected to the territorial assembly on a PDCI ticket, the conflict continued and came close to an open breach in the few months before independence.

The unions throughout French West Africa thus grew directly as a result of the nationalist campaign, but their relationship with the nationalist organizations varied considerably. Where there were no indigenous economic groups above them powerful enough to lead the nationalist parties, the unions played an important part in political campaigns and the drafting of programmes. Otherwise their relationship with the politicians was ambiguous, some leaders finding government posts in cabinets and on party executives, but the weight of the union organization remaining outside and frequently in opposition.

If in the French territories the unions developed out of a dialogue with the French trade union federations and from campaigns waged by African politicians and white-collar workers for equality of opportunity and status, in the Sudan the metropolitan unions were much less active – though, as in other British-controlled territories, the Administration encouraged works committees and other forms of labour-management consultation and attempted to guide the unions in their development. More importantly, the workers on their own initiative created an omnibus organization, the Workers' Affairs Association (WAA), part trade union and part an 'improvement association'. Prior to 1946 there was little labour organization in the Sudan, but following the war three important events deeply affected the course of trade union development. Early in 1946 the tenants of the Gezira cotton growing scheme went on strike, demanding that a reserve fund of £1,300,000 should be paid to them. In June the government began sponsoring works com-

The Rise of Trade Unionism in Africa

mittees, and the Sudan railway workers established the WAA. And in October and November demonstrations occurred in the main towns of Khartoum and Omdurman after negotiations in Cairo over the political future of the Sudan had broken down. With an economic depression following the war, the cost of living rose by over 30 per cent in three years. Existing wage rates in the railways had been fixed as early as 1935 and ranged from £E 1.05 to £E 2.0 a month, but a Government Inquiry in 1948 found that the absolute monthly minimum required to maintain a small family was £E 4.

On 18 May, 1946 the Government Labour Board decided that wage committees should be set up on lines followed in Britain. But 'no attempt was made by the central government to show how the principles involved should be applied in the different conditions of the Sudan.'[14] There was no trained labour specialist in the country to advise on the implementation of the decision; the nearest was the Labour Attaché at the British Embassy in Cairo. Where in the Sudan works committees were to be the first step in establishing industrial relations, in Britain they had been tentatively introduced after many years into an already complex system of industrial relations. In the event the experiment failed because management insisted on dominating all proceedings of the committees, the government was confused in its aims, and – mainly – the committees themselves were planned as 'the basis on which trade unions could subsequently be set up on sound prepared lines.'[15] The railway workers in particular had other ideas.

The Workers' Affairs Association was the successor to several works' clubs, established as early as 1934 – first at Atbara, the main railway junction, and then at Khartoum – with the purpose of grouping together workers for social and cultural activities. The acute economic conditions following the Second World War, as well as the natural homogeneity on the railways caused by working for one employer in a country which had few wage-earners, led to the formation of the WAA. The Association drew up a lengthy constitution – which included trade union functions, mutual help, and cultural activities – and declared its intention to achieve its objectives by strictly legal means. For the next few

African Trade Unions

months the WAA and the railway management entered into prolonged negotiations, but reached deadlock on the main issue of union recognition. After an appeal to the Governor-General, which was curtly rejected, the WAA then announced its intention of staging a demonstration to display its support. On 9 July 1947, as the workers marched to the offices of the railway management, they were intercepted by armed police, and sixty trade unionists, including the entire WAA executive were arrested. Immediately all the railway workers came out on strike. After political leaders had effected a compromise, the strike came to an end on 18 July, and the WAA gained official recognition. But on the issue of collective bargaining, the management was inflexible, and the dispute was referred to the government. From this time onwards, the Association's campaign was increasingly directed against the British colonial régime, and the issues became more political. By November 1947 the WAA was announcing that it

> failed to see how either the railway management or the government could make business gains at the expense of lowering the living standards of human beings to such depths, when it was realized that the greater part of those profits went to the central government to be expended largely on the unduly high salaries earned by British officials who led luxurious lives, and out of which were built magnificent mansions, the construction and maintenance of which required hundreds of thousands of pounds.[16]

When the government failed to respond to these accusations, the Association called two major strikes in January and April 1948. Finally the government was forced to set up a Committee of Inquiry into wages which substantially confirmed the demands put forward by the WAA. A Trade Union Ordinance was introduced which legalized trade unions; but, in the pattern adopted by the British in other colonies, these were subject to registration. Several unions registered themselves in terms of the Ordinance; but in 1950 a Sudan Workers Trade Union Federation was created, and this was refused registration. As a direct reply the SWTUF, which was a direct successor of the WAA, amended its constitution to include among its objectives the defeat of imperialism and the achievement of self-determination

The Rise of Trade Unionism in Africa

for the Sudan; a United Front for the Liberation of the Sudan was set up, and this became an important part of the nationalist campaign. The SWTUF became increasingly militant and co-operated with the pro-Communist Sudan Movement for National Liberation, though there is little evidence that the Sudan unions were themselves Communist-dominated. Both movements shared an opposition to imperialism, and on occasion their tactics and policies coincided; but the unions put more emphasis on the industrial inequalities and always gave primary attention to their industrial role. Strikes with direct political intent were rare, and SWTUF's campaigns were mainly a reaction against the policies of government and employers. Because the unions were not treated as responsible organizations, and because, even after Sudanese political parties began to play an important part in the government of the country, they were not given a place in policy-making, the unions remained militant and outside the wider political movements.

The history of the Sudanese unions – together with that of the militant unions in Nigeria – provides an interesting contrast with developments in French West Africa. In the Sudan and Nigeria, the leaders of the militant unions were industrial and manual workers, and their differences with political leaders were essentially those of a developing proletariat. In French West Africa, on the other hand, the unions were led by white-collar workers jealous of the privileges enjoyed by the Europeans. When nationalist governments were formed in the French territories, unions leaders, as part of a growing indigenous middle class, were more easily absorbed into government posts. The struggle of the industrial workers for recognition was to come after independence. In the Sudan and Nigeria the union leaders tended to remain outside the governments and formed the basis of an opposition against the bourgeois parties and, later in the Sudan, a military régime. But the role of unions in the nationalist movements deserves a little closer attention.

Chapter 4: Notes

1. Quoted Richard L. Sklar, *Nigerian Political Parties*, Princeton U.P., 1963, p. 497, Note 41.
2. Georges Balandier, *Sociologie des Brazavilles Noires*, Armand Colin, 1955.
3. In D. Forde (ed) *Social Implications of Industrialisation and Urbanisation in Africa South of the Sahara*, UNESCO, 1956, p. 120.
4. G. Hunter, *New Societies of Tropical Africa*, O.U.P., 1962, p. 25.
5. Government of Kenya, *Labour Department Report*, 1950, paras. 42–50.
6. *East African Royal Commission Report*, H.M.S.O., 1955, p. 147.
7. *Report of Commission of Inquiry into Strike and Disturbances in Freetown*, H.M.S.O., 1955, para. 68.
8. *Sierra Leone Labour Department, Report*, 1949, para. 15.
9. *Third Congress of All-Nigerian TUF*, 1955, speech by Gogo Chu Nzeribe, Secretary-general.
10. Elliot J. Berg, 'French West Africa', in W. Galenson (ed) *Labour and Economic Development*, John Wiley, 1959, p. 214.
11. *Le Proletaire*, (African CGT Journal), No. 29, October 1953, quoted in ibid., p. 230.
12. R. Schachter-Morgenthau, *Political Parties in French-Speaking West Africa*, O.U.P., 1964, p. 229.
13. Seydou Diallo, quoted ibid., p. 230.
14. Saad ed din Fawzi, *The Labour Movement in Sudan*, O.U.P., 1957, p. 26.
15. Quoted in ibid., p. 32.
16. Ibid., p. 72.

5 Trade Unions and Political Commitment before Independence

The trade unions inevitably became involved in the colonial politics before independence, but as the degree of involvement varied from colony to colony, some attempt to discuss the political role of unions is necessary if the post-independence relationships are to be properly understood. There were three main levels at which the unions could act politically. Initially their attempts to gain recognition through strikes were seen by colonial rulers as political, especially when the strikes were directed against the main employment agency – the government or a public corporation. It did not take much for a colonial government to jump to the conclusion that any strike of government employees was subversive. That many strikes were so categorized, indeed, led African politicians and some trade unionists themselves to see the strike as a political weapon, and therefore some coordinated planning of strikes became part of the nationalist campaign. This constituted a second level of political activity, though in practice its use was restricted; few strikes were political in objective, and frequently unions resisted the attempts of nationalist leaders to use industrial action for their own purposes. But at a later stage politicians and trade union leaders in some colonies created a combined trade union-party movement, in which the struggle for independence was seen as the first priority, and the trade unions adapted their tactics accordingly.

The issues over which trade unions came into conflict with the Administration in the course of seeking recognition or making protests against wage and employment conditions are, of course, too numerous to mention. In every colony the unions were at some stage or other accused of subversion, Communism or simply breaking the law. Most Administrations banned strikes in the public services, so that any industrial action in this sector was calculated to raise the political temperature, and alongside the general intransigence displayed by employers in the private sector this meant that in most cases any organization of workers for routine negotiating rights ran into difficulties. Many strikes which started out as complaints against conditions were readily regarded by employers, governments and nationalist politicians as political. Of course the bare fact of calling a strike against a paternalist and reactionary government was in many ways a political act, though it is doubtful if either France or Britain would have accepted this as a proper definition at home.

The instances where the trade unions early allied themselves with the leading political parties and continued to do so up to independence are few. Guinea, Ghana, Tanganyika, Kenya, Tunisia, Algeria, the Ivory Coast and Mali are almost the only ones that stand up to examination. In Guinea, Ghana, Kenya and Tanganyika there was an early inter-relationship between trade union officials and party leaders, but only in Guinea did the party actually absorb the unions before independence, though Ghana came close to doing so. In all other instances the unions remained quite separate from the parties, seem to have been relatively uninfluenced by party directives, and drew on several external sources for their financial and organizational aid. In only two of these territories – Kenya and Tunisia – do the unions appear to have acted for some time as the basis of the nationalist movement and to have acted as substitutes for political organizations when these were forced underground. But this led in both instances to open disagreement with the political party at independence; both the Kenyan and Tunisian unions produced their own political leaders, who attempted to create alternative political parties or gain control of the nationalist movement themselves.

Elsewhere the unions played some part in the political struggle by supporting groups that were eventually submerged, by dividing worker allegiance among several parties, or by conducting campaigns and strikes which furthered political resistance without the unions themselves becoming tied to a leading political party. In some territories, notably Nigeria, Morocco,

Trade Unions and Political Commitment before Independence

and the French Cameroons, the unions at one time appeared in the vanguard of the nationalist campaign, only later to move into an opposition role. This was also true, to some extent, in most of former French West Africa, where the unions tended to act until 1958 as the industrial wing of the inter-territorial party, the RDA. The secession of Guinea from the French Community, isolating Sekou Touré as Secretary-General of UGTAN, the inter-territorial trade union federation, forced the unions in the remaining states into an ambiguous position. They were forced to choose between continued UGTAN affiliation and a closer relationship with the leading territorial party, and at independence most of them had not yet clearly resolved the dilemma. In Northern Rhodesia the unions never formed an industrial wing of the leading nationalist parties. For a time – in 1950 and 1958 – Lawrence Katilungu, of the mineworkers, formed an alliance with Harry Nkumbula's African National Congress (ANC); but differences between Katilungu and Nkumbula, and later between Katilungu and other union members prevented any effective collaboration. As in Nigeria, this early experience of political activity made the unions chary of any new alignment when Kenneth Kaunda formed the United National Independence Party (UNIP). When Zambia became independent, relationships between UNIP, which emerged as the government, and the Northern Rhodesian TUC were strained and uncertain.

Although the nationalist parties were quick to note the strategic importance of unions, the extent to which they considered them important enough to be included in the party machinery or consulted as allies depended on whether the parties themselves were or became 'mass' or '*élite*' in character.[1] Parties led by *élites* – chiefs, religious leaders or the more wealthy middle class – were inclined to discount the unions as a significant source of strength. The Northern People's Congress in Nigeria or the Kabaka Yekka in Uganda drew their power from the established tribal order, and the leaders were already secure in senior positions of authority; they did not need the unions to bolster their claim to legitimacy, and, given their internal organization and conservative ideology, had little room for unions even as convenient recruiting grounds. (Later, with

97

African Trade Unions

the responsibility of government and the threat to the authority of traditional rulers implicit in the existence of unions, some *élite* parties tried to cultivate or foster their own labour movements, though with limited success.) The history of the earlier parties – the United Gold Coast Convention, the Kenya Africa Union, or the Tunisian Destour – show that parties led mainly by the petty bourgeoisie or businessmen had little interest in workers' organizations unless they aimed also to create parties with a mass following, professional party workers and elaborate local networks. Most of these early *élite* parties, in fact, were ultimately replaced by mass parties which became conscious of the need to cooperate with the unions as the only alternative non-tribal organizations. In some territories, notably in French Equatorial Africa, Nigeria and Sierra Leone, the *élite* parties survived to form the first independent governments.

The relationship of the mass parties to the trade unions depended mainly on local political and social conditions: on the degree of settler resistance to African advancement, the size and cohesion of the wage-earning force, the manner in which the main party was created (e.g. through mergers or the efforts of a central directorate), and the degree of external trade union affiliation. Analysis can best be pursued by establishing three areas of union experience: that area under settler control, the area of multi-party constitutions, and the area where the idea of single-party rule was conceded before independence.

EUROPEAN SETTLER DOMINATION

To describe the area of settler control, three countries provide useful variations: Kenya, Algeria and Southern Rhodesia. In Kenya the idea of settler control was officially resisted, but the settlers themselves, in control of most of the government machinery and the whole economy, were able for a long time to dictate the pace of events. After the 1952 Emergency the major political party was banned, but the trade unions were allowed to function. In Algeria independence was not conceded at all, and a seven-year war was necessary before the Arabs gained control; in the meanwhile, political parties and trade unions were banned.

Trade Unions and Political Commitment before Independence

In Southern Rhodesia the local settlers controlled the entire Administration and outlawed African nationalist organizations (outside a small, 'constitutionalist' opposition party), and though trade unions themselves were not officially banned, their leaders were regularly imprisoned or sent to restricted areas.

Several other states have shared part or all of these experiences. For some years Morocco was situated very like Algeria, but the nationalist struggle did not last as long there, and independence came with the traditional *élite* in control and the political parties badly divided. Tunisia was in many ways like Kenya, with an illegal nationalist party and the main trade union federation acting as its front. And, of course, the South African situation is an extreme case of settler control, with the total suppression of all African political and effective trade union organization.

In Kenya the Federation of Labour took on the role of substitute for the persecuted nationalist party as soon as the Emergency was declared in 1952. Tom Mboya, Secretary of the Local Government Workers' Union, who acted as Director of Information and Treasurer of the Kenya African Union in the last days before it was banned, was elected General Secretary of the KFL in September 1953. In his own words, 'the KFL became the voice of the African people, in the absence of any other African organization to speak for them'.

It spent a great deal of its time attacking the government's emergency measures: the mass eviction of Rift Valley Province farm workers and 700 Kikuyu families from Nairobi; the collective punishments; the introduction of pass book laws; and the lack of provision for destitute children. Because of such activities, the European community demanded the proscription of the KFL, and under 'Operation Anvil' in 1954 most of the union executives were detained and the offices ransacked. Mboya records that the membership of the Local Government Workers' Union was reduced from 1,300 to 500 in one day's round-up. 'Some union offices had to close down as there was no one left to run them.' But in spite of such repression, the KFL survived, and Mboya remained at its head. In no small measure this was due to his astuteness in selecting his allies. As a member of the

Brussels-based International Confederation of Free Trade Unions or ICFTU, the KFL drew on British and American support; Mboya contributed several articles to the ICFTU's 'Free Labour World', wrote a Fabian pamphlet which exposed the nature of the Kenya police state, and was generally able to extend the Kenyan nationalist campaign to the presses and political platforms of the world. At the same time international pressure made it difficult for the Kenyan authorities to maintain and develop their repressive measures. When the KFL was threatened with a ban in 1956, Sir Vincent Tewson of the British TUC argued the union case. 'The ICFTU sent money to help evicted families, they pleaded our case with the ILO, they made strong representations at the Colonial Office and briefed MP's in Britain.'

But although the KFL was more directly involved in political campaigning than were most other national centres in Africa, its survival depended in part on its being a conciliatory industrial body. Had it sponsored a series of strikes with clear political aims, it is difficult to believe that the Administration would have permitted its continued existence, whatever international support it had. As Mboya himself has declared:

I used to tell my colleagues that our job was not to promote strikes, but to try to achieve for the workers their demands. I have always taken the view that the first job was to see how the strike could be resolved, and try for negotiation. In the end you are going to negotiate anyhow, and the less suffering inflicted on the workers themselves and on the country the better. It is only when employers are deliberately provocative and will not agree to negotiate that I think a strike is justified and should be supported.[2]

During the important dockworkers' strike at Mombasa in March 1955 and the Local Government Workers' dispute with the Nairobi City Council in April of the same year, Mboya used his office to mediate between workers and employers. In both instances the right of the unions to represent workers in negotiations as well as substantial wage increases were gained. Mr Justice Windham, who headed the Board of Inquiry into the Nairobi dispute, remarked on 'the responsible and patient attitude' adopted by the KLGWU, and it is clear that the hand-

Trade Unions and Political Commitment before Independence

ling of these disputes did much to gain for the Kenyan unions a bargaining role with the Administration and the private employers.

The strength that the KFL acquired by its political role led Mboya to make a bid for the complete independence of the unions. Certainly it looked in the late 1950s as if the Kenyan unions were powerful enough successfully to dictate their own terms to the developing political parties; at the time, the KFL was the only truly national organization without evident traces of regional or tribal conflict. Repeatedly Mboya returned to the theme of trade union independence, and at times even seemed to suggest that the unions should play an independent political role. In an illuminating policy statement made to the 1960 Annual Conference of the KFL, Mboya argued that 'the trade union movement must have a right to pronounce on political matters and even to take appropriate action to assist during the struggle for independence.'[3] He added that

If the movement must be free and independent of government and employers, that movement must be capable of formulating its own policies on those problems that affect the workers either as employees or as a class that lives and occupies a certain position in the society and community in which it exists.

But if Mboya did think of leading a 'class' party, he dropped the idea when the Kenya African National Union (KANU) under Jomo Kenyatta formed the government. By independence he was arguing that 'most of our governments are working-class governments'[4] and as Minister of Labour was warning the unions that their independence might have to be curtailed in the interests of economic growth. His successor as Secretary of the KFL, Peter Kibisu, tried to create a Labour Party, but by then the chances of any success were lost. In any event, the Kenyan unions no longer seemed as efficient and homogeneous as before.

In Southern Rhodesia the unions were originally not banned but simply denied legal recognition. Then, after 1959, when they were formally allowed to exist, they increased their membership and came out openly in support of the nationalist movement. This support, however, was complicated by three factors. The

African Trade Unions

political movement was forced, after several bannings by the government, to change its title and its tactics. As efforts to change settler attitudes produced only further intransigence, the movement itself then split on tactics. And this split led to a division within the Southern Rhodesian TUC led by Reuben Jamela. Some members urged that, in order to survive, the unions should not commit themselves to either of the nationalist parties; others, and particularly those close to Joshua Nkomo's Zimbabwe African Peoples Union (ZAPU), felt that the unions should give all the support that they could. For some time the unions restricted their political activities, and Jamela refused appeals by ZAPU to conduct political strikes and coordinate activities with the nationalist campaign. Instead, Jamela encouraged all the SRTUC's affiliated unions to register under the 1959 Industrial Conciliation Act and operate within the limits of Southern Rhodesian law. Nkomo, who had himself once been secretary of the SRTUC, encouraged the establishment of a new federation, and in 1962 J. T. Maluleke and other ZAPU supporters formed the Southern Rhodesian African Trade Union Congress. In the past three years, therefore, the African trade unions in the colony have operated on two different systems. The government has been particularly harsh with the SRATUC, and most of its leaders have been detained or imprisoned. Under the circumstances it is difficult to estimate either the strength or effectiveness of the unions; most of the international organizations operating in Rhodesia regularly complain that arrests of union officers make routine organization almost impossible. The role of the international organizations mainly assists the Jamela unions (ICFTU affiliates), but it seems unlikely that this will carry much weight with the Rhodesian government. In situations of extreme restriction and suppression, it is difficult to see what role legal unions can play, either in concert with or in opposition to the political parties.

In Algeria, on the other hand, the unions were banned for most of the war of liberation and based in Tunis. Although this limited their activities within Algeria, they were able all the same to create efficient central machinery and engage in international campaigning for the nationalist cause. They also had

Trade Unions and Political Commitment before Independence

little to fear from governments in developing their international affiliations. The Union Générale des Travailleurs Algériens (UGTA) affiliated at its inception to the ICFTU and made Algerian independence a major theme of the ICFTU's fifth congress held at Tunis in 1957. But its membership of ICFTU was essentially tactical; little that the Confederation did or said won the unconditional approval of the UGTA, which showed greater awareness of the fundamental social issues in Algeria than did the Western unions who drafted policy statements. For these reasons the UGTA increasingly sought assistance from non-ICFTU affiliates; in 1958 it participated in a Conference for the Workers and People of Algeria, held at Cairo and sponsored by the Confederation of Arab Trade Unions and the WFTU, and in 1961 it sent delegates to the Moscow conference of the WFTU.

Throughout all this manoeuvring the UGTA maintained the closest relationship with the FLN or Front of National Liberation, acting as an additional publicity organization for the nationalist campaign. Because of its astute use of international labour organizations, it was able to command an even wider international audience than even the KFL succeeded in doing. Still more important, it evolved a sophisticated theory of the role of trade unionism in a developing country by assimilating the relevant experiences of unions in widely differing societies. For its rank-and-file support, it was supported by a French branch, the Amicale Générale des Travailleurs Algériens, which became responsible for the half-million Algerians working in France, and it managed to collect dues from some 100,000 members in Algeria itself. At independence, in spite of the fact that it had led a clandestine existence for almost all of its seven years, it was in a powerful enough position for the party to accept it as one of the four major political organizations (the others were the FLN itself, the Army, and the Congress of Agricultural Workers). Its vigorous political campaign, alongside the banning of all union federations, meant additionally that the UGTA emerged at independence as the only trade union federation in Algeria.

Together these instances portray the problems that face unions working under strong settler pressure. Cooperation with

African Trade Unions

the political parties of militant nationalism was an accepted fact in all such territories. But where, as in Rhodesia, there was still some constitutional provision for trade unions, the ties were liable to be weakened; the short-term union aim of raising the living standards of its members often seemed preferable to an all-out war of uncertain duration and result. In Tunisia and Kenya, it was possible for the unions to move carefully between political campaigning and constitutional industrial negotiations. Because the road to independence was not entirely blocked, they were able to represent the responsible, organized opinion to which metropolitan governments were forced in time to turn. But where the unions were outlawed altogether, their role became at once militantly political and clandestine.

CONFLICT BETWEEN UNIONS AND PARTIES

In colonies not dominated by settlers, the political affiliation of unions depended on the balance of social forces within the colony and the type of political party produced. Where there were strong traditional and ethnic clusters of power, the pre-independence campaigning was complicated by the struggle for control between the traditionalists and the leaders of the developing mass parties; in such a situation, the unions could hardly form a clear alignment, and their divisions and hesitations often resulted in their operating as an unofficial opposition. Although their campaigns for better working conditions made them as much part of the nationalist movement as were any of the parties, they ended up either by becoming allies of minority parties or by constituting an independent opposition to the programmes of the major ones, which they saw as a threat to the living standards of their members. This was very often because the major party was obviously an electoral alliance between a tribal *élite* from the rural areas and a section of the urban bourgeoisie. The predicament of the unions is neatly instanced in the history of Dahomey between 1956 and 1960.

After the creation of Sekou Touré's UGTAN in 1957, the CGT-Dahomey joined the new federation as the Union Nationale des Syndicats des Travailleurs du Dahomey (UNSTD). Several of its senior officers were also prominent members of the Union Démocratique Dahoméenne (UDD), the territorial branch of the RDA. In the territorial election of March 1957, however, Souron-Migan Apithy's Parti Républicain du Dahomey, in coalition with Hubert Maga's Northern-based party, the Mouvement Démocratique Dahoméen, emerged victorious to form the new government. The UDD under Justice Ahomadegbé, then conducted, with UNSTD support, a campaign of boycotts and strikes against the main employer, the French Societé des Huilleries Modernes du Dahomey, in protest at its policy of reducing the number of workers in its oil mill at Avrankon. In the territorial assembly UDD members attacked the general policy of the management, linking their criticism to a general campaign against the Apithy government. Then, on 3 February 1958, after months of strikes and riots, the Avrankon mill closed down and Apithy resigned. The Governor managed a temporary settlement between employers and unions, and Apithy formed a new government with the promise of various reforms in wages and work conditions. But several months passed before these were implemented, and then only with drastic modifications. In December the UNSTD called for a general strike in protest at Dahomey's membership of the French Community and projected membership of a West African Mali Federation. In January Apithy resigned and announced his opposition to the federation. Though initially some UDD members supported this move, at the ensuing election the UDD itself stood firm against any coalition with Apithy; of the three contending parties, it gained the largest number of votes but the fewest seats. After a state of affairs bordering on civil war, it finally joined the other two parties in a coalition government under Maga. The coalition broke down just before independence, however, when the UDD decided to make a bid for power alone. It issued a series of policy statements and called for a general strike in October 1960. The strike was broken by Maga's use of troops, armed police and archers from the north, and during the election that followed, Maga's new party, the Parti Dahoméen de l'Unité, won all the seats – although one-third of the electorate, mainly in the towns, voted UDD. Strengthened by

African Trade Unions

these results, Maga dissolved the UDD and UNSTD and created a new trade union federation, the Union Générale des Travailleurs du Dahomey, under firm party control. Many of the UGTAN members joined the new unions; but others continued to keep UNSTD in existence as a union with secret affiliates, to emerge in the Cotonou coup of 1963 which overthrew Maga and re-established Apithy as President.

Throughout these years of crisis in Dahomey, the unions were powerful in so far as they were able to underline the programme of the UDD; when the UDD itself collapsed, the unions were easily assimilated into the new structure. The unions had power, but not on their own. They could force governments to resign, but had little public support for pushing through their own programmes. (This is not too surprising, since only 3 per cent of the adult population were wage-earners.) The unions themselves failed to gain the support of the leading political party for four main reasons, which are not untypical of other states in pre-independence Africa.

(i) The UNSTD was allied to a party which confined its attention to the urban areas and the more developed South; it therefore remained an opposition grouping. Similar situations can be found in Nigeria (where the unions initially supported the NCNC); the Sudan (the SWTUF was in fairly close contact with the Communist Party); Senegal (the CGT unions worked closely with the minority Union Democratique Sénégalaise, and later with the Movement Populaire Sénégalaise and the Parti Africain de l'Indépendance (PAI); in Sierra Leone (where prominent trade unionists supported Siaka Stevens' All Peoples' Congress); and in the Ivory Coast (where UGTAN unions conducted strikes against the PDCI, refused to attend the UTCI congress in 1959, and unsuccessfully attempted to create their own political party).

(ii) The UNSTD was allied to inter-territorial federations – first the CGT, later the UGTA – whose political and economic policies were more militant than those of mass parties in Dahomey. The Communist connexion also stressed the danger of alliances with bourgeois nationalist elements (which had a similar practical effect to the ICFTU's insistence on distinguish-

Trade Unions and Political Commitment before Independence

ing between trade union and political loyalties). Again this situation is paralleled across Africa. In all the cases mentioned above, the unions had external affiliations which brought them into conflict with the demands of the nationalist parties.

(iii) The unions represented a section of the population which had different living standards and expectations from the majority. They had little freedom of manoeuvre; either they tried to remain politically neutral, as many of the Christian unions did, or they committed themselves against the threat to living standards implicit in the programmes of the ruling parties. (Within weeks of the banning of the UNSTD, Maga did in fact cut all salaries in the public sector by 10 per cent.)

(iv) The first Apithy government was particularly insensitive to the trade union issue and made few attempts to woo the workers, preferring to base its electoral appeal on the support of chiefs and peasants. In this it contrasted strongly with the leading parties of Ghana, Guinea, Tanganyika or Kenya, which repeatedly emphasized their proletarian character. But again Dahomey was not unique. The NPC in Nigeria, the Umma Party in the Sudan, the Sierra Leone People's Party and the leading parties of French Equatorial Africa all showed themselves indifferent to trade unions. The structure of these parties – often electoral alliances of regional groupings – put the wage earners at a low premium.

But where, as in Dahomey, Congo (Brazzaville) and the Sudan, the unions had backed a political party with its own ideology (whatever its electoral strength), their eventual suppression or absorption into a single party system did not mean their total elimination from political life. After independence they were able to emerge again as powerful factors in the power struggle.

THE TRANSITION TO SINGLE-PARTY RULE

In the few countries where the leading parties showed a great interest in the unions well before independence, the determining factors were ideology, the lack of effectively organized ethnic groups, and the professionalism of the party cadres. In the three

African Trade Unions

instances (outside the settler areas) where the unions entered into close links with the party, there was a general absence of serious regionalism by the late 1950s, and the parties based their claim to leadership on the unity and discipline of the whole people. The countries were also more outspoken than their neighbours in opposition to imperialism and support for African unity, so that trade union attacks on European employers and profits could be readily assimilated into a political philosophy that stressed socialism and self-help. But even if these factors influenced the early appearance of single-party unionism, the mechanics of the merger contained at least as much source of conflict as the situation in other territories.

Although trade unions existed in the Gold Coast before the creation of Nkrumah's CPP in 1949, they were weak, badly organized and scattered. There were in that year fifty-six unions with 17,985 members among them, and a TUC that had existed from 1945 but possessed little power and almost no funds. With the mounting political unrest, the TUC organized a general strike in 1950, and although this had an important effect on the political future of Ghana (CPP leaders were imprisoned, and the administration immediately became aware of the political-industrial strength of the combined CPP-TUC attack), it was almost disastrous for the trade unions themselves. Such union funds as existed were exhausted; the TUC organization disintegrated; and many of the unions lost support. For the next two years attempts to revive the TUC came to little, and two competing centres existed for eighteen months – the original Gold Coast TUC, maintained through the efforts of the United Africa Company Employees Union, and a new Ghana TUC, formed out of a Dismissed Employees Association. The Ghana TUC seems to have had a high proportion of CPP militants, some of whom had had little previous trade union experience. The general secretary, E. C. Turkson-Ocran, was parliamentary secretary of the CPP, personal secretary to Nkrumah and a member of the CPP's Executive Committee. John K. Tettegah, secretary of the Mercantile Workers Union, and also an active member of the CPP, was assistant secretary. In 1953 the two TUC's came together under Turkson-Ocran, but in the same

Trade Unions and Political Commitment before Independence

year he himself was expelled from both the CPP and the TUC for extremism, and Tettegah became secretary-general. From this date the relationship between the TUC and the CPP grew closer, and Tettegah began to canvass his plans for a reorganization of the whole trade union structure. In 1954 the TUC's organization committee suggested the creation of ten national industrial unions (at the time there were nearly eighty small, badly-organized unions, with a combined membership of about 50,000). Tettegah went to Germany and Israel to study trade union organization, and on his return the 1956 Annual Congress called for 'a gigantic labour organization, coordinated and centralized, with a general staff capable of taking decisions and manouevring with monopoly capital in securing for the workers economic independence in an independent Ghana.'[5]

In spite of these moves, the TUC did not gain effective control over the unions before independence. By 1957 only five national unions had been created, as loose federations, and there were now 130 unions with 80,000 members. The TUC's finances were weak (in 1954 it received less than £300 in union dues), and the organization had little power to reinforce reorganization. In 1955 two of the largest unions, the UAC Employees Union and the Dockworkers' Union, led a breakaway movement and formed a Congress of Free Trade Unions based on Sekondi. Although this schism was in part a protest action by political trade unionists, it was part also of the political division that marked Ghanaian politics at the time. The CFTU was named by the opposition National Liberation Movement as one of its auxiliaries, and certainly, as the NLM collapsed, so did the CFTU. By late 1956, after an election had given the CPP an overwhelming majority, the dissident unions reaffiliated with the TUC. The division, however, had underlined the ideological differences within Ghana over the role of unions. The Department of Labour had always fostered the idea of non-political unionism, and in 1950 had been responsible for reorganizing the Gold Coast TUC around non-political elements. The British TUC, with its emphasis on voluntary reorganization and loose political ties, also made some impact on sections of the unions, in particular on the employees of the United Africa Company (who were also

African Trade Unions

subjected to pressures from management to operate on a company-union basis), the railway-workers and dockworkers. Ever since the CPP was formed, these sections attempted to re-establish trade union organization on the traditional model; 1950–3, 1955–6, and the general strike in Sekondi-Takoradi of 1961 are probably the main stages of disagreement. In the early 1950s they still controlled the bulk of the movement; by the mid-1950s they were reduced to a splinter group; and in 1961 protest could only mean an unofficial strike. But up to 1957 the control of the party loyalists over the unions was very uncertain, while the trade union leaders themselves were uncertain of the implications in party affiliation. But whether the UAC employees and the railway- and dockworkers objected more to the party affiliation than to centralization as a separate issue is difficult to establish.

Something rather similar happened in Tanganyika, though there the initial weakness of the unions (none was registered prior to 1947) and the relatively lower level of economic development made the union leadership even more heavily dependent on external support; the Labour Department, TANU, the ICFTU and Mboya's KFL all played a large part in helping with finance and organization. Some union leaders gained large personal followings as a result of industrial disputes, in particular during two long strikes on the railways and sisal plantations in 1959–60, and between 1955 (when the TFL was registered) and 1961, the claimed membership of affiliated unions rose to 203,000 (over twice as many as in Kenya). This growth in organization was directly related to the TFL's identification with the nationalist campaign, so that Rashidi Kawawa and Michael Kamaliza, the senior union officers, became identified in the public mind as national heroes. It was therefore in the interests of the party to see that the unions kept in close touch with the political campaign, and Nyerere made sure that the TFL was adequately financed and staffed to fulfil its political role. In 1960 he remarked that TANU

had an officer in the organization whose special duty it was to stimulate and help the growth of trade unionism. Once firmly established, the trade union movement was, and is, part and parcel of the whole

Trade Unions and Political Commitment before Independence

nationalist movement. In the early days, when a trade union went on strike, for instance, and its members were in direct need of funds to keep them going, we saw no doctrine which would be abrogated by our giving financial support from the political wing to the industrial wing of the same nationalist movement.[6]

Even if this overstates the connexion, the links between the TFL and TANU appeared to be greater than those operating in the majority of African countries. It is therefore not surprising that, as independence approached and a number of senior officers obtained Cabinet posts, attempts were made to make the structure more formal, though – as in Ghana – there was resistance from some union leaders.

The Tanganyika and Ghanaian examples suggest close parallels. In both countries there was some interlocking of personnel; the party and unions provided a common front in the independence campaign; and when disagreements occurred, they came from the members of the more established unions (dock and commercial workers in Ghana, railwaymen in Ghana and Tanganyika alike). When the party moved to establish a firmer control of the unions, it did so in both countries through a federation which aimed to consolidate its power and rationalize the structure of the whole movement. The political philosophy behind these developments was similar – emphasis on national homogeneity, elimination of vested interests, work and self-help as the basis for national reconstruction, and the need for a union structure more in keeping with African realities. But there was one important difference. When CPP members of the TUC decided to reorganize Ghanaian trade unions, they were dealing with a large number of uncoordinated ones, possessing very little central administration. In Tanganyika, on the other hand, the TFL was created almost before its constituent unions, and when TANU tried to bring about a closer relationship, TFL members felt that they already had a rationale for independent action. The conflict in Ghana, therefore, was between the party militants leading the TUC and the leaders of the individual unions; in Tanganyika it was between the party and the federation executive.

The evolution of a trade union movement in close organizational relationship with the major political party was only possible in those territories where the colonial administration ceased to interfere directly in policy matters and was unable to impose its desire for apolitical unionism. Because in most territories a time-limit had been set for independence, the leading political party was already in some control of the situation. If it was able to overcome tendencies for the fragmentation of political movements, it was well placed to assimilate the labour movement. But in very few instances was this easy to accomplish. Guinea is perhaps the only state where the unions became the base for political activity and developed from the early 1950s a close union-party structure; even in the French-speaking territories, where the unions were more overtly political than elsewhere, this was a unique situation. If other trade unionists gained high political office because they were on good terms with the party secretariats, Touré was able to use his position as a trade unionist to establish his own political party and assert the independence of his country. This did not, of course, mean that Guinea became a state dominated by trade unionists, still less a syndicalist one; but it did mean that it was possible for a politician to create a political party using the language of trade unionism and not find this a serious disability.

Chapter 5: Notes

1. For discussion of these terms, T. Hodgkin, *African Political Parties*, Penguin Books, 1961, pp. 68–75.
2. T. Mboya, *Freedom and After*, Deutsch, 1963, p. 41.
3. *Policy Statement by Bro. Tom Mboya*, Kenya Federation of Labour 1960 Annual Conference, Nairobi 1960, p. 3.
4. T. Mboya, *Freedom and After*, Deutsch, 1963, p. 250.
5. Quoted in B. C. Roberts, *Labour in the Tropical Territories of the Commonwealth*, London School of Economics, 1964, p. 50.
6. Julius Nyerere, 'The Task Ahead of Our African Trade Unions', *Labour* (Ghana TUC Journal), June 1961.

6 Towards an African Working Class

Before setting out on an examination of the place of unions in Independent Africa, it is important to make a brief detour into the world of African social differences as they are affected by industrialization. The organization of the peasant or cash-cropping labour force can hardly concern us here, though obviously its part in the economy is of very direct relevance to the political and economic strength of trade unions (and is considered in the final chapter). What must be discussed before the prospects of trade unionism in Africa can properly be measured is the degree to which African wage-earners constitute a class, or a group of people whose activities and political attitudes are motivated by a common economic interest. In view of the growing number of single-party states, many of them claiming to be 'working-class governments', the subject is of more than academic interest; the cohesion of the wage-earners will, to a considerable extent, determine whether opposition groups can develop or on what basis 'workers' governments' can be established. For the trade unions themselves, the issue is important in assessing their potential strength.

The factors working against the establishment of a permanent wage labour force have already been considered,* but in most of Africa various degrees of permanency can, of course, be found. There is the short-term migrant worker who may be employed for up to five years at a stretch, then return to his own area to work for the rest of his life on his farm. A variation of this is found particularly in Southern Africa, where a worker may alternate between wage-earning and subsistence agriculture or cash-cropping. There is also the local worker who works for wages most of his life but at the same time continues to live on his

*See Chapter 1.

land and act as a part-time cultivator. And finally there is that growing category of worker who becomes a more-or-less permanent wage-earner, leaving his land and settling in a town or near a plantation. The reasons for abandoning the land and settling in towns are many, but perhaps the most important are the attitudes of management towards creating a stable work-force, the distances necessary for travelling to work, the extent of Africanization at work, the viability of agriculture as a method of earning a living, and the attraction of the facilities and opportunities provided in the urban areas.

The main problems of accommodation to permanent wage-earning are social rather than industrial, though management in Africa has traditionally valued the African as basically less efficient at work than the European. In fact Africans can rapidly adapt to industrial conditions and accept new rules, restrictions and incentives. 'The African worker behaves as his work situation demands that he should. When he moves from his tribal home to industry he changes his role and it is this role which determines his industrial behaviour.'[1] Such a judgement accords with most of the recent authoritative research into African labour productivity, particularly that conducted under the auspices of the CCTA's Inter-African Labour Institute and by Peter Kilby, M. E. Morgaut and R. Poupart. Although one or two individual factors like the lack of an industrial background and poor nutrition have played some part in affecting the performance of African workers, the most important have been precisely those which are common to the whole industrial world: the effective organization of work-places, worker-management relations, the quality of supervision and training, and the physical nature of the workshop. The responsibilities of management are great, and if performance is bad much of the blame must be laid on the employers. African efficiency responds to good management, smooth industrial relations, better training facilities and decent surroundings.

That Africans may, with better social conditions and more sympathetic management, prefer to become permanent urban dwellers and wage-earners is suggested by experiences in Katanga and Nigeria. The preference in both instances was dictated by the deliberate policy of employers. In Katanga, because local labour was scarce and the costs of recruitment high, Union Minière adopted a stabilization policy in the late 1920s, and despite its many other deficiencies, this system did have the effect of creating a settled labour force. From 1928 (when the new scheme was introduced) to 1957 the percentage of workers recruited annually dropped from 63 per cent to 8 per cent, while the percentage of workers accompanied by their wives rose from 30 per cent to 86 per cent. Significantly Union Minière's policy was accompanied by the provision of housing, social security and higher wages, together with some training for skilled jobs and important wage-incentives, while the Congolese authorities themselves insisted that workers moving to Katanga on long-term contracts should abdicate all rights to land. During the period under review the productivity of Africans rose to equal that of European workers.

In a survey of several industries in Nigeria, Professor F. A. Wells and W. A. Warmington found that 'one of the essential conditions for stability is that management should want it and be prepared to foster it through attention to personnel management, employee services and the provision of incentives'.[2] In the African Timber and Plywood Company at Sepele 'stability is a condition of survival'. The rates of labour turnover were low (though higher than those in Katanga) and workers were anxious to retain their jobs. Promotion depended on efficiency, literacy, and skill, while certain other benefits, like pensions and holidays, were partially dependent on long service and promotion. Other employers – like the Cameroons Development Corporation and one or two groundnuts companies – were moving, because of the rising cost of a high labour turnover, towards a stabilization policy, though at the time when Wells did his research they had not yet introduced any changes that significantly altered the pattern of employment.

The failure of management is most clearly visible in South Africa, though here the resistance to good management techniques comes not so much from the managers and employers themselves but from the policy of the government. In some instances management has even attempted to circumvent the

Towards an African Working Class

Mines and Works Act and the Industrial Conciliation Act by introducing a form of settled labour. In the early 1950s the mining companies themselves decided to establish married quarters for Africans in the developing Free State gold fields, hoping ultimately to bring a permanent African mining force into existence and so improve the output of the mines and the productivity of African labour. The experiment was killed by order of the government, which permitted the mines to provide married quarters for only 3 per cent of their total labour force. Without any attempt to create a settled black working population, therefore, the South African economy is characterized by extremely inefficient use of labour. The government-appointed Tomlinson Commission found that

> Out of a total annual potential of 1,140,000 man-years (one year's labour rendered by one man) available in the Bantu areas (or somewhat less if two to three weeks' leave per year is allowed for), only 480,000 man-years are economically used, and of this latter total only 433,000 man-years are applied in paid employment in the non-Bantu areas. This means that there are always, on the average, 600,000 man-years of labour available which are not economically used.

This figure applies only to African migrants within the Republic, and is an assessment moreover based on the present capacity to work, so that it says little about the productivity potential of African labour.

The human consequences of such a policy are clear. With low wages, few opportunities for African advancement or specialized training, and an authoritarian employment structure, the worker is reluctant to accept his urban condition. Because he is denied success at work, he is likely to direct his interests towards social activities based either on the tribe or on new urban groups. If he does not consider himself to be a permanent town-dweller, his ultimate interests will be in the rural areas, and his work a short-term necessity, 'something like compulsory military service, a period when hardships have to be endured and little mercy can be expected.'[3] The permanent town-dweller, on the other hand, will form new sets of social relationships based on contacts outside work. If, as in East London, the workers are nearly all drawn from the same tribe, the social relationships will reflect tribal ties, but tribal ties confused and complicated by new values; family relationships are less patriarchal, town institutions are accepted as normal in place of country ones, the whole social universe is urban, and English rather than Xhosa may be spoken. But the social life and domestic relationships will contain all ambitions, and work may be simply the essential price to pay for living in town. The price is certainly high; a survey of part of Cape Town found that 36 per cent of the workers were unmarried and that of the remainder, just under half the wives were living out of town.[4] Another survey, of workers in a Dunlop factory, found that only 6 per cent of the married men had their wives in town. Even though higher education may bring with it indifference to tribal relations, it is not surprising that many workers continue to see the tribe and the rural areas as the only real forms of security.

These three examples of work practice in different parts of Africa suggest that where management encourages workers to settle, gain skills and secure chances of promotion, the workers will respond by adapting to the new industrial environment. Where there are no such incentives but wage-earning is a response to the deterioration of agriculture, the expectation of improved living standards, and the development of urban communities, the workers will reluctantly accept the need for wage-labour and at work behave as their situation demands, but otherwise will centre their interests altogether on the community and on obtaining necessary social amenities.

For most of Africa the creation of a stable wage-labour force has not been deliberately promoted either by employers or by governments. If there is a growing middle class in several countries, in very few is there a firmly-established proletariat. And even today few independent African governments consciously plan for a major industrial sector, though the pace of Africanization is likely to bring with it some stabilization of labour. For many years to come trade unions are likely to be dealing with a large percentage of short-term migrants in the work-force, though in very different degrees, as the examples of Uganda, Zambia and Morocco show.

Towards an African Working Class

In his survey of workers in Kampala, Walter Elkan found that most wage-earners

> look upon employment as a means of obtaining the capital which would enable them to enjoy a higher standard of living at home. Consequently they look upon employment as a temporary expedient to amass money and they come to Kampala because the money wages there are higher than in the countryside or in the smaller towns.[5]

To some extent attitudes to wage-earning depend on the distance travelled to work. The Baganda, who live in and around Kampala, have tended to stay longer at work so as to earn higher wages and obtain promotion. They have also been able to enjoy two incomes at the same time because they live on smallholdings round the town from which they commute daily to work. The higher living standards and costs prevailing in Buganda has been a further factor in compelling the Baganda to work; if they have left wage-employment, this has rarely been for a return to subsistence agriculture but for forms of small-scale capitalist enterprise – commercial farming, garages, shops, or the contracting business. In the main, however, the high spending-patterns in Buganda have made the saving required for such capital investment difficult, and the creation of a permanent labour-force is likely to proceed rapidly. Management policies could assist in creating incentives for staying at work, but these are inclined merely to confirm tendencies already present in local work attitudes.

In addition to the Baganda, migrants form an important part of the Ugandan labour force. These include two groups: short-term migrants who come mainly from Rwanda and Burundi to earn savings for some specific purpose, and long-term migrants from Kenya found mainly at Jinja who, like the South African migrants, maintain a dual relationship with town and country. These long-term migrants leave members of their family in charge of their farms, which they periodically visit; but wage-employment is their main source of income. Because of their near-permanency and their important role as a minority group, they have become the most militant organizers of Ugandan unions. Unlike the Baganda workers, who remain socially to a very large extent within traditional tribal groups, the Kenya migrants are partly de-tribalized and may therefore form the basis of the ideal-type proletariat.

In Zambia the picture is entirely different. Apart from having a European wage-force which has until recently dominated the pattern of labour conditions, the towns are created largely for a migrant population, drawn from over seventy tribal groups, covering Zambia itself, Malawi and Tanganyika. Housing in most towns is linked closely with the dominant mining companies, and provides family accommodation as well as single-worker rooms. There are therefore present all those conditions working for and against urbanization which are found in South Africa, except that the employers have conceded more in terms of Africanization and the stabilization of the work force than the South Africans have done, and that today the government of Zambia is African. But since independence the earlier policy of trying to move towards 'equal pay for equal work' has been reversed. Two wage-scales have been introduced, one for Africans and one for 'expatriate staff', although the theory of equal opportunity still stands. There does seem to be a chance, therefore, that companies may prefer to train Africans for higher skilled jobs, as they will have to pay them approximately half that Europeans would get, though certain forms of job reservation for Europeans still exist. In the light of these changes it is difficult to say what kind of labour-force will emerge over the next few years, but one of the interesting social consequences of the earlier growth of mining in Zambia has been the similar degrees of mobility shown by Europeans and Africans. In 1958, 36.7 per cent of European workers had less than two years service, compared with 33.3 per cent of the Africans; 60.6 per cent of the Europeans had worked less than five years, compared with 61.1 per cent of the Africans.[6] The organization of mining in Zambia would therefore seem to suggest that all races find an element of instability in the type of work offered and the accompanying conditions. In spite of this there is clearly an 'increasing commitment of Africans to the urban way of life'. In the Copperbelt towns during the 'fifties, 28.6 per cent of the population in Broken Hill and 24.3 per cent in Ndola had lived over ten years away from the rural areas.[7] The people who stayed in town increasingly came to view their social situation in urban terms: tribal relationships were of secondary importance and gave way to the new loyalties of trade union, political party and the urban court. Even though the tribe continued to have some importance in personal and social relations, social prestige or 'class' assumed increasing significance as a measurement of relationships. Styles of dress, transport, language, religion all contributed to a conscious adoption of 'western' styles and reference points from which town-dwellers assess the social standing of each other. In such an atmosphere it is hardly surprising that the unions rapidly gained the support of the wage-earners during the 1950s; a large proportion of the workers saw wages as their only source of income and the towns as a permanent alternative to the land.

The urban clusters of the Zambian Copperbelt have been based almost entirely on the growth of the mining industry, and this gives towns like Ndola and Luanshya, in spite of segregated housing and other facilities, and the existence of separate mining and government townships, a remarkably homogeneous appearance. They are noticeably industrial in character, with the bulk of housing settled round the main plants and mining areas, and facilities which have conspicuously grown out of industrial development. In contrast, cities like Casablanca in North Africa have been developed from at least three sources: an old *medina*, with a long evolution of trade and small-scale industry; a European quarter brought into existence during the recent colonial period and too obviously favoured and well-spaced; and the new *bidonvilles* and new *medina* comprised mainly of shacks filled with migrants who have swamped the city over the past forty years in search of work. Whatever lack of consistent policy can be noted in Zambia bears no relation to the haphazard development of industry and urbanization in Casablanca.

As among Africans on the Copperbelt, the mobility among Moroccans was strictly limited, but here less on the basis of an open colour bar than on the domination of a European *petite bourgeoisie* which controlled all the important occupations. Southern Morocco lost large numbers to the towns for no other reason

African Trade Unions

than the appearance of opportunity there and the stagnation of local agriculture. No effort was made to train these migrants even in semi-skilled jobs, for in the sluggish economy of protectorate Morocco the half-million Europeans were adequate enough to man even these, and the competition for unskilled work produced a mass of urban unemployed. When the UMT was formed in 1955, it organized unemployed workers as well as the employed, and of its 600,000 members more than half were unable to pay their dues because they were either underemployed or unemployed altogether. The 'proletariat' of Morocco was like the rootless masses described in Algeria by Ahmed Mezerna –

the bands of men, women and children and aged, almost totally naked, whom misery and fear of death have pushed towards the cities and who, each morning, search the garbage pails, disputing with dogs and cats for remnants of food, the rags and the empty tin cans.[8]

Jobs in Morocco were insecure or non-existent; family ties were disrupted by migration and poverty; 'houses' were

made of old packing cases, bits of cloth and discarded gasoline cans ... rooms in the shacks were sublet to new arrivals to the point where it was a rare family that had more than one room. The hazards to health that resulted from overcrowding were further heightened by the absence of sewage disposal facilities and the rarity of water points.[9]

For 95 per cent of the population, the *per capita* income worked out (in 1956–8) at £28 a year, compared with a national average of £63.[10]

In North Africa, cities like Algiers, Oran, Tunis, Tripoli, Cairo and Alexandria all, like Casablanca, have their bands of the displaced and unemployed. And in parts of Tropical Africa the picture takes on a disturbing similarity. At Brazzaville in the late 1950s, it was estimated that out of a total population of 100,000 some 9,000 were 'unemployed' or 'workless', while there was in addition 'a large floating population ... (which) has no definite ties, is unproductive and consequently raises the same problems as those of the unemployed people settling in the town.'[11] A 1962 report calculated that there were between 6,000 and 7,000 unemployed youth in the city. Across the river, in a 1959 survey of Leopoldville squatters, it was found that 73 per cent were unemployed. In their living quarters there was a complete lack of hygiene, sewers and means of refuse disposal, and lack of drinking water forced the squatters to drink from streams. 'Young people are not helped or directed and since they suffer particularly from unemployment they tend to gather in delinquent bands, smoking hemp, thieving, attacking young girls.'[12] Further South, in the capital of Tanganyika, Dar-es-Salaam, and the surrounding urban areas it was calculated in 1962 that 13,500 were unemployed and 11,500 employed only on an intermittent basis; but 'it is thought that the true figures would be much higher.'[13] In neighbouring Kenya, the figures are very high indeed.

Any verdict on the existence of a 'working class' in Africa is consequently confused. Although there are areas like Buganda where urban wage-labour is developing within a tribal structure, and others like the Zambian Copperbelt where industrialization is producing an urban proletariat with its own distinctive patterns of life, the most evident growth overall may be in the ranks of the unemployed, the casually employed and the dispossessed. A few countries in Tropical Africa (Nigeria, Ghana, Senegal, the formerly Belgian Congo and Zambia) now have a wage-earning sector with second or third generation workers, but in most others the wage-labour force is still very small and largely migrant. No clear pattern emerges from these very different conditions, and any comparison with other countries in their earlier stages of industrialization does not help very much. In Britain the workers who moved from the land to the factories in the late eighteenth and early nineteenth centuries were not peasants with a share in communal land but agricultural labourers, who 'stayed in the towns not because they found conditions there attractive but because, unpleasant though town life may have been, it was preferred to the life of an agricultural labourer.'[14] Although they had many adjustments to make when they moved to the towns, these workers were already used to a money economy, to systems of payment by wages and even, in many cases, to the use of elementary machinery. They were moving from one form of employment, or one form of insecurity, to another. The African today who abandons his small-holding may be abandoning what small security he knows or is ever likely to have. In moving he has to balance loss of security against the possibility of a gain in real earnings; the English farm worker made a much simpler economic calculation, in favour of the higher earnings in town. In the end, of course, the early English worker was like the contemporary African in being poor, and out of poverty he and his fellows constructed their own visions of a new society. The English worker looked to a utopian future and produced protest movements and theories of social change that ranged from religious accommodation (Methodism) through 'communitarian yearning' (Owenism) to open revolt (Chartism). In doing so he drew on many different traditions and many industrial experiences, and thus developed his consciousness of class identity. As E. P. Thompson puts it,

class happens when some men, as the result of common experiences (inherited or shared) feel and articulate the identity of their interests as between themselves and as against other men whose interests are different from (and usually opposed to) theirs.[15]

The history of working-class movements in England is a slow dawning of class consciousness, crystallizing 'the identity of interests' into a loosely-federated political party that encompassed various working-men's organizations. The years between the first early failures and the first Labour Government are marked by a multitude of 'movements' led by the more educated members of the class and by 'massive apathy' from many of the workers themselves, especially 'the least skilled, least educated, least organized and therefore least hopeful of the poor.'[16] When trade unions developed in the late nineteenth century they catered only for a small section of the workers; 'the immense mass of semi-proletarians, the floating, irregularly employed paupers, outworkers or hands in small workshops, the half-world of misery ... was for all practical purposes outside the range of unions.'[17]

The contrast with Africa is striking. If the English working class slowly evolved a mixture of institutions and programmes

Towards an African Working Class

that produced some rough semblance of unity, the African working class has had its spontaneous outbursts and its tentative steps towards organization rapidly transformed into centralized institutions. Protest has been quickly 'nationalized' and turned into government formulas for mass organization and national solidarity. If in some countries, like Nigeria and Congo (Leopoldville), there is still 'massive apathy' and a continual succession of messianic movements, splinter political and industrial societies, and persistent tribal loyalties, elsewhere worker discontents have been sluiced into productive agencies. Formally at least, 'mass apathy' has been abolished; recent figures for Ghana's TUC show more dues-paying affiliates than there are wage-earners. The results of such organization are therefore likely to be rather different from anything so far experienced in Western Europe. Either the workers will, as in Eastern Europe, China or North Vietnam, accept the communitarian aims of governments and work out their own role in the new party structures (if sufficiently discontented, pursuing the logical implications of worker control by insurrection, as in the Hungarian revolt of 1956), or just possibly, and particularly if the numbers of unemployed remain large, they will engage in violent anti-constitutional activities, as in parts of Latin America, to be met by 'massacre as a permanent political institution'.[18]

But if the existence of a stable working class is so far uneven and the future of the institutions to which it belongs uncertain, the other aspect of 'class' activity – social differentiation – does have more solid support.

The idea of classes in Africa has, in significant measure, been obscured by the assumptions of colonial administrators, nationalist politicians and some anthropologists, who have either asserted 'the nineteenth-century view of Africa as a bloodsoaked Dark Continent'[19] with total anarchy and lack of political or economic organization, or have reacted against this by stressing the constitutional communalism of pre-colonial Africa. The reality was rather more complex. Certainly there were societies like the Nuer or the Tallensi where 'ordered anarchy' prevailed, with an absence of rigid class divisions, centralized government or any permanent administration; but it is difficult to believe that immediately prior to colonial rule these formed the majority of political groupings. Large empires in many parts of Africa, coupled with the general absence of individual property rights, suggest, as a prominent French Africanist has written,

> the existence of a form of production in the framework of rural communities (which ignore private ownership of land), and the exploitation of man by man inside these communities (patriarchal slavery) and above them (tribal or military aristocracies, dignitaries and state functionaries).[20]

If the traditional Marxist analysis of class by property distinctions did not apply, classes on the basis of political, military and economic advantage certainly existed. When colonial powers gained control they tended to harden the power structure, partly by the system of indirect rule and partly by introducing totally new administrative forms and economic pursuits which created, often out of existing *élites*, a new social superstructure. In the French territories, as in Nigeria and Uganda, the contrast between the new *élites* and the masses tended to be more marked than elsewhere, with the new middle class and the professional occupations drawn primarily from the traditional *élites*; but everywhere, depending on the level of economic development, a new hierarchy of wealth and expertise came into existence, normally taking its values and living standards from the European administrators, traders and settlers. The experience of the French territories is instructive. In Senegal by 1958 the Europeans (less than 2 per cent of the population) absorbed 31–34 per cent of all incomes; in Gabon (1 per cent of the population), 54–56 per cent.[21] Round them, as independence approached, there clustered an African *élite* expecting and to some extent getting a similar standard of living. (The successful agitation by trade unions for higher wages had in French West Africa given them French wage-levels as a basis for negotiation.) One year after independence 60 per cent of Dahomey's budget went on the salaries of government personnel.[22] In the Ivory Coast a middle class, partly indigenous, has

> transformed an egalitarian society into a society of employers and wage-earners. ... The planters increasingly refuse to allow the

Towards an African Working Class

peasants to work or use their adjoining lands, now disinherited. This new affluent class is evidently determined to consolidate its privileges.[23]

But the new class, though well off, is insecure because its economic control is limited; it must accept the requirements laid down by the external trading powers and therefore has to act cautiously, drawing its values from foreign commercial interests and jockeying for power within the state by joining hands with the new political and bureaucratic *élite*. This *élite* is itself very much one of the professional middle class and the growing business sector. In the Ivory Coast in 1960, 75 per cent of the office-holders in the Assembly or government were teachers, civil servants, university-trained professionals or in 'big business'; 29 per cent were self-employed, and there were no small farmers or manual workers. Similar figures obtained in other states: in Nigeria 84 per cent of the members of the Federal Assembly were in professional, academic or business occupational groups; in Senegal, 88 per cent; in Ghana, 90 per cent; and in Kenya, 87 per cent. Except for territories like Northern Nigeria or Buganda, chiefly status is today a secondary consideration in gaining political office, though tribal or family links play a great part. In West Africa there is a tendency for one tribal complex to dominate the main legislative body, while in East Africa there is not.

Like the formerly French territories, the formerly British ones have not rarely thrown up 'governing bureaucratic castes who enrich themselves by looting public funds.'[24] The recent general strike in Nigeria and the debate produced by the Morgan Report on Wages and Salaries revealed striking differences in income. In the state-controlled sector, while unskilled workers were earning between £36 and £78 a year, Ministers and managing directors were drawing between £3,500 and £10,000.

There are twenty-seven Ministers in the Federal Government, with the Prime Minister earning £5,000 a year and the others £3,000 each. On top of their salaries the Ministers are given houses specially built for them at a cost of £32,000 each. They also pay no electricity, telephone or water charges; they get a basic car allowance of £80 a month, and when on an official trip they are also paid 1/3 a mile. In addition

they get cheap petrol from Public Works Department pumps....
Senior civil servants and officials of Corporations fare little worse.
The Federal Parliament meets for only a few weeks in each year,
but on Victoria Island in Lagos there are three blocks of flats especially
for Members. In Lagos there are modern multi-storey hotels, offices
and packed department stores. But there are also acres of slum shanty-
towns where two families may share a home of corrugated iron and
sacking.[25]

During the general strike itself, A. H. Adebola, one of the leading trade unionists, claimed that 'some foreign industrialists are
being scared away because of the allegation that some public
figures demand 10 per cent commission before the industrialists
can establish in Nigeria.' He also attacked 'the appointments of
wives and concubines of Ministers and Permanent Secretaries
who work twenty hours a week in a bank and are paid £840 per
annum.'

Even in Ghana, with its more rigorous control of patronage,
government investigations have revealed the misuse of public
funds and facilities by members of the political *élite*, though on
nothing like as blatant a scale as is found in Nigeria or the
Ivory Coast. From the scandal over Mrs Edusei's gold bed to the
building of a Casino in Accra for those with incomes of over
£1,500 a year, it is obvious that a sizeable *élite* exists, members of
which have a much higher income than the average wage-
earner or peasant. Large-scale corruption was denounced after
the official inquiry by Judge Akainyah in March 1964, and, as
the character of M.P.s shows, the ruling *élite* is far from occupa-
tionally representative of the people. But quite apart from the
issue of high living by the political *élite*, the evolution of Ghana's
social structure suggests something of the way in which distinctions may develop throughout Africa. Because Ghana
already possessed a significant middle class at independence, and
because the ambitious industrialization plans have demanded
new managers, entrepreneurs and other executives, it is not
surprising that a sizeable commercial *élite* has come into being.
According to the 1960 *Survey of High-Level Manpower*, the
'administrative, managerial, professional, technical and skilled
occupations in the country' would increase by one-third between

Towards an African Working Class

1961 and 1965. According to the Seven-Year Plan, managers would increase by 23 per cent between 1963 and 1970, professional groups by 26 per cent, sub-professional and technical grades by 171 per cent, and traders by 50 per cent. The Plan also sees the need substantially to increase salaries at certain higher levels of employment, particularly for teachers and technologists; the proportion of those in such 'high-level' occupations would increase from 4 per cent to 7 per cent of the total. Both in the current figures and in their projections, therefore, it is easy to see the development of new contending categories. If the proportion of people occupying top-level or specialist posts is now 4 per cent, it is also instructive to note that the government's 'middle level' category (clerks, traders, miners, transport workers, service traders and other semi-skilled workers) is already 16 per cent; the 'unskilled' category (petty traders, miscellaneous artisans and labourers), 20 per cent; and employed agricultural workers, 8 per cent. The proportion of people (apart from the cash-cropping peasants) directly engaged in commercial activity is 28 per cent; the contours of occupational, if not class, difference are beginning to emerge. At one extreme are the occupations directly tied to the modern economy; at the other, the self-employed farmers whose production is increasingly geared to the external market. In between are the petty traders, artisans and village labourers, whose activities are dominated by the expanding economy but still attuned to the demands of subsistence agriculture and rural living. Over and above these, there remain the two major forces affecting the direction of the economy and the provision and level of jobs – the government and overseas interests.

Although Ghana is more advanced and ambitious in its programmes than most other African states, it points to the occupations and the 'class' groupings that are emerging all over. Buganda and the former French West African territories provide variations of this pattern and suggest the enormous differences throughout Africa in the distribution of power and occupations. In former French West and Equatorial Africa[26] the proportion of peasants ranges from 95 per cent of the active workers in Mali and Chad, through 80 per cent in Senegal, to 71 per cent in

African Trade Unions

Congo (Brazzaville). The wage-earners range from 29 per cent in Congo and Gabon, through 19 per cent in the Ivory Coast, 14 per cent in the Central African Republic and Guinea, to less than 4 per cent in Togo, Upper Volta, Niger and Mali. In a few states, planters are important; in Senegal 14 per cent of the population cultivate 43 per cent of the land, and a survey of one region in Dahomey revealed that a third of the landowners occupied 60 per cent of the land, while 10 per cent of the peasants owned no land at all and 40 per cent had insufficient with which to support themselves. The differences in income are particularly marked. At one extreme are the peasants, earning 10,000 CFA a year *per head*, and the unskilled wage-earners with 30,000 CFA *per family* a year while at the other are planters in the Ivory Coast and Senegal who make upwards of 175,000 CFA a year and the major political functionaries. The earnings of the politicians are difficult to assess; but in Cameroun, for example, National Assembly deputies have been receiving 185,000 CFA *a month*, as well as various other payments. These staggering income differences between the various sectors of the population are having their effect on the morale of peasants and wage-earners. A recent sociological survey of the Ivory Coast noted 'the birth of feelings of hatred and jealousy towards the *nouveau riche*.'[27] And it seems clear that recent disturbances in Dahomey, Gabon, Congo(Brazzaville) and the Ivory Coast were directly related to tensions produced by the lack of coordinated development and the crude ostentation of the ruling *élite*. As the trials of ex-Presidents Maga and Youlou have shown, new *élites* can hope to legitimize their claim to power by attacking the corruption and acquisitiveness of their predecessors.

In Buganda fairly clear social differences have been produced by the adaptation of a traditional African social system to a modernized economy and administration. An economist[28] has noted several main income categories: those earning over £300 a year; a middle income group earning between £50 and £300 a year; peasants earning about £35, migrant wage-earners with between £10 and £35, and those 'who have fallen, for one reason or another, well below the general level of prosperity,' whose money incomes do not exceed £10 a year. The prosperous group included the land-owning aristocracy and self-made land-owners, businessmen and holders of professional qualifications; some of the incomes were very high (over £2,000 a year), and as a whole showed a remarkable blend of traditional power, canalized into new economic and political roles, with the *nouveau riche* who had risen by their own effort. Below them was

the sub-professional type of employee – medical orderlies, agricultural instructors, primary schoolteachers and the like; the whole race of clerks; the skilled and semi-skilled workers ... several thousand up-country and suburban shopkeepers ... and above all the very numerous farmers who, without achieving any spectacular volume of output, treat agriculture in some degree as a business.

Within the agricultural sector, extreme differences were noticeable: 32 per cent of the peasants were classed as 'poor' (owning less than ten acres each); 20 per cent were landless labourers; and 2 per cent could be classed as large farmers. In a survey of Mailo, a Buganda region, 6 per cent of the total number of land-owners farmed over 300 acres each, while 50 per cent farmed less than twenty acres. Worsley is probably right when he comments on these figures: 'Development of the Buganda kind is capitalist development, and leads to the emergence of property-based classes which sooner or later will express economic interests in political terms.'[29]

The contention that social differences do not exist at all in Africa has clearly little support from the evidence. Apart from the large mass of peasants, many of whom are living at barely subsistence level, the growth of new middle-class occupations and property-owning groups is creating substantial differences in living standards, with African bureaucrats and professional politicians enjoying enormous power and economic strength. But the existence of differences does not necessarily produce a 'class struggle'. As *Présence Africaine* commented in a discussion of the book by Raymond Barbé:

It is difficult to conclude from Barbé's analysis that social classes exist and are antagonistic. ... The fact that there are 'peasant masses', 'wage-earners' and 'young bourgeois Africans' does not prove the existence of this phenomenon, because there can be no social classes without class consciousness and a sense of belonging.[30]

African Trade Unions

This is perhaps the crux of the matter. Classes in the sense of antagonistic social groups are clearly no more than embryonic in Africa today. The new divisions within society have not in any way produced hard categories; there is little evidence that 'class consciousness' has been developed sufficiently among either the peasants or the wage-earners for them to put a class-loyalty before tribalism, regionalism or nationalism. But the areas for tension are there. As *Présence Africaine* concludes: 'If there is no real class consciousness at the moment, it could be born by the crying inequalities that are obstinately practised by our governing bodies.'

Chapter 6: Notes

1. V. L. Allen, 'Management and Labour in Africa', *The Listener*, 15 August 1963, p. 227.
2. F. A. Wells and W. A. Warmington, *Studies in Industrialisation*, O.U.P., 1962, p. 251.
3. P. Meyer, *Townsmen or Tribesmen*, O.U.P., Cape Town, 1961, p. 144.
4. S. van der Horst, *African Workers in Town*, O.U.P., Cape Town, 1964, pp. 42–5.
5. W. Elkan, *Migrants and Proletarians*, O.U.P., 1960, p. 42.
6. P. Mason, *Year of Decision – Rhodesia and Nyasaland*, O.U.P., 1960, p. 144.
7. J. C. Mitchell, 'Urbanisation, Detribalisation and Stabilisation in Southern Africa', in UNESCO, *Social Implications of Urbanisation and Industrialisation in Africa South of the Sahara*, 1956, p. 703.
8. Quoted by Joan Gillespie, *Algeria, Rebellion and Revolution*, Benn, 1960, p. 69.
9. Charles H. Stewart, *The Economy of Morocco, 1912–1962*, Harvard U.P., 1964, p. 142.
10. ibid., p. 143.
11. Roland Devauges, 'Le chomage à Brazzaville', *CCTA Bulletin*, No. 8, 1960, p. 22.
12. Paul Raymaekers, 'Le squatting à Leopoldville', *CCTA Bulletin*, Vol. VIII, No. 4, pp. 34–5.
13. CCTA, *Symposium on Unemployed Youth*, Dar-es-Salaam, 1963, p. 54.
14. W. Elkan, op. cit., p. 138.
15. E. P. Thompson, *The Making of the English Working Class*, Gollancz, 1963, p. 9.
16. E. J. Hobsbawm, *The Age of Revolution*, Weidenfeld and Nicolson, 1962, p. 204.
17. E. J. Hobsbawm, *Labouring Men*, Weidenfeld and Nicolson, 1964, p. 321.
18. E. J. Hobsbawm, 'The Most Critical Area in the World', *The Listener*, 2 May 1963, pp. 735–7.

African Trade Unions

19. P. Worsley, *The Third World*, Weidenfeld and Nicolson, 1964, p. 205.
20. J. Suret-Canale, Review of R. Barbé's 'Classes Sociales', *Présence Africaine*, Vol. 22, No. 50, p. 277.
21. Raymond Barbé, *Les Classes Sociales en Afrique Noire*, Economie et Politique (Paris) 1964, passim.
22. R. Dumont, *L'Afrique Noire est Mal Partie*, du Seuil, 1962, p. 201.
23. E. H. Favrod, *L'Afrique seule*, du Seuil, 1960, p. 156.
24. Suret-Canale in *Présence Africaine*, op. cit., p. 280.
25. John Bulloch, 'Nigeria Anger at Leaders' Rich Living', *Sunday Telegraph*, 21 June 1964.
26. Figures from Barbé, op. cit., passim.
27. B. Holas, *Changements sociaux en Côte d'Ivoire*, Centres des sciences humaines de Côte d'Ivoire, Abidjan, 1963, p. 10.
28. Figures derived from L. A. Fallers (ed), *The King's Men*, O.U.P., 1963, pp. 16–210.
29. P. Worsley, op. cit., p. 220.
30. 'About the Class Struggle in Negro Africa', *Présence Africaine*, Vol. 25, No. 53, p. 249.

7 Trade Unions and Governments –
(i) In Opposition

Today, African governments play an important and expanding part in trade union affairs. This situation is not unique to independence or to Africa itself. As the earlier chapters have shown, the colonial governments were particularly concerned with developing systems of industrial relations that suited their own administrative convenience, and in every colony the trade unions were subjected to a variety of legal restrictions. In most other parts of the world trade unions have either been brought under government control or have had to operate in spite of complex and restrictive legislation. Moreover, in some states where ruling parties have close relationships with the trade unions, they have used the connexion to extract from the unions some of their independent bargaining rights. The important question, therefore, is what kind of relationship do unions in developing countries have with their governments? Indeed, other questions of industrial relations are of far less significance than the role that the unions find for themselves in the state apparatus. This is because, as one socialist has recently noted:

When misery and inequality are the destiny of an entire nation; when there is no technical infra-structure; when there is no literacy or common culture; when there is no civic political tradition; when there is no real national identity the *State* tends to become the sole repository and reality of the society as a society. 'Civil society' is so protoplasmic, disarticulated, amorphous, impalpable that its only tangible existence is its crystallization in the State.[1]

The place given to the unions in the State (or the place that they manage to carve out for themselves) becomes an important indication of social cohesion and of the extent to which something like a 'civil society' is developing on a broad national front.

African Trade Unions

In the developed world, three situations seem to have emerged. Some states have simply banned the existing trade union movements and attempted to replace them with national union fronts which have little industrial importance and in practice little political effectiveness (the old unions have simply gone underground). Perhaps Portugal (not too developed a country herself) and Spain provide the clearest examples today. Secondly, some unions are merged into the party front unions, but the whole trade union movement, however closely controlled through legislation, is able to play an influential part in the machinery of industrial negotiations and management. Trade unions in most Communist countries are advanced cases of this tendency. Finally there are the situations, mainly in the industrial capitalist states, where the ruling parties have close working relationships with the trade unions (Sweden, Norway, Israel and Britain under Labour) or where the party of the unions is in opposition and the unions themselves have to accept severe state limitations on their activities (Germany, Australia, Japan, France). Outside these situations there are a few countries where the unions are not controlled by the state, where they do not have alliances with political parties, and where there is no voluntary control of wage claims (as in Sweden). The most important of these are the United States and Canada, but here the trade unions themselves are highly bureaucratic in structure and have come to fairly close working arrangements with the state bureaucracy (as opposed to individual parties). In the British case the fact that the Labour Party sometimes holds office does not seem to give it much control over the organization of unions and the determination of wage claims; but this is a situation which is under increasing attack both from Labour Cabinet Ministers and, recently and more significantly, from the Conservative Opposition, whose leaders would like to see union 'powers' drastically curtailed.

But these variations simply illustrate that everywhere the governments either control unions or have evolved various means of coming to terms with them while introducing certain restrictions and obligations. In developing countries the effect and extent of government intervention may be equally varied.

Trade Unions and Governments – (i) In Opposition

In Latin America, for example, where unions have had a chequered history, the governments have never hesitated to use fierce legal measures to control them. (One interesting consequence is that 'in education programmes organized by Latin American unions, the study of labour law almost invariably predominates'.[2]) But even here the unions have had a variety of relationships with governments and political parties. At one extreme, in Argentina under Peron, the Secretary-General of the Argentine Confederation of Labour attended Cabinet meetings and helped to make the unions part of government machinery; at the other, the Chilean Federation (CUTCH: Central Unica de Trabajaderes de Chile) is divided among Communists, Popular Socialists, Centre Radicals, the Catholic Falange, the Socialists of Chile and the Anarchists. In between these is a range of relationships: Mexico's almost mechanical structure, linking the Institutional Revolutionary Party and the Confederación de Trabajadores de México; the existence of two rival confederations in Colombia supporting the two major political parties; and the current anti-union legislation and imprisonment of union officials under the Castello Branco régime in Brazil. These differences are possible even though in almost every Latin American country the state

> controls the content of union by-laws, specifies the qualification of candidates for office, supervises elections, scrutinizes the conduct of meetings, audits union funds, defines the scope of union activities, requires the submission of a variety of reports concerning composition, officers and administration, and decrees what the structure of unions shall be and whether or not federations and confederations of unions shall be permitted.[3]

Uruguay seems the only important exception to this generalization.

The experiences of Latin America confirm two features that reappear in Africa. In a developing country the government is particularly prone to impose strict limits on the activities of unions and is inclined to assume a proprietorial role over the technicalities of union organization. At present in Africa there seem to be two main tendencies in union-government relations. First there is the attempt to assimilate unions into a centralized political structure, with the unions functioning as the 'industrial wing' of the ruling party. Second, the unions are independent of the ruling *élite* and pursue policies in opposition to those of the government. But in practice, of course, the situation is a lot more fluid. For example, in Morocco the unions have been inside the government machinery and are now outside; in Dahomey the unions were integrated only to further a *coup d'état* in 1963; in Ghana and Tunisia the unions have long been part of the one-party complex, but both have been allowed considerable autonomy in developing their own external affiliations and policies (though in Tunisia the autonomy looked like being lost during major policy changes in mid-1965); and although Zambian unions are outside the ruling party structure, they are subjected to strict legislative controls over administration. Even where unions act as an opposition, they still find that the government is ubiquitous. It will appoint labour officers to supervise the registration of unions; it may control union appointments; will almost certainly audit union funds; and will attempt to get unions to accept wage policies which they have had no part in drafting.

In such states the unions are normally in opposition to *élites* or political parties that represent elements of traditional rule, the growing bourgeoisie and possibly the army. In many cases the ruling party is in fact a federation (or the leading element in a federation), making a political consensus difficult to achieve and thus giving the unions freedom to manoeuvre between the various interest groups. The most important examples are Morocco, Nigeria, the Sudan and Congo(Leopoldville), but variations are also found in Sierra Leone and the Cameroons. Although in all of these territories trade unions perform an opposition role, they are by no means united over what that role ought to be. In Nigeria, for example, the unions are divided into several different federations, each supporting different political groups, and a large number of individual unions, not affiliated to federations, who eclectically support no political line or even a number in turn. The causes of division are somewhat similar to those suggested for unions in areas of European settlement; while some chance remains of achieving change through con-

Trade Unions and Governments – (i) In Opposition

stitutional methods, trade unions will differ over the tactics to be employed. There are always the 'constitutionalist' unions working as far as possible with the government and claiming to be non-political, and the 'opposition' unions who see the only alternative in militant action and the creation of radical opposition parties.

MOROCCO AND THE SUDAN

Since independence the major trade union federation in Morocco, the Union Marocaine du Travail, has had three phases of action. Up to 1959, when the major political party, the Istiqlal, split into two factions, the UMT was the only trade union federation in Morocco. Affiliated to the party of the independence struggle, it was also frequently consulted by Mohammed V on major economic policy decisions, and gained a place on most central planning committees. Its political caution, considering the conservative nature of the régime, was impressive.

More than any other group in Morocco the UMT succeeded in gaining legal and social benefits for its members.... Strikes could have been used with political effect, but the union leaders exercised restraint. The union leaders understood that no redistribution of existing wealth would noticeably ameliorate the workers' conditions; such a vitally needed change in conditions would require sizeable increases in total national production.[4]

But the split in Istiqlal and the death of Mohammed V reduced the UMT's consultative status. After 1959 it allied itself with the UNFP (Union Nationale des Forces Populaires) led by Mehdi Ben Barka, Abderrahim Bouabid, and the former Istiqlal prime minister Abdallah Ibrahim. Istiqlal was pushed out of office, and Morocco came increasingly under the combined rule of the royal household, senior businessmen, and the Army. Under Hassan II and his chief minister, Reda Guedira, important measures of land reform and social security, initiated under the government of Ibrahim, were blocked, while the power of the growing Moroccan commercial class and the state bureaucracy increased. Hassan II paid less and less attention to the UMT (though its numerical strength increased, particularly after

139

African Trade Unions

1961 with the extensive organization of the agricultural workers). Although the Istiqlal formed a rival trade union centre, the Union Générale des Travailleurs Marocaines, in 1960, this has never posed a serious threat to the UMT and has likewise been little involved in national economic policy. The change in government tactics has had its effect on union militancy. If there were few strikes before 1960, there has been increasing agitation since. In 1961 the number of man-days lost through strikes increased by 150 per cent over the previous year, and the unions have taken the lead in opposing the Hassan régime. At military courts in November 1963, Ben Barka and Hamid Berrada (president of the Moroccan Students Union) were condemned to death *in absentia* (both had fled into exile before the trial began) and the UNFP and the left-wing of the Istiqlal were both compelled to operate clandestinely beyond the vigilance of the police. In the face of Hassan's attempts to set up a Gaullist-type régime, the political parties have been isolated and divided. Few attempts to raise the standard of living of the peasantry or the city workers have been made, and the government has repeatedly acted out of deference to the landowners' Moroccan Agricultural Union and the various commercial organizations while blocking all agrarian reform and reconstruction of industry. The unions are now caught in a vicious dilemma. The cost of living has continued to rise while productivity has fallen. External pressure from the Common Market, which absorbs over two-thirds of Morocco's trade, and internal recessions have brought government austerity programmes. Without any government support or interest, the UMT has mounted campaigns for increased participation in planning councils and, latterly, organized militant strike activity. By 1965 the trade unions and the government were in open conflict. On 22 and 23 March, major demonstrations and strikes in Casablanca and other cities were held by students and trade unionists. Police and soldiers fired on the crowds, killing 100 people and injuring 450. Sixty-one trade unionists and student leaders were sentenced to imprisonment.

The trade union movement in the Sudan was granted legal permission to create federations only in 1957, one year after independence, seven years after the Sudan Workers' Trade

Trade Unions and Governments – (i) In Opposition

Union Federation had been formed, and ten years after the colonial government had recognized the first union, the railwaymen's Workers' Affairs Association. At that time two federations existed – the SWTUF and the ICFTU affiliate, the Sudan Government Workers' Trade Union Federation. The SWTUF was by far the larger group and was in close contact with the WFTU (Shafia Ahdem Ahmed el Sheikh, its secretary-general, was a vice-president of the WFTU). But of these only the SGWTUF applied for registration, and throughout 1958 the SWTUF was engaged in protracted court cases to prevent the government from having it declared illegal. A military *coup d'état* in November 1958 was followed by the suspension of trade unions and the right to strike. The offices of the SWTUF were raided, its newspapers closed, and several of its leaders arrested and imprisoned. For eighteen months no trade union activity was permitted (though from abroad members of the SWTUF were active as publicists, and one, Ibrahim Zakaria, became a secretary of the WFTU). Then, in 1960, the Abboud government introduced a Trade Unions Ordinance (Amendment) Act which allowed unions to function once more, though under even more stringent restrictions than those that had been imposed by the British. Federations of unions were prohibited; no union could be formed except where more than fifty workers were employed in the same firm; white-collar workers and government employees were forbidden to organize; all unions had to be registered and approved by the Ministry of Information and Labour. The effect of this Act was to exclude at least 60 per cent of workers from all trade union organizations (about half of the wage earners worked for employers using less than fifty workers) and to prevent effective coordination of policies by the unions. Paradoxically, however, it also increased the strategic importance of the railway workers, who had always been the backbone of Sudanese trade unionism. Because of its geographical position, Khartoum, which dominates the economy and administration of the Sudan, can be isolated and all but paralysed by any railway stoppage. In 1961, after only one year under the new Act, the railway workers stopped all rail traffic in protest against the military junta's rejection of a memorandum calling for a return

African Trade Unions

to civilian government. This was accompanied by demonstrations and riots; the strikers were finally met by the Minister of the Interior; and though one very unpopular general was deposed, the junta resisted any further pressures. But if the immediate result of this campaign was failure, it prepared the way for the successful *coup* of 1964. Another, better-planned railway strike succeeded in cutting Khartoum off from the outside world and forcing the military junta to resign. Backed by discontented soldiers and some leaders of the banned political parties, a coalition government was formed, including Shafia Ahdem Ahmed el Sheikh as Minister without Portfolio and workers' representative. But the success was short-lived. Within six months of the *coup* a right-wing government had been elected to power, and the unions returned to their pre-1958 role of political-industrial opposition.

In both of these countries the unions, representing mainly the urban workers, have proved themselves important focal points of discontent. But their political success has been limited by the membership and appeal of the unions, confined as they are mainly to the urban areas, and in Sudan to the Arab North. Although the UMT has recently been successful in organizing an agricultural workers' union, the impact of UMT campaigns is still felt primarily in the cities. In both countries, therefore, the unions have been unable to transfer direct action into long-term political change. Although strikes and demonstrations can succeed in gaining the support of most town-dwellers, ruling *élites* are able to appeal to tradesmen, farmers and the military by evoking traditional nationalist and religious sentiments. Nor have the dissenting political parties succeeded in creating a broad enough social base for successful opposition. As they divide on social, regional and religious lines, the unions can only work to improve their membership in the agricultural areas, so as to begin to look like a political alternative.

NIGERIA

These problems apply in large measure to Nigeria, though the role of the military there is not a serious factor in political

Trade Unions and Governments – (i) In Opposition

decisions and the existence of three major political parties has made the creation of a united trade union movement even more difficult. At independence in 1962 there were four major union centres, reflecting both international and national political differences: the United Labour Congress of Nigeria, affiliated to the ICFTU and ATUC; the Nigerian Trades' Union Congress, supporting the AATUF; and two smaller centres, the Nigerian Workers' Council, maintaining close relations with the IFCTU, and the Northern Federation of Labour, an off-shoot of the NTUC but developing close relations with the Northern People's Congress. In 1963 a fifth centre appeared, the Labour Unity Front, formed originally by some of the larger industrial unions who had disaffiliated from the ULC and NTUC, and now sought to effect a reconciliation of the existing four centres. Unity of a kind was at last achieved in September 1963, when a Joint Action Committee was established to stage a general strike during the Republic celebrations in protest against a wage freeze. This included members of all centres except the NFL and managed to retain its cohesion until Janury 1965.

In the face of the disorganization of the unions, the Federal Government ignored the demands of union leaders for better working conditions and higher wages. It banned all public trade union demonstrations and meetings, and restricted the right to strike. Under the Six-Year Development Plan, launched in 1962, wages were pegged to allow for greater investment, but prices allowed to increase. Between 1960 and 1963 the cost of living index for Lagos rose from 132 to 142.5; for Ibadan, from 117 to 136.8; and for Enugu, from 119 to 150.7.[5] The government recognized only the ULC as a negotiating body, and refused in principle to negotiate wages. In September 1963, as a prelude to the threatened general strike, a national strike was called throughout the public services which lasted three days. After failing to break it, the government set up a Commission under Mr Justice Morgan to make a general study of wages and salaries. The strike was called off, and the JAC turned its attention towards making representations to the commission. In their evidence the unions produced a comprehensive analysis of the social and economic conditions of the country and made radical recommendations for political and economic reforms. Two kinds of claim were submitted: for a national wage policy (including national minimum wage levels), and for structural changes in the country's economy. In particular the JAC called for the nationalization of petrol, mining, the banks and insurance companies, with control over the export of profits by foreign investors. ('In our view nationalization is a post-colonial measure to restore the national economy from old and neo-colonialists ... and to give a democratic basis to our independence.') The employers and the government submitted that free wage negotiation, rather than a central policy, was a prerequisite for economic development; the government went even further and argued that limiting higher incomes, raising lower incomes and establishing a minimum wage were utopian claims.

In the event the Morgan Commission went some way towards meeting the trade union demands, though it rejected the structural proposals and reduced the JAC's minimum wage claim by 20 per cent. It proposed the fixing of guaranteed inter-professional minimum wages; the stabilization of the floating labour force; a general increase in low wages; the freezing of middle and higher incomes, with the exclusion of any rises for incomes above £600 a year; and a large reduction in the incomes of higher officials, as well as the curtailment of fringe benefits. The effect of the proposals would have been to increase wages near the guaranteed minimum (fixed according to region) by an average of 25 per cent, and those in the higher ranges (below £600) by an average of between 2 per cent and 7 per cent. Some wages would have gone up by 60 per cent, and some down by 100 per cent. The whole basis of Nigeria's political system might have been challenged by the more equal distribution. This the government was quick to see. It was not prepared to accept a levelling-off of higher wages, and saw the Commission's recommendations as endangering foreign investment. In a White Paper it recommended some wage increases (totalling about one-quarter of the Commission's) but totally ignored the Morgan proposals for an inter-professional guaranteed minimum, the stabilizing of the labour force, and the reduction of higher salaries and expenses.

Trade Unions and Governments – (i) In Opposition

The government received the Morgan Report at the end of April 1964, but delayed publication (although union leaders were given copies for their private information in the middle of May). On 26 May the JAC demanded publication of the Report and of the government's own proposals within seventy-two hours, or a general strike would be called. The government remained silent. On 31 May, after demonstrations and the arrest of leading unionists, the strike began. Initially support was concentrated in the South, but within hours the North, led by Ibrahim Nock, secretary of the NFL, joined as well, and there was an almost total work stoppage in the country. On 3 June the government finally published the report along with its own White Paper, and the effect, as even the government might have imagined, was to further unite the unions. The strike now became a protest against the government's own proposals, and some unions which had held back joined in. By 4 June over 500,000 workers were on strike. On 8 June the government threatened to dismiss all government employees who did not return to work, and some private companies issued orders dismissing their whole staff. This had some effect in the North, where Nock's NFL entered into negotiations with the regional government. But elsewhere the strike continued without much loss of support. The police were active in trying to smash demonstrations, but since these were few, incidents were not common. Ultimately on 13 June the strike ended with a compromise. The government and employers agreed to withdraw dismissal notices; there was to be no victimization; and negotiations would take place on the basis of the Morgan Report. Ultimately this meant wage increases half-way between the Morgan and White Paper proposals, no reduction in higher salaries, and some provision for industrial courts, low-cost housing and improvements in urban transport. The unions lost nothing, but did not gain guaranteed wage increases before returning to work.

The strike was economically as successful as any general strike has been. Politically it had far-reaching implications. Early in the course of the strike 'the demands of the crowd and the speeches of the trade union leaders made it clear that they

African Trade Unions

were questioning the whole social structure of Nigeria.'[6] The exposure of extravagant living by government officials, Ministers, MPs and high-grade businessmen, with the undertones of corruption and nepotism, helped to accentuate a division on class lines, while the government's ham-fisted tactics brought authority into disrepute among the workers. As one commentary noted:

It is impossible to avoid the charge against the government that it did not take the situation seriously until it was too late. There was one occasion at least when the Federal Minister of Labour, Chief J. M. Johnson, was due to hold a meeting with leaders which might have led to negotiations that would have avoided the strike; instead he went to the airport to meet the Prime Minister on his return from leave.[7]

Throughout May the government issued vague promises about the Report and, by its own leaks to the union leaders, ensured that most people knew approximately what the Report said. With Morgan's exposure of Nigerian social differences, the nation-wide rallying of wage earners and the crudeness of government tactics, it is not surprising that the strike also became an important focus of political discontent. One trade union leader, Goodluck, put it bluntly: 'Although the cause of the strike was based on economic demands, yet in its development it has raised possible political action which, with a developed Marxist-Leninist party, could have led to a proletarian revolution.'[8] Other trade unionists were less dogmatic, but the overall effect of the exercise was to heighten demands for the establishment of a socialist party and encourage the use of a general strike as a political weapon. Almost immediately the strike was over, however, the fissiparous tendencies of the Nigerian labour movement began to make themselves felt. Some of the leading trade unionists supported two new political parties, the Socialist Workers' and Farmers' Party led by Dr Otegbeye and founded in August 1963, and the Nigerian Labour Party formed after the strike in July 1964 by Michael Imoudou. But many continued to support the established groups – Adebola and Borha remained in the NCNC, Nock in the NPC – and some like Gogo Chu Nzeribe stood as independents in the federal elections later that year. As the elections them-

Trade Unions and Governments – (i) In Opposition

selves approached, it was clear that the new-found unity of the trade unions was disintegrating through factionalism. On 29 December Goodluck called for a sitdown strike on election day in protest against alleged irregularities in electoral arrangements, and this finally succeeded in destroying the unity of the JAC. A fortnight later Adebola, Borha and Chukwura led several ICFTU-aligned unions out of the JAC to form a Supreme Council of Trade Unions. As a result two Confederations existed in early 1965, and five national labour centres. Once again the Federal Government recognized the ULC as the 'only Central Labour Movement'. As *West Africa* commented:

The Nigerian labour leaders returned to their habitual postures of warfare among themselves. ... The feeling of triumph that many workers experienced after last June's general strike is no longer nearly so powerful. This stems mainly from the inability of those who want to give the labour movement political teeth to do so.... We are a long way from the Battle of Carter Bridge where Alhaji Adebola shed blood alongside Michael Imoudou. Part of the trouble has been that the movement has thrown up too many 'personalities', too individualistic to work together.[9]

But although individualism is an important issue, the main problem is that the unions have had to work in the face of government and employer opposition, while they are themselves divided along lines of external affiliation. Although the government showed some interest, through the Ministry of Labour, in assisting trade unions with training schemes, this was very much in the paternalist tradition of the former British administration. With no major opposition party to put their case, the unions have differed widely amongst each other on the issue of tactics. Although they have displayed greater organizational ability and political sense than most other unions in Africa, the Nigerians have suffered from the political-ethnic divisions of their country. One of the most impressive features of the general strike was that it forced all sections of Nigerian society, as well as the foreign companies, to take the unions seriously.

The mere fact that it was a joint movement with a major role being played by the ICFTU-inspired unions was enough to exclude [the possibility of insurrectional activity]. The government press naturally talked about plots and subversion but nobody seems to have taken this seriously; even the many American observers in Lagos did not uncover any sign of 'the hand of Moscow'.[10]

The only sign of a plot was a rather absurd attempt to implicate a British lecturer, Dr Victor Allen, who was collecting material for a study on African industrialization, as the main figure behind an alleged attempted *coup*. Together with four Nigerians, including Sidi Khayam, deputy president of the NTUC, he was arrested and charged with attempted subversion. Following a prolonged trial, he was then given twelve months' imprisonment on three counts, but was subsequently acquitted on appeal after serving four months of his sentence. The whole incident suggested the panic of the Nigerian authorities, but even more it marked the resentment of some police officers (led by a newly-recruited White South African CID officer) against any European who identified himself with African workers. (Allen, rather than find accommodation with Europeans or at an *élite* hotel, had been staying with Khayam.) The attempt to indict Allen failed, but two of the trade unionists arrested with him remained in prison.

CONCLUSION: TRADE UNIONS AS THE OPPOSITION

The role of trade unions in countries where they do not share in the mass party apparatus increasingly turns on the pace of modernization and the extent to which the government can persuade wage earners that austerity programmes are ultimately in their interest. As the unions have little reason to identify themselves with the *élite* once the solidarity of the independence campaign is spent, they view with suspicion all attempts to control incomes. They may even question the legitimacy of the new rulers. As Gogo Chu Nzeribe remarked on the independence struggle in Nigeria, 'people who had done nothing took over the country, and [the workers] were relegated to the background.'[11] But although the unions may have a strategic political position because of their membership in the crucial industries and services, this is unlikely at present to

Trade Unions and Governments – (i) In Opposition

result in the creation of viable opposition parties, unless the existing opposition groups are able to reorganize themselves and develop a programme appealing to both the wage earners and the peasants. At present only the UMT seems to be coming close to this. In Nigeria the wage earners represent only 5 per cent of all workers; in the Sudan less than 10 per cent; and in Morocco, around 20 per cent. In other countries where the unions do not form part of the ruling political complex, the proportions vary from 4 per cent in parts of French-speaking Equatorial Africa to around 25 per cent in Congo (Leopoldville). The effective political role of unions has so far been limited to occasional forays into politics by politically-directed strike action, unsuccessful attempts to create socialist parties, or, in extreme cases, by engineering a *coup d'état*. In two instances, Morocco and Sierra Leone, the unions have played important parts in major opposition parties, and in both countries trade union leaders have been encouraged by their unions to hold senior municipal posts in the leading cities. Indeed, in Morocco the UMT has directed much of its attention recently towards putting its officers into strategic local government positions, while in Sierra Leone the opposition All People's Party controls Freetown with strong trade union support. But these are exceptions. Elsewhere the unions suffer from serious political divisions as in Nigeria, the Sudan and Congo (Leopoldville), and have been unable to establish a permanent political presence through other institutions. Where they have been able to back *coups*, as in Dahomey, Congo (Brazzaville) and the Sudan, their efforts have not been followed up by consolidated gains. In Dahomey and Brazzaville general strikes and demonstrations helped to overthrow the governments of Maga and Youlou respectively and some recognition was granted to the unions by giving their leaders government posts. But in neither instance was a government created on the basis of a coherent ideology, and the new political leaders found difficulty in attempting to create mass parties. Within months of the Dahomey *coup*, the unions were insisting that the government was not representative and that they themselves would preserve their autonomy. Inevitably in most of such instances any struggle for power is in the nature of a palace revolution. The unions may provide a convenient base for a takeover, but unless there is a coherent plan for developing the economy and organizing support through a mass party, the workers will once again find themselves excluded from power.

Because ruling *élites* are so easily able to expose union demands as sectional selfishness, the unions can only make their case heard by speaking for a wider working class, including the peasants and cash-croppers, and calling for major structural changes in the economy. Senghor suggested something of this kind in 1960:

As the best educated and therefore the most conscious group, the wage earners must transcend their own group interests as well as their strictly professional preoccupations. Placing themselves on a higher level, they will embrace all the interests of all social groups and, first, those of the underprivileged – the peasants, shepherds, fishermen and artisans.[12]

From a somewhat different political standpoint, this is precisely what some trade unions have been trying to do. The arguments advanced by strike leaders in Brazzaville in 1963, in Nigeria in 1963-4, and continuously since 1960 in Morocco were along these lines, but linked with demands (not mentioned by Senghor) for austerity cuts in the earnings of senior administrators and politicians. During the government crisis in Leopoldville in 1962-3, several of the unions demanded severe cuts in government spending and an austerity wages programme to bring the country back to efficiency.

The long-term effects of such campaigns are difficult to establish, but it is clear from the examples of Morocco and Nigeria that persistent constructive criticism of government policies alongside direct appeals to peasants, artisans and other sections of the underprivileged can make life extremely difficult for the ruling *élites* and thereby raise the level of political debate and the pressure to redistribute the wealth. In fact the most fruitful role that unions in these states can play for the foreseeable future may simply be to act as outlets for dissenting views on political policy and the organization of economic growth, so preparing the way for popular mass movements capable of replacing present self-centred *élites*.

Chapter 7: Notes

1. Perry Anderson, 'Problems of Socialist Strategy', in P. Anderson and R. Blackburn (eds) *Towards Socialism*, Fontana Library/New Left Review, 1965, p. 228.
2. Miles E. Galvin, *Unionism in Latin America*, New York, Cornell U.P., 1962, p. 42.
3. ibid., p. 25.
4. D. Ashford, *Political Change in Morocco*, Princeton U.P., 1960, pp. 241 and 271.
5. *Digest of Statistics*, Nigerian Federal Office of Statistics, Lagos, Vol. 12-2, April 1963. Other details from *Report of Commission on Wages and Salaries*, Federal Office, Lagos, 1964.
6. Emile R. Braundi and Antonio Lettieri, 'The General Strike in Nigeria', *International Socialist Journal*, Vol. 1/5-6, September-December 1964, p. 698.
7. *West Africa*, 6 June 1964, p. 619.
8. Wahab Goodluck, Address to Conference of U.S.S.R. Academy of Sciences Institute of World Economy and International Relations, reprinted in *African Communist*, No. 19, October-December 1964, pp. 49-59.
9. *West Africa*, 15 May 1965, p. 533.
10. Braundi and Lettieri, op. cit., p. 609.
11. *West Africa*, 15 May 1965, p. 533.
12. L. S. Senghor, *Nationhood and the African Road to Socialism*, Prèsence Africaine, 1961, p. 124.

8 Trade Unions and Governments –
(ii) Socialism and the One-Party State

If in territories controlled by military juntas or '*élite*' parties the trade unions have to cast themselves in an opposition role, in the one-party states they have to accept a place that involves them directly in the apparatus of economic planning. Their freedom to manoeuvre is limited, possibly circumscribed by law, and they find that their tactics have at most stages to take account of government directives and the nuances of party policy. In practice the scope of trade union activity will depend on several factors, of which the proportion of wage earners in the labour force, the past history of union-party relations, the size of the public sector, and the party structure and ideology are the most important. In all instances the unions tend to become agencies for increasing national production, in contrast to the more normal tendency in Europe where they are agencies for greater consumption and consequently act as pressure groups on governments and employers for higher wages and better conditions. This distinction between 'productionist' and 'consumptionist' unions[1], though it helps to mark a tendency in modern African trade unionism, does not take us more than part of the way in explaining the ideologies of African governments and the part that the labour movement is beginning to play in social policy. In some states productionism represents almost the only function of the unions; their existence is found useful by politicians only in so far as they can help to raise economic output in growth industries and maintain discipline and efficiency in the public services. In others, while the productionist function of unions is stressed by politicians and leading trade unionists, the unions are able to maintain some degree of autonomy through the business enterprises and welfare services which they are encouraged to provide for themselves. And in a third group the

Socialism and the One-Party State

strength of the unions comes from their ideological role in the party, the fact that they represent a 'left opposition', have a powerful semi-autonomous machinery of their own and can bargain with the government over strategy, particularly in industries of the private sector. Any comparison on these lines, of course, implies hard categories where in reality there are simply subtle shades of difference; but if European or Latin American experiences are of any value, the categories are likely to become clearer as African political patterns become more firmly established.

UNIONS AS AGENTS OF INCREASED PRODUCTION

In several of the states which now have one-party structures, there was no working agreement between the unions and the major party before independence, and the establishment of a single-party régime necessitated a new examination of the union's role in the state. In addition there are two major territories where unions have deliberately been given a productionist role and placed under the direct control of Ministries of Labour – Egypt and Tanganyika; in the first, the military junta established its own trade union organization as part of the process of giving a popular base to the régime, and in the second the government decided drastically to overhaul the organization and programme of its own affiliate.

In French-speaking West Africa the unions developed in a multi-party context and were often allied to political ideologies and movements outside the nationalist mainstream. The history of the unions was influenced to a great degree by the nature of external affiliations. Because half of the trade union membership of French West Africa was originally under the direct influence of CGT, the Communist-controlled metropolitan federation, and later under UGTAN, the African Marxist federation of Sekou Touré, many of the French-speaking unions saw their struggle as one against the common enemy of capitalism and colonialism. The identification with purely nationalist movements existed, but there were also wider identifications. Although the French government dismembered the West African Federation through the *loi cadre*, with its specifically territorial reforms, the unions attempted to retain their pan-African commitment. UGTAN and the CATC both projected loyalties above nationalism and were consequently threats to the internal unity of the new states. UGTAN, in particular, was seen by the governments of Senegal, the Ivory Coast, Niger and Dahomey as a disruptive, virtually seditious body. The reasons for this were many; but most important of all was the fact that, after the break-up of the RDA, UGTAN was the only body constantly to campaign across state frontiers for a militant anti-colonialism. In the 1958 referendum, UGTAN – led by Sekou Touré's Guinean members – recommended a vote against de Gaulle's Community proposals, and when Guinea alone voted '*non*', UGTAN became a symbol to governments throughout the French territories of dangerous French-baiting. In many states UGTAN members had led the campaign against Community status, and in the debate that followed most of them allied themselves with or created opposition parties. In addition, UGTAN began to criticize the definitions of African Socialism advanced by many proponents of Negritude. Its advocacy of a continuous revolution until capitalism and colonialism had been removed from Africa did not recommend itself to governments whose existence depended on signing military and economic treaties with France. Between 1957 and 1960 UGTAN was deliberately isolated in most of the former French colonies. In 1958 the governing Senegalese party, the Union Progressiste Sénégalaise, assisted in the formation of UGTAN-Autonome, under the leadership of Abbas Guèye, a UPS deputy and former member of the CGT, and in 1959 a breakaway from UGTAN established UGTAN-Unitaire under Alioune Cissé, former UGTAN secretary-general. The two Senegalese centres then came together in 1959 to form the Union Générale des Travailleurs Sénégalaise, and in 1962 merged with the Christian federation, CATC-Senegal, to form the Union National des Travailleurs du Sénégal, with a large proportion of UPS deputies on the executive committee and firm support for UPS political policies. Many of the UGTAN officers remained outside the new centre, and several supported the illegal pro-

Socialism and the One-Party State

Communist Parti Africain d'Independence led by Majemout Diop and based in Mali.

Although the UPS saw the need to retain trade union support, its labour philosophy has never been very clear and does not now seem to have much room for the unions as part of the political apparatus. In his books on African Socialism, Senghor – the President of Senegal – went out of his way to attack UGTAN and the whole outlook of socialist-minded unionists. Union leaders were the representatives of a hypocritical, privileged *élite*.

> Their average monthly wage is about 36,000 francs CFA, which is higher than the *per capita* income of the inhabitants of France, whereas our peasants and shepherds, who constitute 90 per cent of the population, make less than 2,000 francs CFA. Are not the latter the true proletarians?[2]

He called for the unions to 'transcend their own group interests ... and embrace the interests of all social groups'; but it was clear that this meant 'Wages will be blocked' and that the unions could not expect, as they demanded, 'participation in the management of economic and social affairs'. No concession was made to UGTAN's demands for increased Africanization or the development of a publicly-owned sector of the economy. The economy was to be openly capitalist; 'there is no difference between a capitalist and a socialist state',[3] and 'there can be no question of nationalization in an underdeveloped nation'. But subsequently, after Father Lebret had produced his five-year plan in 1961, moves were made to nationalize key public services and increase the industrialization programme. In the conflict between Mamadou Dia and Senghor in 1962–3, union members became slightly more prominent under the patronage of Dia, and several of them, including David Soumah, attained senior posts.

The trade unions were similarly integrated into the political machinery of the Ivory Coast, though here the conflict between unions and party has been more prolonged and the ultimate fate of unionists in the Cabinet less happy. Initially the relations between the major union centre, the Union Nationale des Travailleurs de Côte d'Ivoire (the territorial section of UGTAN) and the nationalist party, the Parti Démocratique de Côte d'Ivoire were closer than in many other West African states. But during the 1958 referendum the UNTCI was divided over the '*non*' vote, with the executive supporting Houphouet-Boigny's government and a majority of individual unions led by the civil servants supporting UGTAN. The leadership of the PDCI immediately reacted by threatening the unions with legislative action. Philippe Yacé, general secretary of the party, stated at the 1959 party congress that it was dangerous for Ivory Coast unions to take directives from abroad, because the central federation might not take account of the country's own social and economic problems. The party's President, Auguste Denise, warned the unions 'to set aside their particular interests for the general interests of the nation'.[4] During the UNTCI congress in June the main supporters of UGTAN had stayed away, and for the next few months they worked to establish a relationship with the CATC which had also kept clear of the PDCI, creating in August an Intersyndicat des Travailleurs de la Fonction Publique under the secretaryship of Blaise Yao Ngo. The UNTCI members, headed by Amon Tanoh, who was also a deputy and member of the PDCI national executive, hoped that by working with the party they would be able to influence the development of industrial relations policy. Their hope was rudely shattered, however, when the Statut de la Fonction Publique was published on 28 August 1959, outlining labour relations policies for the four West African Community states. The right to strike in the public service was severely curtailed, and the government was given power to requisition employees for the performance of vital services. Vacation time was reduced from three months every two years to one month every year, and family allowances were cut. Joint councils of workers and employers were given more restricted functions than before, and most decisions were left to the government.

The *statut*, which became law on 3 September, served to confuse the UNTCI and fortify the Intersyndicat in its militancy. The government of Houphouet-Boigny was denounced as 'worse than any form of colonialism', and mass demonstrations and meetings were held in Abidjan, which the police attempted to ban. After warning the Intersyndicat that any union which maintained relations with a 'hostile' country would be outlawed, Houphouet deported Yao Ngo to Guinea on 7 October. On 8 October the Intersyndicat called a strike which was supported by just over one quarter of the government workers. For three days Abidjan was in chaos. A protest march resulted in police baton charges and the use of tear gas. Twelve union leaders were arrested, 200 government employees were sacked and over 300 were suspended without pay. The UNTCI, while sympathizing with 'innocent victims', generally supported the government action.

The result of the strike was further government control of civil service workers and renewed attempts to bring all unions into a national centre. The official government journal *Fraternité* called for 'the restoration of psychological health in the public service', and Philippe Yacé, attacking UGTAN unions – he called their failure to support the nationalist movement 'a kind of class selfishness' – declared 'we cannot tolerate that ... a part of the nation remains a foreign particle within the whole.'[5] Attempts were made to create special party committees for civil servants which effectively replaced the trade unions both as policy-making bodies and as negotiators. The union leaders arrested during the strike were released without being brought to trial, most of the workers were re-employed, and the secretary of the CATC was elected to the National Assembly on the party ticket. Houphouet granted increased labour representation in the Assembly (from two to four) and gave the unions the Ministry of Labour and one ambassadorial post. In 1961 plans were drafted for creating one single union centre with close government ties, and in 1962 the Union Générale des Travailleurs de la Côte d'Ivoire officially came into being. Although it was made responsible for all workers in the Ivory Coast, it was not conceded any powers for negotiating the check-off, and its financial position remained weak. Any chances that it might become an influential ideological wing of the party disappeared in September 1963, when seven Ministers were dismissed from their posts and imprisoned

African Trade Unions

following an official announcement that a plot had been discovered to overthrow the government. Altogether sixty people were arrested, including several trade unionists, and at the trial, held in January 1965, four former Ministers and two local politicians were sentenced to death on charges of high treason. One of these was Camille Gris, former leader of UGTAN and Minister of Labour. The unions have consequently lost what place they were acquiring in the overall apparatus of rule.

The Ivory Coast and Senegal represent the most important steps taken in former French territories to reduce the trade unions to purely productionist functions. With local differences, the pattern was similar in other West African territories – Niger, Upper Volta, Dahomey, Mauretania; the government attempted to influence trade union leadership at federation level, precipitated a show-down with the militants, and isolated UGTAN as a 'foreign' influence. Prominent party workers were encouraged to be active in the new union centre, and one of these became Minister of Labour with direct responsibility for union discipline. In all cases the national centres became active in the anti-Accra ATUC, and some were allowed to continue their membership of the ICFTU or IFCTU. The unions now have few bargaining powers, develop little of their own education programmes (though some send officers to occasional international courses), and are seen strictly as adjuncts of the party machine. In the short run such a policy can only succeed if the living standards of the whole population rise and if the union officers really do have a chance to participate in party councils where the real decisions are made. But as the 1963 upheavals in the Ivory Coast and Dahomey suggest, this is not an easy matter; the Ministers of Labour, who are most closely in touch with the feelings of the unions, may be the first to rebel.

The attitudes displayed by the governments of Tanganyika and Egypt differ from these in the important respect that they recognize the significance of a strong labour movement, partly as an aid to mass organization and partly as a method of improving the efficiency of the work force. But in neither state have the unions developed any significant autonomous role, and their control by the administration is virtually complete. In Egypt the

Socialism and the One-Party State

Revolutionary Council of 1952 inherited a Labour Unions Act passed in 1942 by the Wafd government under British influence. This had given formal recognition to the unions of industrial workers alone and had provided for their very close supervision; had forbidden intellectuals or other non-employees to hold union posts; and had made it impossible for union officers to be employed full-time on union jobs. Political and religious activities by trade unionists had been banned; the Minister of Social Affairs had been given power to dissolve any union which infringed the 1942 Act; and the check-off had been forbidden. The Revolutionary Council of 1952 immediately set about revising the labour law. Agricultural workers were allowed to form unions; the check-off was permitted in firms where three-fifths of the workers already belonged to a union; and no union could be dissolved without an appeal to the courts. But political activity continued to be banned and strikes remained illegal, while intellectuals and other 'outsiders' were still prevented from working with unions. The unions were seen as primarily concerned with providing welfare services for their members, and only secondarily with negotiating wage increases and improvements in working conditions.

The 1952 amendment to the Labour Act also provided for a national federation, but no moves to establish one were made until 1955, and it was not until 1957 that the Egyptian Confederation of Labour was created and recognized by the government. One of the difficulties involved in establishing any federation was the existence of a large number of unions (increasing from 472 in 1952 to 1,154 in 1955) based mainly on individual work places, and although industrial federations grouping these 'place' unions were permitted after 1952, they had little power because each union remained autonomous. The remaining legal restrictions on office holders as full-time officials effectively prevented the creation of central organizations, and for some years the Egyptian Confederation of Labour remained weak and unimportant. The weakness of the Egyptian unions was also due to their ambiguous role between management and the government. In some companies the unions had to work closely with management for any union to exist at all.

African Trade Unions

Their power to negotiate was limited, and the election of officers frequently supervised by management officials. This was particularly true in private Egyptian companies. In foreign-owned companies, the unions were able to play off the state and the management against one another. In general the Ministry of Labour used the unions as a kind of watch-dog to ensure that policies were pro-Egyptian. But the relationship was characterized by a truce between unions and management, and unions had to fight hard to gain any major concessions. In the state-controlled industries (for example, the transport services), however, the position was rather different, with fairly powerful trade unions and more cooperative management.

Since 1957 the Egyptian unions have slowly reorganized their structure under government supervision, with greater power entrusted to the industrial federations. In 1960 the whole of the organization was recast, with an Egyptian Federation of Labour replacing the old Confederation and some full-time appointments made possible. Certain workers in the nationalized industries (in contrast to state-controlled private industry, where they could already organize) were allowed to form unions, and by 1962 the total number of members claimed throughout Egypt was 1,250,000 in 65 main union federations. This membership figure showed a spectacular increase on the 275,000 reported in 1958 and the 116,735 in 1952, and was due largely to the introduction of the check-off throughout Egyptian industry, as well as to the rapid increase in petroleum production, the manufacture of consumer goods, and mining and steel investments. The major reforms announced in July 1961, when nationalization was expanded and some land redistributed, also strengthened the position of the unions by giving them a more direct share in the administration of industry. All company boards were to include two Workers' Representatives (out of a maximum of seven directors), and the workers were to get 25 per cent of all company profits (either by wage rises or by increased social benefits), while a seven hour working day was introduced throughout the public sector. Following the recommendations of a special committee set up in November 1961 to define the 'popular forces' in the country, a National Congress of Popular

Socialism and the One-Party State

Forces was held in February 1962, with 1,500 members of whom 25 per cent were peasants and small farmers, 20 per cent industrial workers, 15 per cent trade unionists, 10 per cent businessmen, 7 per cent teachers, 7 per cent students, and 7 per cent women. Through this Congress Nasser was attempting to create institutions that would form the basis for 'scientific socialism' and the extension of popular control. But with a highly-centralized rule, and an uncertainty over the possible role of the 'people' in government, Egypt has still a long way to go in creating a democratic socialist state. As for the unions, they are certainly treated more sympathetically and given more encouragement under Nasser's régime than ever before. And it may be true that 'the labour movement, weak as it may be at present, is a force pushing in the direction of more democracy in a society which in the past has had very little exposure to free political institutions.'[6] But up to now their independent role has been confined largely to the politically safe regions of external activity, through the Confederation of Arab Trade Unions and the AATUF.

The Tanganyikan unions have been brought under party control by yet another route. Unlike the unions in former French West Africa, the Tanganyikan Federation of Labour was in close working relationship with TANU – the single nationalist force – long before independence, and there was certainly some interlocking of personnel between the two organizations. After independence the second Prime Minister, Rashidi Kawawa, also became the second African head of government (after Sékou Touré) who had risen to power through the trade union movement, and Michael Kamaliza, his successor as President of the TFL, became the first Minister of Labour in independent Tanganyika. But in many ways these union successes brought to an abrupt end the close relationships that had existed between the TFL and TANU. The unions began to agitate for increased minimum wages and quicker Africanization, and shortly after independence a series of strikes began to shake the foundations of the union-party alliance. In particular a serious railway strike in February 1962 threatened to disrupt the new government's plans for economic development. Kawawa denounced the

African Trade Unions

strike leaders in a speech on 9 February, but two of the leading trade unionists, Victor Mkello, President of the TFL, and C. S. K. Tumbo, actively campaigned for much faster Africanization. In mid-1962 Tumbo was appointed High Commissioner in London, while Kamaliza pushed through a Trades Disputes Settlement Bill, which made strikes and lock-outs illegal except where the Ministry of Labour decided against putting the dispute before an arbitration tribunal. The Bill had features close to Ghana's 1958 Industrial Relations Act, but immediately ran into difficulties because the union leaders were not prepared to make it work. Tumbo resigned his post in London and moved to Kenya from where he attempted to create a new political party, while Mkello and other union leaders supported him openly. In January 1963, two members of the TFL executive including Mkello were placed in restriction near the Northern Rhodesian border. This action followed several militant speeches by union leaders and a large number of unofficial strikes on the sisal plantations (Mkello was also general secretary of the Plantation Workers' Union). The outbreak of a mutiny in the army in January 1964 was the signal for a further reorganization of the trade union movement. Mkello (now free) was re-arrested with almost the entire executive committee of the TFL and various other union leaders, and once again sent into restriction. Then, on 24 February, the government published the National Union of Tanganyikan Workers (Establishment) Act, which dissolved the TFL and its eleven affiliated unions, and created instead one central union with eleven sections. The new union was affiliated to TANU ('and shall do everything in its power to promote the policies of TANU') with the main officers appointed by the President of the Republic. The first secretary-general was Kamaliza, the Minister of Labour, and for all practical purposes the union became a constituent party of the Ministry of Labour. The projected functions of the union were collaboration with government and employers in the development of a national wages policy; 'to enforce and to assist in the enforcement of collective agreements and awards and a disciplinary code'; and to provide benefits for its members. The union was expressly

Socialism and the One-Party State

forbidden to use its funds for other than trade union purposes, and in turn was guaranteed the closed shop in all industrial locations where more than 50 per cent of the workers belonged to the union. (This is similar to the practice in Egypt and significantly different from practice in Senegal or the Ivory Coast.) No mention was made of education, and shortly after the passing of the Act all Tanganyikan students were withdrawn from the ICFTU college at Kampala.

In spite of the panic that accompanied them, the Tanganyikan labour reforms were more coherent and reasoned than much found in either the Ivory Coast or Senegal. In his speeches defining African Socialism, President Nyerere sees the wage earners as a potentially privileged class whose members must be persuaded to direct their energies towards raising productivity and the living standards of the whole people. Addressing a TANU conference on socialism in 1962, he argued:

There are bound to be certain groups which, by virtue of the market value of their particular industry's products, *will* contribute more to the nation's income than others. But the others may actually be producing goods or services which are of equal, or greater, *intrinsic* value although they do not happen to command such a high *artificial* value. For example, the food produced by the peasant farmer is of greater social value than the diamonds mined at Mwadui. But the mineworkers of Mwadui could claim, quite correctly, that their labour was yielding greater financial profits to the community than that of the farmers. If, however, they went on to demand that they should therefore be given most of that extra profit for themselves, and that no share of it should be spent on helping farmers, they would be potential capitalists.

This is exactly where the attitude of mind comes in. It is one of the purposes of trade unions to ensure for the workers a fair share of the profits of their labour. But a 'fair' share must be fair in relation to the whole society. If it is greater than the country can afford without having to penalize some other section of society, then it is *not* a fair share. Trade union leaders and their followers, as long as they are true socialists, will not need to be coerced by the government into keeping their demands within the limits imposed by the needs of the society as a whole. Only if there are potential capitalists among them will the

African Trade Unions

socialist government have to step in and prevent them from putting their capitalist ideas into practice.[7]

In traditional African socialism 'it was taken for granted that every member of society ... contributed his fair share of effort towards the production of its wealth.... Work was part and parcel, was indeed the very basis and justification of this socialist achievement.' So today work and a communitarian spirit must be the basis of Tanganyika's reconstruction.

The implications of this philosophy of labour are spelled out by Kamaliza.[8] The unions must cooperate in development plans by securing for their members 'their fair share of increasing national prosperity', and by undertaking 'that their members cooperate wholeheartedly in implementing the agreed plan.' They must undertake the 'unpopular and difficult work of advocating and securing increases in productivity and working efficiency'. Because unions are weak and led 'by persons of conflicting personalities, each advocating programmes which are sometimes contradictory and contrary to the best interests of the worker or the nation', the government is obliged to create a centralized structure with Presidential appointments at the top. 'The union is required to educate wage earners in the need for harder work and the need for discipline and efficiency at the place of employment.'

This theory, like Senghor's, may represent the basis for a form of union autonomy within the single party structure and may even provide adequate ideological grounds for the development of a theoretical left opposition there. But at present there are few signs of such development. The union (NUTA) is given little chance to conduct a dialogue with the party over the management of industry and has few commercial activities of its own to give it an economic stake as a bargaining counter with the government, though NUTA is setting up a Tanganyika Workers' Investment Corporation which could possibly be the prelude to other business activity. It is, however, probably true that there is greater flexibility in Tanganyika than in the French-speaking West African states or in Egypt. The unions have great prestige, for all their setbacks, and a very large membership, with a measure of financial security.

Socialism and the One-Party State

UNIONS AS BUSINESS PARTNERS OF THE GOVERNMENT

Where the unions are linked closely to the ruling political party, the government may either allow them to develop their commercial activities and welfare services or grant them some part in the administration of industry and consequently an ideological role in the state. The Tunisian and Kenyan unions represent an attempt to make the unions sponsors of development programmes, and consequently suggest one way in which the governments can solve the problems of union militancy while at the same time allowing them some room for manoeuvre.

The Tunisian unions, after the early phases of political militancy under Ferhat Hached and Ahmed Ben Salah, were rapidly absorbed into the political machinery of the Neo-Destour. At independence in 1956 the UGTT was led by Ben Salah, thirty years old and perhaps as popular a political figure in the towns as Bourguiba. Refusing a minor Ministry in Bourguiba's first government, he attacked the lack of socialist theory in the Neo-Destour and called for a complete overhaul of the party's aims. Although Bourguiba had already guaranteed the continuation of private investment policies, Ben Salah put forward a scheme for a National Economic Plan which would include large-scale nationalization of the major industries and services together with rapid industrialization. In reply Bourguiba encouraged a veteran trade unionist, Habib Achour, to advocate a new trade union federation completely divorced from politics, and this federation was created in October 1956 with a constitution which specifically mentioned reunification with the UGTT on condition that Ben Salah resigned. After continued attacks by Bourguiba, who accused him of 'sowing the seeds of division under cover of foreign doctrines and principles that we would be ill-advised to want to apply in our country', Ben Salah resigned in December and was replaced by Ahmed Tlili, a member of the Neo-Destour Political Bureau, who had earlier made his way to political prominence through the trade union movement. In 1957 the two federations were merged. Three months later Ben Salah reappeared as Minister of Public Health and, in 1961, as Minister of Planning and Finance, when he introduced a drastically amended version of his original economic plan.

The effect of the Tlili-Achour *coup* in the UGTT was to deprive the unions of an independent political role and firmly commit them to party policy. The unions were instructed to limit their attention to workers' affairs. That there were difficulties even then is suggested by the passage of a social security bill in 1959–60. The bill was aimed at extending social security benefits to all wage earners, including agricultural workers for the first time, and was drafted and put to the Cabinet by Ben Salah in early 1959. For eighteen months it was stalled in the National Assembly, redrafted in the Cabinet and subjected to repeated objections by all the major interested parties, notably the Industrial and Commercial Employers Union, the Chambers of Commerce, European businessmen and the doctors. By October 1960 an amended form had been passed by a final Cabinet council; but because it had lost one or two significant clauses, UGTT representatives and Ben Salah made one or two amendments, precipitating another prolonged debate in the Assembly. At long last the Bill became law in December 1960, and in that shape clearly represented a tactical concession by Bourguiba. Salaries and wages had been blocked or reduced since 1954, and in June 1960 the employers had succeeded in pushing through a law facilitating the dismissal of incompetent workers. A commentator has put it:

Bourguiba thus seems to have carefully balanced the demands of workers and employers. When he had once decided upon general principles of the new legislation, the national organizations were allowed to participate in its detailed elaboration. The single-party régime thus allows in modest measure for the articulation of professional interests through the national organizations; these interests are balanced and effectively subordinated to the national interest by virtue of the party's control of the organization.[9]

But with so little scope for action either in promoting higher wages or in direct political action, the UGTT has learned to direct its attention elsewhere. It has had little choice. Between 1956 and 1962 its membership dropped from 182,000 to 83,000 (there is no check-off agreement in Tunisia). Tlili has rational-

Socialism and the One-Party State

ized the situation accordingly: 'The UGTT has made a point of seeing that the legislation on trade unions guarantees the workers all the freedoms, including that of the free choice of trade union.'[10] It has consequently developed a range of extra-union activities – cooperatives, investments, stores – and in 1965 opened a Banque du Peuple in Tunis aimed, as Habib Achour proclaimed at the opening ceremony, 'to increase the UGTT's budget for its many projects and thus contribute towards the economic development of the country.' In its role of entrepreneur the union mirrors tendencies prevalent elsewhere in the world, notably in Israel, Sweden, the United States and, recently, Britain, where similar schemes have been initiated particularly by the General & Municipal Workers' Union and the Electrical Trades Union. But there is a difference. While other unions supplement their other interests with commercial ones, the UGTT has virtually no other activity.

In many respects the Kenya trade union movement is moving in the same direction. A centralized body is outlined in the recent White Paper on Socialism and Economic Planning, 'in the interest of economic stability and good industrial relations'; legislation is planned 'providing for compulsory arbitration of major issues not resolved through the regular bargaining process, together with any other measures that may be needed to prevent strikes'; and the 'government will assist trade unions to become involved in economic activities such as cooperatives, housing schemes, training schemes, workers' discipline and productivity.'[11] But the tendency towards party control of the unions has been accompanied by greater misgivings among politicians than in most other parts of Africa – largely because Tom Mboya, while secretary-general of the Kenya Federation of Labour, established his reputation through the independence and militancy of the Kenya unions. Addressing the Sixth World Congress of the ICFTU, he declared:

The existence of a strong, free, and healthy trade union movement is an essential factor in creating a healthy democracy on sound economic foundations. By building up their organization on a sound basis, by giving an example to the rest of the community of how democratic bodies should function, and by pursuing their normal trade union

African Trade Unions

aims without being unresponsive to the community as a whole, the free trade unions can have a very great influence in the moulding of their country.[12]

Unfortunately for such principles, the KFL displayed few of these qualities. Between 1960 and 1965 it was in regular conflict with KANU, the major nationalist party; became so deficient in organization that, despite a subsidy of £1,000 a month from the ICFTU, it was £5,000 in debt by 1962–3; and was not too successful in implementing the model Industrial Relations Charter of October 1962. During 1962 and 1963 several prolonged strikes rocked Kenya, and Mboya, the Minister of Labour, told the Legislative Council 'If the right to strike is abused, it will be removed. The government cannot see the country held to ransom and do nothing about it.'[13] But the trade unionists, as in Tanganyika, were militant in their attitudes on Africanization and saw KANU as a threat to trade union freedom. Several of them supported the opposition party, KADU; in the May 1963 general election Peter Kibisu, secretary-general of the KFL, and four other union leaders ran as independent candidates against official KANU nominees, but all were heavily defeated. Kibisu was compelled to resign his post and, for a time, KANU played an active part in influencing a trade union election. Clement Lubembe, a KANU senator and president of the Commercial Workers' Union, succeeded in gaining control, and from now on the KFL came under increasing government influence.

But the government still refrained from taking action as strong as that in Tanganyika. It had already encouraged the setting up of a complex network of negotiating bodies through the 1962 Industrial Relations Charter. Two committees – both equally balanced between employers and workers, and each with a government chairman – were set up to deal with demarcation issues and negotiating apparatus. These covered union recognition, introduction of the check-off, disputes machinery, wage agreements, and any break-down in agreements. A permanent Industrial Court was planned as well as arbitration tribunals and boards of inquiry. The emphasis throughout was on joint union-employer agreements and negotiations at top industry level. The role of government was made minimal, while the trade unions accepted responsibility for supervising the conduct of their members at work and discouraging

such practices as (a) negligence of duty (b) careless operation (c) damage to property (d) interference with or disturbance to normal work (e) insubordination (f) abusive and intemperate language, and generally to respect the provisions of ILO Convention No. 98.

In many ways the charter was an ambitious document, though scarcely as progressive as the Fabian Society thought ('splendidly outlining principles which should and possibly could be applied in Britain after negotiations between the TUC and the British Employers' Confederation.')[14] The prospects of realization were slight; many employers in Kenya, despite the moderate front presented by the Federation of Kenya Employers, persisted in wildly illiberal practices while the unions, despite their ICFTU grants and education schemes, could not organize themselves sufficiently to be representative of their members, let alone supervise their behaviour at work. The Agricultural Workers, with a mass of unemployed members, had been consistently dissident and militant. Employers were reluctant to introduce the check-off, and the unions remained financially weak. With the draining away of prominent trade unionists to management and government posts, and the anti-KANU activities of the KFL executive, the obligations of the unions under the Charter were wildly impractical. (Above all, the Charter demanded more from the unions and less from management than any trade union organization could reasonably tolerate.) It was after this failure that Mboya recommended government control in his White Paper.

The party's plans for the unions had been clear for many years. While he was secretary-general of the KFL, Mboya repeatedly advocated the growth of business activities as an adjunct to trade union organization. In his autobiography he returned to the theme in detail. The future of the unions as government partners was not to depend on their role as ideological shock-troops nor as agents for management in the growing public sector; there was little recognizable public sector, and it was not planned to create one, except 'if the need is urgent ...

African Trade Unions

and if it is understood that most industries nationalized will not be operated at a loss.' Unlike Ghana, Algeria, Guinea, Mali or even Egypt, Kenya has today no apparent ideological machine (the Lumumba Institute has been virtually closed), nor an integrated foreign policy. Instead the KFL was to 'be involved as an economic interest, running its own cooperatives and even running large companies and banks.'[15] In 1962, with assistance from Israel's Histadrut, the KFL announced its intention to establish a consumers' cooperative, and its wish to follow this up with 'a construction company, the sponsoring of a fisherman's cooperative on Lake Victoria, and, the encouragement of cooperatives among peasant farmers.' In fact by 1964 nothing tangible was evident, though plans were advanced for sponsoring a cooperative store and establishing a printing works. If the government succeeds in putting the KFL's house in order, it seems likely that, following the UGTT's example, the Kenya trade union movement will be further encouraged to direct its attention to extra-union business pursuits, leaving the settlement of wages and working conditions to central negotiating bodies that will operate within the national economic plan. In the field of social security and 'fringe' benefits, Lubembe has advocated greater cooperation with management:

Today in Kenya there are many international companies which are operating world wide. It is known that these companies have stock purchase plans and/or profit sharing plans in operation for their employees outside the continent of Africa, and our unions intend insisting that these companies develop appropriate profit-sharing schemes for the African workers. We intend to approach those industries which we believe are in a position also to establish comparable plans and demand that they incorporate them in our bargaining agreements. We also intend approaching industry on pensions, health, insurance plans and workers credit after careful studies through African experts who know these schemes well.[16]

The governments of both Tunisia and Kenya, inheriting countries which were dominated by a European settler minority, have been at pains to stress that within the limits of a nationalist programme, European economic control must continue. Consequently in both countries little stress has been placed on the

Socialism and the One-Party State

importance of the public sector, though after 1962 Tunisia made some moves to extend the area of state control. The unions have been consequently obliged to turn their activities towards fringe benefits (negotiated with industry and rarely obtained through government effort, thus increasing the power of the foreign employer) and commercial enterprises. But although the union may get some temporary autonomy from such activities, this does not appear to be long-lasting. In 1965 both the Kenya and Tunisian trade unions were put under stronger government control. In June 1965 Bourguiba arrested several trade union leaders and put the union cooperatives under state control, in response to mounting agitation for wage increases. In fact, during the first decade of Tunisian independence the Tunisian unions could do almost nothing to raise the level of wages in the country, and their main achievements were the Social Security Bill and the Banque du Peuple. The lessons are clear: unless the unions in a one-party state are given a prominent place in the national committees for economic planning and wage determination (as may happen in Kenya), they are likely to seem increasingly impotent to their own members and increasingly expendable to the government.

TRADE UNIONS AS THE LEFT OPPOSITION

There remain the unions with a role in the single-party state that is partly ideological, partly productionist, and partly managerial. In some cases the unions may also have some commercial activities of their own, but mainly they are a conscious ideological wing of the party, with a political life, publications and education schemes of their own. Four countries come clearly into this group – Ghana, Algeria, Mali and Guinea – though the reasons for the particular role of the unions in each differ, as does the extent of their activities.

In his campaign for independence Sekou Touré, as President of the Confédération National des Travailleurs de Guinée (formerly the Union Syndicale des Travailleurs de Guinée) carefully developed the workers' movement as an integral part of the anti-colonialist campaign and a wing of the political party. As

African Trade Unions

President of UGTAN, furthermore, he assumed a personal role as spokesman for the African workers of other French-speaking territories as well, in contrast to the *élite* leaders who approved de Gaulle's plans for the French Community. During the early days of isolation, Guinea's unions were an important vehicle for creating the communitarian state. Sekou Touré himself argued that they were not to be divided on the basis of class differences and must work with the peasants towards 'the creation of new conditions, calculated both to raise the living standards of the labouring masses and to find a just solution for the conflicts that manifest themselves within African society.'[17] This was easier to achieve in Guinea than in the other French-speaking West African territories because the issue of Africanization did not arise; almost all French civil servants, technicians and skilled workers left as soon as Guinea became independent. The civil servants, elsewhere the centre of union resistance to government take-overs, were in Guinea the backbone of Touré's plans for reconstruction. In the independence crisis of 1958, it was easier to introduce drastic salary reductions and give the public sector workers a part in economic planning.

As long as Guinea was engaged in the struggle to achieve and then preserve independence, the unions flourished as an important part of the country's African identity. Conakry became the centre for UGTAN's debate on the role of trade unions in independent states; the CNTG published pamphlets and journals challenging the conventional wisdom of the pro-French unions and parties; and attempts were made to work out the precise role of the unions in a single party state. In all these activities Touré was both participant and tolerant spectator. He told the unions: 'In the trade union movement there can be members and adversaries of the PDG; we must therefore recognize the right of this movement to organize independently and be free to define its own means of action.'[18] In 1960 an UGTAN training college was established at Conakry with the close co-operation of the East German unions.

But the economic difficulties that Guinea encountered after her first three years of independence began to have their effect on industrial relations. With growing disorder in the new state

Socialism and the One-Party State

monopolies, and the growing deficit in foreign balances, there was increasing disquiet among wage earners. In 1961 the CNTG began to look like an uneasy coalition of interest groups rather than the coherent and dynamic union centre of 1958. Despite its earlier promise of becoming a nation-wide movement encompassing peasants and wage earners, it now looked like a pressure group of the urban *élite*. In response to deteriorating wage-scales and fringe benefits, the teachers' union began a campaign in 1961 for a review of salaries by circulating a memorandum among party leaders and UGTAN/AATUF officers. Some copies also reached the Eastern European embassies. The 1961 national convention of the CNTG was dominated by discussion of the teachers' complaints. Then, in November, the teachers' union executive was suspended by government order: two of the leaders were sentenced to ten years' imprisonment, and three others to five years, on charges of conducting subversive activities. The party threatened to make the union headquarters into a youth centre, and severely restricted the international activities of the CNTG and the individual unions. Plans to introduce the check-off were abandoned, and in 1962 the UGTAN centre at Conakry was nationalized. It was directly out of the events in late 1961 that the Guinea government expelled Danil Solod, the Soviet Ambassador.

Since then, the role of the unions in Guinea has been much more closely supervised by the PDG, and the practice by which non-PDG members could hold union office has been abandoned (some of the teachers' leaders were members of the Parti Afrique d'Independence, the pro-Communist group based on Mali). But the management role of unions has survived; several union officers continue to sit on the boards of nationalized industries, and there are various forms of union-managed small industry. The ideological role of the CNTG has not been entirely lost, and the union continues to publish its own journal, *Le Travailleur de Guinée*, which acts as a forum for union debate and as a major educational organ of the party. The Guinean unions are also remarkable in Africa for organizing the police as well as all sections of the civil service. Since 1962 they have also increased their activities among the agricultural workers, and the check-off has been introduced to cover 100,000 of the 107,000 wage earners. The 1961 strike taught an important lesson. The teacher claims displayed a failure in communication between the party and the unions, and suggested that lack of coordination was producing a union *élite* out of touch with the conditions of the peasantry. The government simply pointed to the difference in earnings between the peasants and the teachers to expose the unions as representative of an enraged vested interest. If the unions want to retain their role as an internal opposition to the party programmes, the 1961 debate has clearly shown them that their tactics have to be much more sophisticated.

But although Guinea is an interesting case study in the problems of union-party relations, both Ghana and Algeria are likely to provide more important models for other African states wanting to experiment with union democracy. In many respects Ghana's industrial relations procedure has already influenced Africa, but the debate that has raged for several years within the party has not yet had its full impact on other countries. In Ghana the trade union movement has been consciously accepted as a participant in formulating the ideology of the state, and the unions have been granted formal equality of status along with the Cocoa Farmers Council and the governing CPP, while the CPP's idea of African Socialism is based not only on the development of socialism out of traditional African society but on the importance of an ideologically-conscious working class as an active force in creating the secular state. In his major statement on trade union policy in Ghana[19], John Tettegah, then secretary-general of the Ghana TUC, held that 'the working class possesses, even at this stage of our development, many of the qualities that characterize the citizens of a socialist state', but that in Ghana and throughout Africa 'class enemies' exist. 'Many Ghanaian businessmen, owing to their greedy intention to get rich quickly, do not pay full wages to their workers or do not pay at the proper rate stipulated by law' ... and elsewhere there are 'African bourgeois leaders who continue to aid [the colonialists] in retaining their hegemony over the economic reserves.' The worker's struggle is therefore directed as much against these class enemies as against the colonialists themselves, who continue to take

Socialism and the One-Party State

tribute from African states, and in this struggle the CPP and the GTUC are close allies. The aims of the CPP – 'to create a state based upon the socialist pattern of society adapted to suit Ghanaian conditions' – are identical with the aims of the GTUC, Tettegah therefore insists that the unions work 'consciously for the development and strengthening of the new socialist sector of the national economy', raising the level of literacy, helping to establish a national wages policy and 'being alert to possible rises in the cost of living', while developing an effective organization that is able to communicate ideas and programmes from one level of the movement to another. Trade unions are responsible organizations which must be vigilant and militant in the interests of their own members and the future of Ghanaian socialism. Their officers must be scrupulous in their private lives and clear-sighted in their public functions; the corrupt and the self-indulgent must be instantly dismissed. Throughout the trade union movement a pyramid structure of closely-interrelated bodies should ensure that discipline is maintained, grievances are aired, programmes discussed and implemented. Internally the top of the pyramid is the Cabinet (on which the secretary-general of the GTUC has a seat as Ambassador Plenipotentiary); externally, the executive committee of the AATUF. The aims of the GTUC must be to consolidate socialist gains in Ghana and assist the African trade union movement 'to exist authentically and defend its unity on national and continental levels'.

But if this theory appeared more comprehensive and articulate than most, in practice the relationship between unions and party has been subjected to at least as many strains in Ghana as in any other African state. The 1958 Industrial Relations Act, on which the present structure of trade unionism is based, was the result of four years of hard negotiation with the Ghana unions, and at the 1958 Congress of the GTUC opposition to the proposed changes was voiced by the Miners', the Railwaymen's and the United Africa Company unions. But in December 1958 the Industrial Relations Act was passed, based substantially on the findings of Tettegah's commision of inquiry. Under the Act a Trades Union Congress was established with twenty-four constituent unions (in an Amendment of August 1959 no other unions were permitted to exist outside the twenty-four authorized). All negotiations – for registration of unions, failure of collective bargaining procedures, introduction of the 'union shop' and 'check-off' – were to be conducted through the GTUC, thus making it directly responsible for the conduct of all trade union affairs in Ghana. Strikes in the private sector were to be legal only after an elaborate negotiating machinery had been exhausted – and then could only be called with the approval of the TUC. In the public sector strikes were forbidden altogether. A later government document explained the attitude to strikers and wage claims:

In a socialist Ghana, the distribution of the national income can no longer be the chance outcome of a chaotic struggle between antagonistic classes. Rather it should be based on scientific decisions regarding the utilization of increases in the nation's wealth in such a way as to advance the welfare of the worker and the growth of the economy and to maintain an adequate level of employment within a framework of economic stability.[20]

Throughout the debate on the creation of a new industrial relations charter, three tendencies were marked: the desire of the government to harness the unions to the productive effort and the general task of social reorganization; the demand of the TUC Executive for a more powerful trade union movement with increased finances, membership and authority; and the resistance by the leaders of some industrial unions, members of the opposition and employers' organizations to the scope of the measures. Initially the government was neutral in the debate; as late as January 1958 the Minister of Labour, N. A. Welbeck, warned that 'the government would be acting wrongly and exceeding its proper function if it attempted to impose these changes on individual unions by legislative action.'[21] But then, probably following the reluctance of employers to introduce the check-off and the union shop as well as collective agreements, the government changed its attitude; the important amendment of August 1959 compelled 'company unions' to amalgamate or be wound up, and strengthened the hand of the GTUC in enforcing compliance with the 1958 Act.

For the next three or four years, however, employers, recalci-

Socialism and the One-Party State

trant unions and opposition leaders showed that they were not happy with the implications of the Act. In 1960 the Commercial and Allied Workers' Union staged a demonstration in Accra before the GTUC headquarters in protest against a delay in appointing an arbitrator. The government reacted immediately by increasing all wages by 1/- a day and introducing an amendment to the 1958 Act which provided for quicker arbitration and empowered the TUC to discipline member unions. But this amendment was hardly sufficient to meet the next crisis. Following a severe budget in 1961 (which introduced a compulsory savings scheme and a new system of purchase tax) prices rose. In September 1961 a major strike occurred in Sekondi-Takoradi among the railway and harbour workers, lasting over two weeks. A State of Emergency was declared; violent clashes broke out between strikers and the police; and a number of workers, sympathetic market women and leaders of the opposition (including J. B. Danquah, Joe Appiah and P. K. K. Quaidoo) were arrested.

These tensions indicated the fundamental difficulties of operating a trade union movement in close liasion with the party in power. Quite apart from the differences in attitude among various union leaders over the degree of centralization, the political commitment of a federation like the GTUC raises the major issue of the distinction between the TUC's syndicalist activity, its purely economic function, and its political one. The crisis of 1961 showed that this had by no means been resolved and, despite the radical theories of the CPP, the methods employed to handle crisis situations were not dissimilar to those in less-syndically minded states like the Ivory Coast, Senegal or Upper Volta, though the government's speedy accession to wage demands suggested greater sensitivity to union pressures than elsewhere. The unions may also have been able to exert some pressure on the government and employers to maintain general wage levels; certainly wages have been higher in Ghana than in many other African states. But the relative strength of the unions and the relationship between political theory and practice are worth scrutiny.

Because of the introduction of the check-off and the union

African Trade Unions

shop, almost all wage earners in Ghana are now dues-paying members of the TUC and its sixteen constituent unions (the number was revised in 1960), giving a total membership in 1962 of some 500,000 workers, which, next to the Moroccan and Egyptian makes the Ghanaian trade union movement the largest in Africa. 45 per cent of the dues (2/- a month) go directly to the GTUC, and the remainder to local branches and national industrial union headquarters; 50 per cent of the dues that it gets are used by the TUC for its own administrative expenses and education programmes; 20 per cent for a social welfare and insurance fund; 10 per cent for investment in business enterprises; and 10 per cent for a central strike fund. Educational activities are of five kinds: basic education, often organized in conjunction with the Institute of Public Education; education in trade union organization (mainly evening and Sunday classes arranged by the GTUC's education and publicity department); vocational education, either run by unions on their own initiative or more generally in cooperation with firms and the government; political education under the direction of the Kwame Nkrumah Ideological Institute at Winneba; and various courses abroad (including the U.S.A., Eastern Europe, Russia, Israel, West Germany, Sweden and China). In addition the GTUC has its own publications, *Labour* and *TUC News Bulletin*, and helps to publish *The African Worker*, bi-monthly of the AATUF. Some union officers also contribute to the semi-official theoretical journal, *Spark*, while individual unions publish occasional journals and publicity material.

The industrial efficiency of the Ghanaian unions is not in dispute. Even a hostile commentator has remarked:

In the industrial relations field the GTUC has acted with a considerable degree of responsibility; its relations with the Ghana Employers' Confederation have developed well, and together these two organizations have agreed on important advances in the scope of collective bargaining and joint consultation.[22]

It is almost certainly true, as the GTUC remarked in reply to one of its critics, that before the 1958 Act was introduced there 'had been the wanton refusal of certain employers to recognize or

Socialism and the One-Party State

meet their workers for negotiation',[23] and that afterwards employers were compelled to deal with unions and negotiate industrial agreements. It is difficult to see how employers could have been made to recognize unions, and negotiate with them, or how the unions themselves could have developed adequate strength, unless the government had given the TUC wider powers. In view of the rapid economic changes in Ghana and the introduction of several austerity budgets, it is remarkable how rare have been the industrial disputes and how effectively the system has worked.

But the problems of union-party relations remain. Unlike the UGTT in Tunisia, the GTUC has not compromised away its wage-bargaining functions for a semi-autonomy based on independent commercial activity. It has rather accepted a moratorium on strikes in favour of continuing collective bargaining within a framework of checks and balances. In addition it accepts the importance of a political dialogue with the party on ideology, has developed some commercial activity of its own, and in a number of instances has elected members to the management committees of state enterprises. All the features of a triangular debate among party, unions and workers' management (as found in Yugoslavia or Algeria) are therefore present, though the element of self-management has not so far developed far enough in Ghana for it to become a major issue in political life. What has become important is a debate on the foundations of democracy within the trade union movement. As an example of this, an article in *Spark* by S. G. Ikoku,[24] former leader of the Action Group in the Eastern Nigeria House of Assembly and now lecturer at the Kwame Nkrumah Institute, explored the nature of union-party relations. It attacked party appointments to senior office, advocating instead union elections for leaders throughout, and a three-member party commission to ensure effective liasion. Because the trade union movement was young and controlled primarily by white-collar workers, it was necessary for the party to influence its development; later the manual labourer would come to control his own organization. Although this view did reflect some unsubstantiated optimism, it also indicated the extent of the debate now proceeding openly in Ghana and the fluidity of trade union theory. Interestingly enough, Ikoku also paid attention to the self-management enterprises and concluded that a balanced relationship in the triangle was essential, though 'self-management must have the last word where production is concerned.'

These issues, tentatively raised in Ghana, have become the central preoccupation of the Algerian unions since independence. As the French *colons* fled from the land on the signing of the Evian Agreements, peasant workers took over production in many areas, forming communal *assembléés d'autogestion* (self-management assemblies) and electing from these *comités d'autogestion*. By March 1963, when the government issued a decree outlining its policy for self-management, some 3,600,000 acres had been expropriated, and in October Ben Bella nationalized and turned over to self-management the remaining 3,000,000 acres formerly owned by French settlers, together with an additional 750,000 acres belonging to rich Algerians. The importance of this agrarian revolution was threefold. Self-management prevented the fragmentation of the big estates; it opened up the possibility of introducing the mass of the agricultural workers and peasants to a full and practical part in the economic life of the country; and it demonstrated more clearly than anywhere else in Africa the revolutionary power of the peasant worker. *Autogestion* meant simply that the peasants had organized themselves, and put in their claim for a political role in the country by collectively seizing the most important part of the Algerian economy. But even so, *autogestion* in agriculture meant, by 1965, employment for only 350,000 of the 2,630,000 rural workers; some 2,000,000 were unemployed or barely employed on small uneconomic farms of an average $1\frac{1}{2}$ acres each in size. When the first *Congrès des Fellahs* was held in October 1963, one of its most important tasks was to accelerate the integration of the unemployed into the permanent work-force by discouraging the use of casual labour and putting all agricultural work on a permanent basis. Further, the 1964 FLN Congress outlined plans for placing a ceiling of 120 acres on the private ownership of land, thus making a further 10,000,000 acres available for self-management and increasing the acreage of large-scale farming.

Socialism and the One-Party State

(By 1965, some 7,000,000 acres of larger farms had still to be nationalized.)

The expropriation of the land initiated by the land workers had some parallel in industry. Several firms which had been abandoned by the *colons* were taken over by employees on their own initiative, and after 1963 Ben Bella encouraged others to set up self-management committees even where there was little obvious local initiative. By 1964 some 70,000 workers were managing their own small factories and services, while in addition the government had nationalized (under state capitalist enterprises) several major industries including the Tamzali oilworks, several transport companies, and the automobile industry. Some 80 per cent of industrial and commercial undertakings still remained in private hands, but the government had declared its intention of nationalizing more industry and made sure that it controlled every new enterprise itself. The take-over of the industrial concerns resulted from an even greater upheaval than occurred on the land. Out of the 900,000 *colons* who scuttled to France in 1962–3, 650,000 had lived and worked in the towns. They took with them almost the entire professional class, the managers, doctors, teachers, and skilled workers, together with their savings and purchasing power. Machinery from factories and offices was either transported to France or smashed; stocks were run down and bank accounts emptied; taxes and debts remained unpaid. In a short time the industrial sector had become a gigantic slum, with a large number of factories, plants and services out of action. The only capital left was human labour. The FLN, itself divided and with no clear policy for the emergency, was unable to provide an effective plan for managing the abandoned firms. It was consequently presented with the workers' own solution – *autogestion*. As on the land, this was no comprehensive and planned campaign, but local if widespread initiative by groups of employees. Little guidance was necessary; without production the people starved, and there was no one else to organize the production.

When the FLN had sufficiently reorganized itself to act at last as a party of social reconstruction, it had little option but to recognize the initiative of the workers as a necessary step in the

African Trade Unions

revolution. Ben Bella declared that *autogestion* underlined 'the effectiveness of the Algerian Revolution by the spontaneous and conscientious action of the labouring masses', and was 'the distinguishing characteristic of Algerian socialism'. In spite of opposition from many FLN leaders to the movement, sheer pragmatism dictated acceptance of what had been done. The problem now was how the 'distinguishing characteristic of Algerian socialism' was to be incorporated into the evolving economic and political programmes. Within the government itself two major tendencies co-existed. One saw *autogestion* as a useful short-cut towards putting the country back on an economic footing in the absence of an indigenous bourgeoisie, while the other saw workers' control as in itself a desirable objective, even though it might in the short run cause a lowering of efficiency and productivity. While the first group wanted to replace the workers' movement as soon as possible by the usual type of bureaucracy-run nationalized industry or even by capitalist enterprise, the second saw it as something to be consolidated and extended. In the event, a compromise was reached. Ben Bella himself tended to lend his support to the second group (the extension of self-management); but the lack of any nationwide policy aimed at consolidating the workers' gains compelled the FLN to introduce measures for incorporating *autogestion* into the plan for extended state control and nationalization. The Decrees of March 1963 established a Director (appointed by the State) at the head of each self-managed enterprise who had wide administrative powers as representing the state economic plan. The *comités d'autogestion* retained a large degree of their early powers over the day-to-day organization of the enterprises, but the respective spheres of influence of the director and the committee were poorly outlined. Conflicts of method and aims were therefore inevitable, and provided the basis for much of the political controversy within the FLN and its affiliated organizations for the next two years.

The Decrees also specified a further level of workers' control organization – councils representing all members of the *comités d'autogestion* as well as the FLN and the unions – but up to the time of the Boumedienne *coup* this necessary bridge between

Socialism and the One-Party State

local enterprises and the state machinery had not emerged satisfactorily. Two major congresses were, however, held, the first of agricultural workers in October 1963 and the second of industrial workers in December 1964. The *Congrès des Fellahs* in particular showed a remarkable grasp by the workers of the complex technical economic and power issues at stake, and rebuffed allegations that the new managers were 'backward'. But the paramount issues remained unsolved. At one extreme political power was highly centralized in the hands of men who had emerged to leadership during the war, many not fully committed to the socialist aims of the revolution and some of whom gained control of the entire machinery when Boumedienne staged his *coup* in June 1965. At the other extreme, the awakened sense of responsibility among the urban and peasant workers has not developed the necessary political and social organizations. During the FLN Congress in April 1964 an advanced charter (*Le Chartre d'Alger*) was composed, probably expressing the demands of most of the workers but beyond the scope of the existing state machinery. To implement it, a dialogue between the party and state leaders and the various groups of workers was necessary. The 1965 Congress of the UGTA showed that this was possible, but there was little sign of the emergence of new national leaders.

In spite of a massive demonstration in favour of solving the political crisis in late 1962 which eventually gave power to Ben Bella, the UGTA was not committed in any sense to the political policies of the FLN. The activities of the Political Bureau and particularly Ben Bella and Khider were soon savagely attacked by the UGTA. On 1 November 1962 the union's journal, *L'Ouvrier Algérien*, published an article 'The UGTA confronts the party' which led to the issue being confiscated. For the next few months a struggle between the Political Bureau and the UGTA Executive for control of the movement intensified. The union agitated for increased nationalization, the introduction of an austerity salary range for political leaders, and the replacement of the Political Bureau with a new organization representing the various worker organizations and the party. The Bureau, struggling to maintain its authority in face of potential military threats and the continued opposition of some rural areas, decided that the UGTA must be firmly controlled. The preparations for the first union conference in January 1963 were taken over by the Political Bureau. On the third day of the conference delegates appointed by the Bureau took their seats and a new Executive Committee was nominated with only the secretary-general, a Ben Bella supporter, retained. After the conference had broken up in disorder, a party spokesman said that 'The UGTA has become, under the aegis of the party, the FLN, one of its national organizations.'

For the next two years the battle between the unions and the party was conducted on two fronts: the unions campaigning for more comprehensive planning and social ownership, greater democracy in industry and freedom of debate within the FLN, and Ben Bella attempting to integrate the unions more firmly into the party structure. Paradoxically the attempt to integrate the unions only made them more important if Ben Bella's programmes were to take effect. In view of his commitment to increased social ownership of industry and *autogestion* and the hostility of sections of the FLN to radical social measures, Ben Bella found that the unions and the agricultural workers were among the most important potential supporters. With the *Chartre d'Alger* in April 1964, the UGTA became even more an essential part of the revolution. It contained some of the few available managers for the public sector in a struggling economy, it was almost the only effective mass organization, and with its social policies provided an imperative ideological base for Ben Bella's power. The second UGTA congress (in March 1965) was consequently more fruitful and constructive than the first had been. Ben Bella went out of his way to court the workers and a vigorous debate throughout the congress suggested a more democratic approach to union affairs. But stringent criticism from the floor was levelled against the government for fitful policies, inability to distribute earnings fairly, and for putting *autogestion* in an administrative straight-jacket.

But if Ben Bella was just beginning to see the importance of the unions as the necessary link between the political leadership and the mass of the workers, the problems of creating a middle

Socialism and the One-Party State

level of leadership remained. Col. Hourari Boumedienne's *coup d'etat* in June 1965 exposed the weakness of a régime that had not yet managed to develop a powerful enough mass-movement to gain total confidence. The trade unions were caught off-guard. Not yet sure of Ben Bella's objectives, they were beginning nevertheless to work out for themselves a role in the new society. The future under Boumedienne was, at best, uncertain, and at worst might involve the reversal of the gains the unions had made. Strikes were called immediately following the *coup* and a general strike was planned a week later. But Boumedienne was able to play on the differences between Ben Bella and the workers and promise a further loosening of restrictions on trade union activity. The expected clash between the UGTA and the new régime did not take place and towards the end of the year it seemed possible that the unions would continue their role as part cooperators and part opposers within the government structure. Unlike unions in most of Africa, they were powerful enough to directly influence government policy. Unless it was prepared to engage in a prolonged terror campaign, no Algerian government could afford to ignore the very strategic role of the unions. And no African trade union movement, struggling for its place in a one-party structure, can afford to ignore the very important lessons of the UGTA.

Chapter 8: Notes

1. Terms used by Isaac Deutscher, 'Russia', in W. Galenson (ed) *Comparative Labour Movements*, N.Y. Prentice Hall, 1953, p. 505. See discussion in W. H. Friedland, 'Basic Social Trends' in *African Socialism*, (edited Friedland & C. G. Rosberg), Stanford U.P., 1964, pp. 15-34.
2. L. S. Senghor, *Nationhood and the African Road to Socialism*, Présence Africaine, 1962, p. 129, and pp. 122-6.
3. ibid., p. 77.
4. Aristide Zolberg, *One-Party Government in the Ivory Coast*, Princeton U.P., 1964, pp. 297-8.
5. ibid., pp. 304-5.
6. F. Harbison, 'Egypt', in W. Galenson (ed) *Labor and Economic Development*, Wiley, 1959, p. 184.
7. J. Nyerere, 'Ujamaa, the basis of African Socialism', *Présence Africaine*, No. 47, pp. 15-16.
8. Michael Kamaliza, 'Tanganyika's View of Labour's Role', *East African Journal*, November 1964, pp. 9-16.
9. Charles A. Micaud, *Tunisia – the Politics of Modernisation*, Pall Mall, 1964.
10. Statement by Tlili, Appendix B to *Kenya Federation of Labour Policy Statement*, June 1960, Nairobi.
11. Government White Paper, *Socialism and Economic Planning*, Nairobi, 1965, p. 56.
12. *Sixth World Congress of ICFTU*, Brussels, 3-11 December 1959, Published Report, 1960, p. 403.
13. Quoted Tony Hughes, 'The Strike Weapon in East Africa', *Venture*, Vol. 14, No. 9, October 1962, p. 6-7.
14. *Venture*, Vol. 15, No. 1, January 1963, p. 3.
15. T. Mboya, *Freedom and After*, Deutsch, 1963, p. 200.
16. Clement K. Lubembe, 'Trade Unions and Nation-Building', *East African Journal*, April 1964, p. 21.
17. *First Congress of UGTAN*, Présence Africaine, 1959, p. 50.

18. Sekou Touré, *L'action du PDG au lutte pour l'emancipation Africaine'*, Présence Africaine, 1959, p. 244.
19. John K. Tettegah, *Towards Nkrumahism, The Role and Tasks of the Trade Unions: Report on Doctrine and Orientation*. GTUC Education and Publicity Department, 1962.
20. *Seven Year Development Plan, 1963–4 – 1969–70*. Office of the Planning Commission, Accra, January 1964, p. 171.
21. Quoted D. Rimmer, 'The New Industrial Relations in Ghana', *Industrial and Labour Relations Review*, Vol. 14, No. 2, January 1961, p. 212.
22. B. C. Roberts, *Labour in the Tropical Territories of the Commonwealth*, London School of Economics, 1964, p. 145.
23. 'The Views of the Ghana TUC on Mr J. I. Roper's analysis of the Industrial Relations Act, 1958', *CCTA Bulletin*, Vol. 7, No. 4, July 1960, pp. 46–66.
24. 'Trade Unions and Socialism in Ghana', *Spark*, 15 May 1964.

9 The Politics of International Trade Unionism

THE EARLY YEARS

While they were sure of control over their colonies, the imperial powers were able to resist any external interference in labour problems. Early international organizations like the International Federation of Trade Unions and the Red International of Labour Unions played almost no part in the politics of colonial labour, and the only outside bodies to show any interest were the metropolitan trade union federations which, after 1930, began indicating their support for the development of trade unions in the colonies and the implementation of ILO conventions. The signing of the Geneva Labour Agreements posed the first serious challenge to the assumed privileges of the colonial governments. But even here the European unions (in particular the TUC and its affiliates in Britain) were slow to advocate the cause of African labour. The Commonwealth Labour Conferences held between 1925 and 1935 included only white South Africans as representatives from Africa, and in debates on issues in countries like India and the West Indies, the British delegates showed themselves unable to understand the point of view put by the coloured representatives. This lack even of communication is starkly illustrated by the TUC's first venture into colonial issues, when it sent a delegation to India in 1927–8.

The trade unionists whom the TUC met in India saw the industrial struggle as part of the fight for independence; some of them were communists, but most were allied to one or other of the various socialist and nationalist organizations that existed at the time. The TUC, however, saw its role as mediator between rival groups and advocate of minimal wage conditions; it was unable to accept the political nature of Indian labour. When an Indian Trades Disputes Act was passed in 1929, modelled on the repressive British Act of 1927, the TUC supported it with minor reservations. When thirty-two Indian trade unionists were imprisoned after the Meerut trial in 1930, Walter Citrine dismissed the whole issue as 'political' and unrelated to trade union affairs.[1]

Until the outbreak of the Second World War, the British trade unions continued to support all-white unions in South Africa, while the French organized their affiliated white unions in North and West Africa, and the Belgians permitted white workers to organize in the Congo. The internationalism of labour existed only for the European race.

These attitudes were shaken by the war, just as were the *laissez-faire* policies of the imperial powers. Despite the indifference of the British unions and the paternalism of the French and Belgian ones, Africans were beginning to organize. Moreover, the decision of the British and French governments to permit trade union organization put the metropolitan unions on the spot; there is little evidence that they had themselves much agitated for such a decision, but now the federations obviously had to accept the implications. When, in the first flush of victory and social reconstruction the World Federation of Trade Unions (WFTU) was founded in 1945, the British introduced delegates from Nigeria, Sierra Leone, Gambia, and the Gold Coast, together with Europeans from Northern Rhodesia as observers. In the assembly hall they found themselves seated alongside such improbable comrades as the Central Council of Soviet Trade Unions, the American Committee of Industrial Organizations, and the Swedish Landsorganisationen. No French colonial federation was represented, and the French CGT was without a single African delegate. The Africans themselves found ranged against them the remarkable alliance of French Stalinists (who, while glorying in their anti-colonialism, questioned the credentials of African trade unions in the interests of international working-class solidarity) and imperialist Britons (who were at pains to excuse the record of colonialism in the name of responsible 'trusteeship'). For a while the Americans alone seemed interested in linking the development of colonial trade unions to the liberation struggle. But even this support soon turned sour; the Americans were less concerned to develop a labour movement than to recruit troops for an anti-communist crusade.

The years of the 'united' WFTU marked the development of two policies towards African trade unionism that were greatly to influence action throughout the 'fifties and 'sixties. The first, and more positive, was the attempt to create an African regional body to coordinate activities in the continent. A conference was held at Dakar in April 1947, and this collected some useful information on African unions and labour problems; the fact that it was held at all suggested the increasing influence of the militants (U.S.S.R., U.S.A.) over the imperialists (Britain, France, Belgium) in WFTU councils and the more positive role that a section of the WFTU was trying to take in the anti-colonial campaign. But in the same year an attempt by Russian and American delegates to set up a fund that would help colonial trade unions was vetoed by Britain's Arthur Deakin, then President of the WFTU. The trade union centres of the colonial powers insisted on their own prerogatives in areas for which they claimed responsibility. The British TUC (controlling the Presidency) and the French CGT, with Louis Saillant as Secretary-General, were able to determine the direction of policies, particularly at Executive Bureau level. The effect of this remarkable alliance is most clearly displayed in the dispute over the Tunisian national federation, the UGTT.[2]

After two earlier attempts had failed, a Tunisian national trade union centre was established in 1946 by Ferhat Hached. In its objectives, it proclaimed that 'the fight against colonialism and foreign companies comes first; the fight for improving the economic situation after', and it accordingly affiliated to Bourguiba's nationalist movement, the Neo-Destour. Up to that time all trade unionists in Tunisia had been members of the French CGT's local section, and when the UGTT applied for WFTU affiliation, the CGT moved on two fronts. It reorganized its Tunisian section under Tunisian leadership as the Union Syndicale des Travailleurs de Tunisie, and Saillant moved a resolution in the WFTU's Executive Bureau (carried with minor amendments) rejecting the UGTT's application and urging it to reunite with the CGT in the new USTT. The USTT was automatically affiliated to WFTU, and Saillant justified the discrimination against Hached's federation in the following terms:

> It is the Neo-Destour Party which cannot be integrated in the WFTU. The UGTT is a nationalist and not a national organization; it enjoys the support of occult, religious, political and economic forces; its leaders mislead the workers, indulge in demagogy and may be termed neo-fascists; the legitimate aspirations of some of its members are incompatible with the political objectives of its leaders.... There are in Tunisia several organizations which for thirty years have taken part in the international trade union movement through CGT. French unions have always backed them, since both in theory and practice they accord CGT conceptions.... It will be necessary to bring home the fact that unity must be achieved around the traditional organizations already integrated in the WFTU.

In the debate following this statement, the Russians and Italians expressed doubts about the general argument, but Deakin supported Saillant on the grounds that the WFTU should not encourage breakaway unions and that unity should be achieved on the basis of organizations already affiliated.

At the first congress of the UGTT, a British observer representing the WFTU attacked the Tunisian federation for being a nationalist and not a class organization, and at the June 1947 Executive Committee meeting of the WFTU, Benoit Franchon, General Secretary of the CGT, said that 'there is no doubt that imperialist appetites have no hesitation in using national movements for imperialist purposes and there can be no question of backing them.' A UGTT-called strike at Sfax that August, in which workers were killed and injured, was dismissed by the CGT as 'demagogic and provocative'. In turn Ferhat Hached criticized Saillant for his pro-colonial attitude and for taking 'the enormous responsibility of imputing to our organization the blame for killings which have painted our working class in blood.'

Yet a few days after the non-communist unions had walked out of a session of the WFTU's Executive Bureau in January 1949 (subsequently to form the International Confederation of Free Trade Unions, or ICFTU), the UGTT was admitted to membership. This volte-face marked the WFTU's increasing interest in colonial labour movements and was the first sign of a change in

African Trade Unions

policy towards unions not directly fostered by WFTU affiliates. The lesson, however, had only in part been learned. At the second world congress of the WFTU in July 1949, it was decided that the Secretary-General of the USTT should represent North Africa on the Executive Committee. In spite of Ferhat Hached's protests and the fact that the UGTT had over three times as many members as the USTT, Saillant justified the decisions on the grounds that it was acceptable to the CGT as well as to the Algerian and Moroccan unions, both of which were local sections of the CGT. In response the UGTT decided in June 1950 to leave the WFTU, and it was accepted in July 1951 as an affiliate of the ICFTU.

The experiences of the UGTT constitute a convenient backcloth to the complex history of the international labour movements and their African policies in the 1950s, and mark an important stage in the evolution of international labour attitudes. If the united WFTU had been controlled administratively by the British and French unions, the rump WFTU and the ICFTU were increasingly dominated by the Russians and the Americans who attempted to create international organizations that mirrored their national foreign policy preoccupations. That they were not very successful was due to continued differences within the organizations on policy, their failure to understand the details of African conditions, and the irrelevance of their political categories for the weak and embryonic structures of the new unions.

DISCORD IN THE ICFTU

The members of the ICFTU included four distinct interest groups – the Americans; the federations from France, Britain and Belgium; a 'neutralist' mainly North Atlantic group (Sweden, Norway, Denmark, Israel, Austria and Canada); and the unions from the developing countries. For the first few years African policy was essentially based on a dialogue between the Americans and the British. Learning perhaps from the Tunisian episode, the Americans argued for identification with liberation movements and support for national trade union federations; but this conflicted sharply with the British view that the growth of trade unions in the colonies should not be linked with the anti-colonial struggle and that national federations should not become the major agencies for union development. The TUC was in a strong position to bargain; over half of the African labour movements seeking affiliation in the 1950s came from British colonies. (The French influence was small because most trade union centres in their colonies were CGT affiliates or members of Christian organizations and hence affiliated to the International Federation of Christian Trade Unions, while the Socialist Force Ouvrière mainly represented Frenchmen working in Africa.) Throughout the tedious debates of the 1950s, the TUC representatives repeatedly stressed the problems of 'trusteeship', a key word in British statements. What mattered was not 'merely the granting of complete independence to the people in the colonies', but 'the consequences of the transfer of power'.[3] The TUC believed in approaching 'this matter from a trade union point of view.... We believe that if there can be developed an effective trade union movement, the principles of democracy can be practised and learnt in order to serve the purposes of self-government.'[4] Time and again TUC spokesmen stressed the responsible nature of British rule and proudly indicated their part in it. The Labour Government of 1945–51 had laid the ground for colonial liberation; it was disheartening to attend an ICFTU Congress 'and find that in a sweeping generalization it is all dismissed under the expression "colonial domination"'.

For some time these protestations of virtue had their effect. Resolutions passed at ICFTU congresses and at meetings of the General Council or the Executive Board were restrained in their criticism of colonial rule. For example a General Council meeting in 1952 noted that independence did not automatically lead to improved working conditions, but that 'the establishment of self-government is capable of giving workers a fighting instrument in addition to meeting moral requirements.'[5] And the 1953 World Congress could only 'express anxiety at the present situation in Kenya', hoping that 'a peaceful state of affairs will soon be re-established and that in the meantime the British government will apply a progressive policy.'[6] But this politeness was the prelude to a storm that threatened to destroy the whole movement. Between 1953 and 1957 the Americans worked behind the scenes to erode the influence of the British in African affairs by increasing their own independent activity throughout Africa. During 1953 and 1954 the 'Mau Mau' war in Kenya provided them with an excellent opportunity.

Although the British TUC looked with sympathy on the plight of the Kenya workers, it was prevented from effectively intervening by conditions of its own making. By its membership of the Colonial Labour Advisory Committee, it was more or less obliged to act through the colonial machinery, and while massive repression was conducted by the British government, the TUC made representations to the Colonial Office with the object of ensuring trade union liberties, but produced little open protest. A British trade unionist was employed in Kenya as an adviser in the Labour Department, but in 1952 he was advising workers that 'a trade union is not an organization with political aims: it is an association which has as its object the regulation of relations between workers and their employers.'[7] This advice fell heavily on the ears of Kenyans whose political parties were banned and whose leaders were in detention, so that the only legal organization able to make political comments was the Kenya Federation of Labour. The British TUC was also insisting that the development of a central trade union federation should take second place to the encouragement of individual unions, works councils and 'probationary' unions under Labour Department control. With such paternalistic advice, the TUC left the field wide-open for American activity.

From the Kenya labour leaders themselves the Americans possessed some distinct advantages. As representatives of the major non-communist power, they were in a position to compel respect from the British authorities. They had money, possessed no scruples about developing a central federation, and had an impressive network of publications and platforms which would enable the Kenya Africans to put their case before world opinion. Tom Mboya pulled out all the stops, using the international trade union press for his articles on conditions in Kenya and astutely drawing on the help of the AFL, the ICFTU, and the TUC to develop the organizational strength of the KFL and avoid a ban on its activities. For its own part the TUC, which had always been inclined to assume all responsibilities for labour movements in British colonies, found that the Kenya unions were drawing at least as much on American support and also appealing directly to the ICFTU. The influence of the TUC was further reduced when the KFL developed its own forms of organization – the development of unions on industrial lines, adoption of the 'check-off' system of collecting dues, growth of union business enterprises – all of which owed nothing to the British model. The AFL made large grants towards KFL administrative costs, provided scholarships for study in the United States, and ultimately paid for the building of a splendid Federation Headquarters in Nairobi. An ICFTU representative was stationed in Nairobi from 1953, and the British role was reduced to an intervention by Sir Vincent Tewson in 1956 to help prevent suspension of the KFL's registration. Even when Mboya visited Ruskin College at Oxford in 1955, his most fruitful contacts were not with British trade unionists but with Fabians, academics and West Indians. On his way home from Ruskin he spent two months in the United States, expanding his trade union contacts and arranging educational programmes and financial aid in which the British had shown such little interest.

The effect of the Mboya campaign and the American response to it marked the end of British influence on the ICFTU's colonial activities. It was not difficult to show that the TUC represented a conservative view of colonial affairs. Every time a British delegate spoke at Congresses, he included warnings against Pan-African 'dominance' and 'political unionism', and made his pathetic plea for an understanding of Britain's colonial mission. And every time he was attacked vigorously by the delegate from some developing country. Cubans, Tunisians, Indians, Ghanaians united in condemning the TUC for not making 'an explicit and concrete declaration that it will support with all its strength the desires for independence of all colonial or non-self-governing countries'.[8] Between 1957 and 1961 the Americans clashed frequently and openly with the British. In 1957 the AFL-CIO decided not to contribute to the ICFTU's newly-created 'Solidarity Fund' because it was dominated by 'imperialists' and

African Trade Unions

'socialists' (the Americans particularly objected to J. H. Oldenbrook, the Dutch Secretary-General of the ICFTU). The TUC on the other hand made a donation of £500,000 for a three-year period, but reserved its right to independent activity in British colonies and Commonwealth countries. The AFL-CIO in its publications and at Congresses spared no pains in attacking the TUC and linking it with British colonial domination. The colonial labour advisers were 'saboteurs' of trade union development because they acted as spies for the colonial government and hindered union growth;[9] the British TUC had not resolved the problems of trade union organization and education, and was mistrusted by the new unions because of its colonial outlook; it was 'essential that free trade unions should view Pan-Africanism in its true light, as a movement which developed against the colonialism of European powers'.[10] In 1960 the AFL-CIO resolved to improve its overseas organization and extend its activities to other parts of Africa, notably the former French territories. The TUC could only emphasize its fears of opportunism. Above all, it deplored

a growing tendency for African trade unions to be subordinated to the aims of political Pan-Africanism, to the detriment of genuine trade union activity; and this tendency is being wittingly or unwittingly encouraged by some non-African trade union organizations.[11]

American policy was a response to a real situation; no foreign labour movement could hope to influence African unions if it was unsympathetic to the major political movement on the continent. And the ICFTU, to survive in Africa, had to make the same adjustment. In 1956 the decision was taken to set up a regional organization for Africa with headquarters at Accra, following the establishment of an Information Centre at Accra in 1953 and the basing of an ICFTU representative at Nairobi in 1955. Because of the movement towards developing an African Federation under Sekou Touré, African members pressed for their own organization, and the ICFTU was compelled to convene its first African Regional Conference in 1957. The intention was to use the Ghana TUC with its Pan-African appeal as the basis for activities in tropical Africa and the Tunisian UGTT as the

The Politics of International Trade Unionism

centre for North African action. John Tettegah was elected Chairman of the Conference, and Nkrumah welcomed the delegates by suggesting how the trade unions could assist in developing the economic potential of new nations – a new theme for the ICFTU. The proceedings were also marked by the continuing disagreement between the Americans and the British, each party reiterating its own position on trade union organization and colonialism. The French Force Ouvrière delegate attacked the AFL-CIO for having 'contributed nothing to the expenses' of the conference and for 'airing their views on general political problems'.[12] Despite these conflicts, however, it was decided to establish three ICFTU area committees in Africa and ultimately a semi-autonomous regional organization with its own secretariat and control of funds. The resolutions passed were noticeably more militant than any at a World Congress of the ICFTU, and the importance of the Pan-African ideal was paramount.

But if the ICFTU thought that it had effectively latched on to the nationalist movement, the first conference of the All-African Peoples' Organization at Accra in December 1958 disillusioned it. A resolution was passed urging the creation of an All-African Trade Union Federation, and there began that new battle for African trade union loyalties that has marked the history of the past seven years. If the ICFTU's efforts were going to prove almost completely fruitless, it might have expected this from the experiences of the WFTU and the pro-Communist unions in French-speaking Africa.

UGTAN AND THE BIRTH OF PAN-AFRICAN UNIONISM

After the split in the WFTU, almost the only African affiliates left were in the French colonies, though the Sudan Workers Trade Union Federation and the non-racial South African Congress of Trade Unions were for some years sympathetic outsiders. (Two prominent Sudanese unionists, Ibrahim Zakaria and Shafi Ahmed el Sheikh, were elected to senior executive positions in the WFTU in the late 1950s.) Following the experiences of the UGTT, the Algerians and Moroccans created federations in the early 1950s that were outside CGT control, and in a short time

African Trade Unions

the strength of the pro-Communist unions was drastically reduced. Both the Algerian UGTA and the Moroccan UMT affiliated to the ICFTU because they felt that the issue of colonial independence would be given a fairer and more profitable hearing there (along the lines that the Kenya Federation of Labour had pioneered). But because both of these federations were obliged to operate as underground movements until independence, their strength was difficult to assess, and the CGT was able to show a paper strength of mainly European support.

The WFTU's major crisis came with the disaffiliation of the CGT unions in French West Africa. Disagreement between the CGT and its affiliates began as far back as 1950, when Félix Houphouet-Boigny led the inter-territorial political movement, the RDA, out of its affiliation with the French Communist Party. ('We were wrong in allowing the use of the *communist pretext* as a justification for retrograde policy and for division among Africans.... The battle continues but without the pretext of Communism'.)[13] Although one or two prominent unionists like Abbas Guèye of Senegal and the entire Union des Syndicats de Haut Volta made the break, most trade unionists insisted on retaining their CGT affiliations. Thus an important division occurred within the anti-colonial movement between its trade union members, like Sekou Touré of Guinea, Kissi Gris Camille of the Ivory Coast and Abdoulaye Diallo of Soudan, and the other political leaders under Houphouet-Boigny. Many of the trade unionists kept outside the RDA and even joined or created splinter political parties, and for five years the close working relationship between the RDA and the CGT unions was broken by 'the splitting up of the African movement into groups which were in no way consonant with African reality'.[14]

But two factors brought the CGT affiliation to an end. Many of the leading RDA politicians worked actively to promote an independent African federation, and the growth of a trade union movement in Guinea closely linked to the main political party created new tensions with the French communists and moved the African CGT towards a more militant nationalist position. In 1955 the central committee of the CGT in Senegal and Mauretania decided to disaffiliate from both the French CGT and the WFTU, and form instead an autonomous African group. This was immediately followed by a split at the West African CGT Co-ordinating Committee meeting held at Dakar in February 1956. Sekou Touré of Guinea and Diallo Seydou of Senegal urged separation, but Abdoulaye Diallo, leader of the Soudan CGT and a Vice-President of the WFTU, argued cogently for the advantages of continued affiliation and was supported by Cissé Alioune of Senegal and Gris Camille of the Ivory Coast. The inevitable rupture occurred; Touré and his supporters withdrew from the CGT and formed the Confédération Générale des Travailleurs d'Afrique. But, at a second conference held at Cotonou in January 1957, the two wings agreed to merge into a new interterritorial federation, the Union Générale des Travailleurs d'Afrique Noire (UGTAN), which was affiliated to neither the CGT nor WFTU.

Thus within twelve months the WFTU lost all its affiliates in French West Africa. However, this did not mean that it was entirely without support in the former French colonies. Apart from some individual sections of UGTAN which continued to support the WFTU in general policy questions, the CGT affiliates in French Equatorial Africa, the Cameroons, Madagascar and the Belgian Congo were rather differently affected by the movements in West Africa. In Madagascar the CGT was in 1956 active in promoting the creation of a new federation, Foraison'ny Sendika eron'i Madagaskara, as the major rival to the well-established Christian Federation. In the Cameroons the major federation, the Union des Syndicats Confédérés du Cameroon, was deeply divided over issues similar to those affecting the West African unions. Jacques N'gom, the secretary of USCC, was in favour of continued WFTU affiliation, but was bitterly opposed by Mayoa Beck who wanted links with UGTAN. After a series of conflicts and temporary rapprochements, two major unions appeared – the Confédération Générale Cameroonaise du Travail led by Beck and without international affiliation, and N'gom's Union Générale des Travailleurs du Cameroon, affiliated to the WFTU. In other French-speaking territories similar divisions occurred, often resulting in three or four federations, and so leaving the Christian unions with some advantage over the others. But what-

African Trade Unions

ever the form of conflict, the direct influence of WFTU was appreciably reduced.

The effect of these divisions and defections was to make the WFTU review its entire strategy in Africa. Pro-Communist federations directly affiliated to the WFTU were discouraged in favour of close cooperation with non-aligned national and Pan-African centres. In opposition to its earlier stand of not supporting 'nationalist' unions, it now advised its members to merge with the new central bodies. In 1956, for example, when the CGT affiliate in Tunisia, the USTT, decided to merge with the UGTT, the WFTU congratulated itself on the decision and declared that it encouraged trade union unity everywhere. Similarly the Algerian section of CGT merged with the UGTA in 1957, and WFTU intervention may have assisted in the creation of UGTAN in 1957. Between 1957 and 1962 the WFTU came out strongly in favour of the two major non-aligned federations operating in Africa – the Confederation of Arab Trade Unions, based on Cairo and covering North Africa and the Middle East, and the All-African Trade Union Federation – while it took a series of major policy decisions in favour of assisting trade unions who were not affiliated to it. By adapting rapidly to the changed situation, the WFTU was able to cut its losses and certainly avoid a disaster similar to that which overtook the ICFTU's relations in the early 1960s. Where it did fail was that its aid was even less geared to African conditions than the ICFTU's, and the emphasis on prestige visits to Eastern Europe brought it many tourists but produced few qualified trade unionists.

PAN-AFRICANISM AND THE DECLINE IN ICFTU INFLUENCE

The formation of UGTAN provided the catalyst necessary for launching a Pan-African trade union movement. The support came from two other powerful sources: politicians who saw the move as a necessary step towards establishing a Pan-African political federation (and in some cases also of ridding their states of external trade union advisers), and trade union leaders like John Tettegah of Ghana and Majoub Ben Seddik of

The Politics of International Trade Unionism

Morocco who were increasingly disturbed by much of the ICFTU's activity in Africa, particularly the persistent attempts by American affiliates to make the organization part of their cold war campaign. Although the Americans had provided much needed support for African unions in their battles with the British and French administrations and the 'imperialism' of the TUC, the CGT, the Force Ouvrière and the Belgian unions, their hostility to all forms of socialism and non-alignment became during the late 1950s more evident than their support for African nationalism and trade union growth. It was difficult to avoid the conclusion that the AFL-CIO, the American Department of State and the Central Intelligence Agency were working together closely in a common offensive. Any such suspicions were more than justified by the evidence.

The history of government-union cooperation in the United States dates back to the First World War when Samuel Gompers, head of the American Federation of Labor, created a Pan-American movement financed with funds supplied by President Woodrow Wilson. After the war Gompers was worried that the Red International and the IFTU might try and extend their activities to Latin America. To forestall this he arranged for the AFL and the Mexican trade union centre to sign a trade union 'Monroe Doctrine' in 1923 which proclaimed their opposition to 'the efforts of European trade unions to encroach upon trade union sovereignty in the Western Hemisphere'. This precedent for government-union collusion was followed during the Second World War by the creation of more comprehensive machinery for pursuing a common policy in developing countries throughout the world. Anti-Communism became an important objective of trade union foreign policy, and the AFL-CIO (the AFL merged with the rival CIO in 1955) obtained as Director of its Department of International Affairs Jay Lovestone, former General Secretary of the American Communist Party and now a professional anti-Communist, who was one of the Central Intelligence Agency's most important contact men.[15] The American Government itself began to see trade unionism as a major element in promoting its policies; by the early 1960s it was spending over $13,000,000 a year on international labour affairs, with forty-eight labour attachés in developing countries supported by a host of trade union advisers. For its own part, the AFL-CIO devoted 8 per cent of its budget in 1960–1 to international activities, and other sums were spent indirectly and by individual unions. In his book on U.S. labour policy abroad,[16] the former Assistant Secretary of Labour for International Affairs, George Lodge (son of the Republican leader Henry Cabot Lodge) demonstrated how close the relationship between government and labour was and how 'American labor, management and government must urgently improve their approach.' He urged Americans to be more active.

Let us not be bashful about setting forth our purposes.... We should use our vast influence, as appropriate, to encourage the régimes of newly developing countries to foster those actions and programs which will encourage the growth of strong, non-communist worker organizations.

But if Lodge, in 1962, believed that not enough had been done, many Africans believed that far too much had been done already. Several leading American trade unionists had gone out of their way to attack the neutralism of developing countries. In 1956 George Meany assailed Nehru for his opposition to SEATO, alleging that he had been converted to Communism, and in 1960 Harry Goldberg, former AFL representative in Indonesia, attacked Ghana and Guinea trade union leaders for opening their movements to communist control by their neutralist ideas. At the 1962 World Congress of the ICFTU, as a member of the U.S. Department of Labor staff noted, 'a subtle attempt was made through the very presence of the Congress in Berlin to strengthen the commitments of Afro-Asian participants against the Soviet bloc.'[17] Even Lodge in his book showed some concern at the ham-fisted tactics of some American unionists and their coolness to nationalist movements in Africa and Asia.

Against the obvious pressures of Americans to commit African unions to rigid cold war positions, it is not surprising that several trade union leaders and politicians found it necessary to establish their independence. The resolution passed by the first All-African Peoples' Conference marked a new phase in the struggle for trade union autonomy, and between this conference and the second, at Tunis in January 1960, two different approaches took shape. The militants, led by John Tettegah and Abdoulaye Diallo, campaigned vigorously for a federation independent of both the WFTU and the ICFTU. They argued that the two internationals were obviously committed to conflicting sides in the cold war and that African unions should refuse to be sacrificed in a prolonged struggle for control. The others, though claiming to be equally non-aligned, countered that the ICFTU was a useful forum for airing African views, that the Americans had not succeeded in dominating the policies of the organization, and that the ICFTU's stand on such issues as Algeria, South Africa, the Congo, Angola and the Federation of Rhodesia and Nyasaland had been in the mainstream of Pan-African objectives. The conflict began to take organizational shape in late 1959. The Ghana TUC announced its disaffiliation from the ICFTU and called a meeting at Accra to inaugurate an All-African Trade Union Federation at the same time as the African Regional Conference of the ICFTU was to be held in Lagos (November 1959). This decision was made independently of the All-African Peoples Organization and it immediately produced the expected collision. Most of the ICFTU affiliates attended the Lagos conference but sent observers to Accra, and there a Steering Committee was set up by the Ghana TUC, the CNT de Guinée, the Egyptian Confederation of Labour, the UMT, and the Imoudou wing of the TUC of Nigeria to prepare the way for creating an AATUF. Between these two conferences and the first major AATUF conference at Casablanca in May 1961 various efforts were made to bring the sides together, but several factors worked against any united action, in particular the ICFTU links and the question of political affiliation.

In November 1960 the third ICFTU Regional Conference established an African Regional Organisation (AFRO) with a secretariat in Lagos. Several resolutions were also passed and principles of action outlined which made pointed criticisms of the AATUF Steering Committee. The most serious of these declared that the AATUF trade unions were 'arms of government administration' and that the governments concerned were 'vigorously employing money and questionable forms of inducements to force similar arrangements upon other African states'.[18] Though these accusations contained some truth (several AATUF affiliates *were* closely allied to governments, and the Ghana TUC had conducted a war of attrition against some African trade union centres), they carefully concealed the ambiguities in the ICFTU's own position. Although the African Regional Organisation included one or two unions which were not directly linked with governments, the majority of its affiliates were as firmly tied to political parties and the administration of labour as any in the AATUF. After they had suppressed the UGTAN sections, the governments of French-speaking West Africa did not object to their 'industrial wings' joining the ICFTU (indeed it was diplomatically convenient for them to do so), and besides these, other federations were represented in AFRO whose 'freedom' (as conceived in ICFTU and AFL-CIO charters) was at least as doubtful as that of their Ghanaian or Egyptian counterparts. In particular Tunisia, with its 'complete cohesion and unity between the trade union movement and national policies', as Bourguiba himself described it,[19] and Tanganyika hardly provided models of unions operating free of party controls.

It is not surprising that AFRO's claims to represent 'free democratic trade unionism' were greeted with scepticism by AATUF supporters and by the more genuinely free Christian unions who had since 1959 been grouped in the Union Pan-Africaine des Travailleurs Croyants, an affiliate of the International Federation of Christian Trade Unions. As was by now clear, the real issue in African trade unionism for the majority of countries was not *whether* trade unions should be linked to ruling parties, but *how*. The decision of the ICFTU to establish an African Regional Organisation based in Nigeria (whose industrial relations were hardly typical of Africa) and having as members the representatives of some one-party states and territories which were not yet independent, merely delayed the necessary process of adjustment. The next contribution to the debate, the 1961 AATUF conference at Casablanca, stressed the need for reappraisal but showed how far the African unions still had to go before they could effectively promote their own federal organization. The conference was messy and inconsequential. Confusion over the credentials of delegates, resentment by many union centres at not having been included in the preparatory stages, lack of any real debate over the major issues exercising African unions, and a tendency for the members of the Steering Committee to allocate to themselves a higher proportion of votes than were granted to other unions, all served to add to the frustrations of delegates. It was remarkable that so many unions came – even the Tunisians and Kenyans were there – but before the conference ended, a third of the delegates had left. The inclusion of Tom Mboya on a Central Council headed by the UMT's Ben Seddik and Ghana's Tettegah was hardly an adequate compensation.

The fundamental issue at stake during this conference was much less that of international affiliation than that of the tactics to be adopted in the creation of African unions. Most of the unions belonging to the ICFTU either came from countries where governments were unsympathetic to trade unions or from colonies not yet independent; their problem was how to grow and survive bans and suspension. Precisely because the ICFTU was basically Western in character, there was some hope that governments would be more tolerant towards its affiliates than to members of a more militant federation. Such was the lesson suggested by the Kenya experience on the one hand and the banning of the Sudan Workers' Trade Union Federation on the other. The Tunisian unions maintained their affiliation because survival depended on their curbing the militants. After the purge of Ben Salah in 1957, Tlili and Achour were obliged to move cautiously; it was most unlikely that Bourguiba would tolerate any fresh declaration of political independence. This was especially true of territories in former French West Africa where party-controlled unions struggled desperately for survival against indifferent or hostile governments. The members of the AATUF Steering Committee, on the other hand, all came from independent countries and, with the exception of Nigeria, from countries where unions either worked closely with the government or where they were seeking an important place in economic planning. Their perspective was therefore rather different. They

African Trade Unions

were already operating detailed schemes of cooperation with governments that, by and large, accepted the importance of a large trade union movement – even if, as in Egypt, the area of trade union activity was limited. Their tactical problems were consequently those of working with governments already outspoken in their Pan-Africanism and of establishing their own political and economic strength in the face of efforts by the ICFTU (and particularly the AFL-CIO) to attach African unions to cold war positions. In fact, the combined membership of the AATUF founder-members[20] at the Casablanca conference was already higher than that claimed by the members of AFRO (2,675,000 contrasted with 1,663,087), and the ICFTU figure included over 800,000 members from Algeria and Morocco who would soon disaffiliate.

Against this background the issue of international affiliation simply underlined the differences between unions struggling under hostile or unsympathetic governments and those which saw their future in working out a social policy within the single-party state. The events of the next few years served to underline the distinction. In January 1962 – twenty-three affiliates of the ICFTU and twelve of the IFCTU, as well as sixteen unions without international affiliation, met at Dakar to establish an African Trade Union Confederation. The stimulus for this came from the leaders of the Tunisian, Kenyan and Senegalese centres. Although the conference drew up a charter, this did not differ significantly from that adopted at the Casablanca conference, except that it allowed national centres to decide on their own international affiliations. ATUC itself was not to be affiliated to any centre. (AATUF reserved the right to affiliate impartially to all international organizations, while proscribing national affiliations.)

But, however loud the demonstration by the members of ATUC, the whole exercise was clearly a holding operation. In 1961 John Tettegah had declared 'total war' on non-AATUF unions: the Dakar conference was both an attempt by ICFTU and IFCTU affiliates to demonstrate their equal desire for an independent African movement and, in the words of Tom Mboya, 'an act of mutual protection in the face of this "declaration of war"'.[21]

The Politics of International Trade Unionism

But as more colonies became independent and unions were absorbed into party machinery, the face of African trade union politics accordingly changed. The AATUF, far from weakening under the competition from ATUC, grew in support. At its second congress at Bamako in June 1964, several new centres were represented, and between 1962 and 1965 the trade union centres of Algeria, Morocco, Tanganyika, Zanzibar and Kenya disaffiliated from the ICFTU, while the TUC in Zambia was brought under closer government supervision and looked, in July 1965, like becoming another deserter. The Kenya unions, which had maintained close ties with the ICFTU before independence, were increasingly embarrassed by the American tag, and as industrial relations in the country moved into patterns more typical of other African states, so the ICFTU connexion became less relevant. The disaffiliation of the KFL in November 1964 brought to an end the ICFTU decade in Africa. Except for the UGTT, the ULC of Nigeria and the Uganda TUC, no major trade union organization remained affiliated, and, as was admitted in the Report on Activities submitted to the ICFTU's eighth Congress at Amsterdam in 1965, 'the intensive effort earlier displayed by the ICFTU has had to be reduced.' ICFTU officers found their work shrunk from supervising operations throughout the continent to organizing a few educational programmes in French-speaking West Africa, Southern Rhodesia and Congo (Leopoldville); maintaining 'in conditions of great difficulty' a Labour College in Uganda; and fostering union development in such unlikely places as Liberia and Ethiopia. With the ICFTU's declining influence, the Americans began to lose interest in it as a weapon for the anti-communist crusade. At the March 1965 Executive Board meeting an open breach between the AFL-CIO and Omer Becu, Secretary-General of the ICFTU, became apparent. George Meany attacked the ICFTU as 'a complete and absolute bureaucracy, inept in the way it functions', and complained that money donated by the AFL-CIO to the organization was lying unused in banks. The main issue, however, was that the ICFTU was not sufficiently committed to the war against Communism.

It is imperative that the ICFTU should devote more attention to the

Communist problem as it manifests itself today.... The study of Communist propaganda and infiltration tactics should be included in all ICFTU training courses. The anti-Communist campaign should be stepped up in all fields of activity.... It might be advisable to establish a new ICFTU department devoted to the struggle against Communism.[22]

To this Becu replied that 'there is no doubt about that, we are against Communism, but we were not created solely for this reason.' It might also be added that Communists in Africa have had little apparent success with trade unions. Although some union centres have used Eastern European and Cuban training schemes, it would be very difficult to prove that these have had any lasting influence on either the ideologies or organization of the unions.

The remarkable spectacle of the AFL-CIO, itself one of the most centralized and bureaucratic labour structures in the world, launching an attack on the ICFTU's bureaucracy indicates the American disillusionment with European labour movements and the complete failure of ICFTU policy in Africa. The attempt to intervene directly in African labour politics had succeeded only in alienating the majority of African unions and in putting African governments on guard against ICFTU activity. The split between the AFL-CIO and the European centres was nowhere more effectively displayed than in Lodge's discussion of the aims of American policy in developing countries. While the Europeans continually emphasized that unions must be independent of government machinery and not subject to political party control, Lodge thought otherwise.

In many developing countries today there are authoritarian régimes, and these countries are probably going to require strong leadership for some time to come.... In several countries whose continued strength is of the utmost importance to the free world, trade unions are under the firm hand of government. If they were not so, it is more than likely that they would either disintegrate or be taken over by fanatical and destructive elements.[23]

If the Europeans rather desperately tried to insist on trade union principles, the Americans were disposed to sink these in a struggle to prevent 'Communist subversion and takeover'. To do this the whole apparatus of the state, management, and the unions must be harnessed in a common effort, the government and unions by giving advice and aid, and American business by regarding

> a strong, democratic and militant worker organization ... as useful for the survival of its enterprise. It must see such an organization as its hope for evolving a stable economic relationship in the country, protecting it against political upheaval and expropriation, as well as preserving the country against communism.

A practical illustration of this conflict was given at the 1965 ICFTU Congress, when the Americans supported the credentials of the Tunisian delegation although Habib Achour and almost the whole committee of the UGTT had been imprisoned and replaced by Neo-Destour nominees. Several of the European delegates, led by Britain's George Woodcock, protested against the move and abstained or opposed the proposal. But American pragmatism won; the Neo-Destour nominees were accredited, and Ahmed Tlili, as Achour's delegate, was given observer status.

INTERNATIONAL AID AND TRADE UNIONS

With the reduced importance of the ICFTU and WFTU as collective agents in African trade union contacts, the type of aid given has assumed greater significance. In practice this has been of five kinds – educational programmes at home and abroad, funds allocated to union centres for use at their own discretion, gifts in kind, provision of labour advisers, and sponsorship of cooperative and commercial projects. The main agencies for these efforts have been the international organizations and their international industrial affiliates, national trade union centres, the ILO, and foreign governments. Generally the aid directed through the WFTU, ICFTU, foreign governments and national centres has been motivated primarily by political considerations, while individual unions, the ILO and the International Trade Secretariats have been more concerned with union organization and practical aid programmes. There are, of course, exceptions

African Trade Unions

to these rules – some national trade union centres are more impartial in their aid than others, and some International Trade Secretariats, under American influence, are becoming more directly political in their activities.

Until the creation of the AATUF, most African trade unions were affiliated to one or other of the international organizations and therefore able to take advantage of the various forms of aid these offered. The ICFTU, indeed, insisted on affiliation as a condition for receiving aid; the WFTU was more adroit. In the late 1950s both organizations established labour colleges for training African trade union leaders – the ICFTU, at Kampala in 1958; and the WFTU, at Budapest in 1959. In addition various other training centres were set up by national affiliates of these organizations which included a large proportion of Africans among the students. The Israeli trade union federation, the Histadrut, established an Afro-Asian Labour Institute at Tel-Aviv in 1960 with substantial help from the AFL-CIO and some from the British TUC; several American Labour Institutes and university faculties of Industrial Relations provided places for African trade unionists; the East Germans offered training to Africans in three institutions at Bernau, East Berlin and Leipzig, while the Czechs did the same at a Trade Union College in Prague. Other scholarships are available for courses at Britain's Ruskin College, the Swedish Trade Union centre Runöskolan, and centres in France, Germany, Italy, Canada and Austria. In 1960 UGTAN established a Labour College at Conakry with some support from East German unions.

Most of such institutions have been frankly ideological centres, and only two, at Kampala and Conakry, were placed under the control of Africans and geared in any way to African needs and conditions. The centre at Prague, for example, deals primarily with 'the world socialist system' and the 'role of trade unions in a capitalist society.', while the Histadrut institute is concerned mainly with the relationship between trade unions and cooperative enterprises, drawing substantially on Israeli experience. The drawback of these types of institution is that they demand a high level of education before students actually arrive; most foreign colleges insist that students should possess secondary school education, and so most of the training is for existing union *élites*, tending to widen the gulf between rank-and-file members (who are in most cases illiterate) and the union officials. In addition, as most of the courses are abroad, union offices are deprived of their main organizers for long periods, with a consequent serious effect on union efficiency. Some unions have actually closed while their secretaries studied abroad.

The ICFTU's decision to create an African Labour College at Kampala was mainly excited by the demand of African trade unionists for more practical training in Africa itself. Certainly the College has been one of the more impressive results of ICFTU activity, demonstrating that it is quite possible to staff a college with African tutors and develop courses more closely related to African realities. In particular the establishment of a research division in the college, concerned with training trade union research officers and providing statistics on African working conditions, was an important landmark in African trade union organization. But the two problems that have troubled both the WFTU and the ICFTU in Africa – political commitment and the training of junior officials – have not been seriously tackled. The college has come under very heavy fire from the governments of Uganda and Tanganyika as well as from the Uganda TUC, which has accused it of interference in local affairs. Currently, indeed, the college is operating under the threat of 'nationalization' by the Uganda government. On selection procedures the college has taken students with at least five years activity in unions, a command of English, and some secondary education.[24] But almost all the students so far admitted were already holding senior union posts, so that the college is guilty, as are most institutions operated by international organizations, of only training the *élite*. The effects of this policy are seen in Professor Zack's statistics on employment taken by Kampala students two years after graduation. Although 9 per cent retained the same union job as they had held before their training, 58 per cent had taken a higher union job, and 27 per cent had, within this short space of time, moved into management or government posts.[25] In part these figures reflect the shortage of trained administrators in developing countries, but they also indicate the important emphasis at Kampala on training for senior positions. In view of its struggle for survival, the college could more easily justify its existence to governments by extending its activities to untrained junior officials and by including some industrial training courses in its programmes. Certainly the relative success of the college suggests the crying need for several other such centres, though closer to the mainstream of the African labour movement.

This tendency to concentrate on *élite* training and so produce a bureaucracy without developing effective leadership lower down the union scale has been reinforced by methods of distributing aid. The establishment of the ICFTU's Solidarity Fund in 1957 was an attempt to create a central pool of money from which aid could be allocated without national centres having to compete against each other for influence. Although to some extent it did have this result, it also strengthened the tendency to make grants only to national union centres. Some national federations received regular subsidies which were swallowed up by administrative costs and the provision of large buildings without noticeably improving the organization of the unions themselves. Centres like the Tanganyikan and the Kenyan (which by 1962 was receiving £12,000 a year from the ICFTU alone) produced large bureaucracies which gradually lost the efficiency and dynamism of their earlier days. Governments and workers began to notice the high proportion of income that went on administrative costs and the expenses of federation officers. It was not difficult for the resistance of union executives to disaffiliation from the ICFTU to be linked with the comfortable standards of living that ICFTU funds had made possible for them.

The failure of the Solidarity Fund's policies and the disaffiliation of the major national centres in Africa have presented new possibilities for foreign union centres and the International Trade Secretariats, whose activities are less suspect than the ICFTU's. The ITSs, indeed, have always prided themselves on their independence from the ICFTU. While the main organization insisted that communist unions could not affiliate, the Miners' International Federation and the International Federation of Builders and Woodworkers both admitted Yugolsav unions to membership, and in 1965 an Italian printing union, affiliated through its national centre to the WFTU, was accepted as a member of the International Graphical Federation. Also, though many African centres have disaffiliated from the ICFTU, several of their industrial unions have retained their membership of the appropriate ITS. Thus, despite their affiliation to the ICFTU, most of the Secretariats have tried to retain their freedom to organize their own activities. Some of their work is directed towards advising unions on the spot and organizing local courses for union officers. Most of the aid they grant is more specific than that given by the ICFTU; it is for office equipment, cars and the part-payment of some salaries. Some of them have representatives living in Africa who work in closer cooperation with unions than ICFTU officials have seemed able to do. Certainly the provision of funds for stated items of expenditure is a more rational way of assisting unions; it helps to contain bureaucracy, tends to limit interference in the policy of African unions, and avoids misappropriation of funds. Even so, the International Trade Secretariats have two major problems to contend with – not entirely of their own making. Several of them are heavily dependent on grants from the ICFTU's Solidarity Fund and the major American unions; this, of necessity, has qualified their scope, for the ICFTU is only too keen to influence their activities in political directions. There are also signs that the Americans, disappointed in the ICFTU as a medium for activity, are increasingly using the Secretariats to further their own aims. If the tendency continues it is likely that the impartial nature of these bodies will be even further compromised. The second problem facing the Secretariats is that their activity is, by nature, sectional. As an ITS is dealing only with part of the labour force, the advice it gives will be limited to one category of labour. It may therefore concentrate on raising the organizational level of a group of workers – and hence possibly their militancy – and so run foul of the central federation which is attempting to co-ordinate policies with the government. A conflict between a capitalist-style free-for-all and a planned economy is inherent in the work done by most Trade Secretariats. Their problem will always be how to raise the level of union organization and militancy and at the same time encourage a philosophy of public service and responsibility. At present, however, there are few signs that the Secretariats are aware of the need to reconcile these positions in a general theory of labour for developing countries.

The other form of aid, too rarely practised, that can be of benefit to unions, is found in the forms of cooperative enterprise established between some union centres in Africa and Europe. The establishment of banks, insurance schemes and cooperatives, while in themselves secondary to the main functions of industrial relations, can be useful for giving unions a stake in the economic organization of their country. The technical and financial help given by some individual national centres (including the American) can be useful in strengthening an African centre. Africans, however, have to be careful that such activity does not, as it appears to have done in Tunisia, become a substitute either for organizing the workers on a national basis or for establishing the workers' strategic role in the distribution of resources and the economic control of industry. The danger is that, with their lack of syndicalist perspective, many Western unions will see such commercial activity as an end in itself. Again, as Tunisia has demonstrated, this end can be an unfortunate one.

CONCLUSION

The tendency of international organizations (Western and Communist alike) has been to give aid that makes the recipients financially and politically dependent on the donors, so reducing the cohesion and strength of the African unions. Africa has not only become a battleground for rival interests; it has become a kind of laboratory where various experiments are being conducted for their own sake. The organizations have rarely set out to analyse African conditions and meet African needs; they have been concerned to further their own ends, to propose programmes, education schemes and activities that fit into preconceived political categories. The paternalism of the outside world has not often shown such a degree of folly and ignorance as in its handling of African labour questions. And while the

The Politics of International Trade Unionism

ICFTU, WFTU, British TUC, AFL-CIO, CGT or Czech and East German unions conspire and wrangle, pass pious resolutions and distribute aid, the living standard of the African worker remains abysmally low.

It is true that one or two organizations have been prepared to support impartial research on African labour problems, but on the whole the international movements have preferred to rely on reports from their own representatives, though these are generally biased, uncoordinated and superficial. It would be useful if some of the $1,278,000 which the AFL-CIO accuses the ICFTU of hoarding could be spent on investigating the problems of the African worker and the effectiveness of various types of union and industrial agreement. Even such bodies as the British TUC, the Swedish LO or the Confederation of Yugoslav Trade Unions, which have little reason to support the political peddling of the major power centres, have been notably backward in sponsoring field research and acting on it. And the ILO, caught in the crossfire from its constituent members and still dominated by a British conception of industrial relations, has been able to produce few reports of value on working conditions and no impartial analysis of trade unionism in Africa. (One report on East Africa, commissioned in 1958-9 remains unpublished.) Any documentation of significance has been done by a few academics working in the field and by the very few African trade unionists who have set out their own experiences in published form. In some respects the novels of Chinua Achebe, Peter Abrahams or Sembene Ousmane have greater value in describing the problems of African labour than all the reports of the ICFTU and the WFTU together.

The history of international activity in Africa shows how European and American labour movements have engaged in fruitless political and prestige competition for influence. But it also shows the fairly successful struggle of Africans to control their own organization. Both the ICFTU and the WFTU have been compelled to accept the fact that Africans will not be parties to alien cold war disputes and will accept no dictation from foreign political centres. As ICFTU influence diminishes, and the WFTU splits up into various national factions, the

African Trade Unions

divisions within Africa look more like the divisions created by different social and political conditions than by artificially-induced external affiliations. There is therefore just a chance that, left to themselves, Africans will be able to develop the kind of unions that suit their particular stages of development. Aid from outside will obviously be required for a long time to come, but it must be granted impartially and on the basis of African needs. It is perhaps not too much to hope that the international labour movements and the interested governments will be able now to swallow their pride and their ambitions, and begin at last to tackle the real issues.

Chapter 9: Notes

1. R. Palme Dutt, *India Today*, Gollancz, 1940, p. 375 and pp. 380-1.
2. Analysed: Fischer, op. cit., pp. 138-44; and Willard A. Beling, 'The WFTU and Decolonisation, A Tunisian Case Study', *Journal of Modern African Studies*, Vol. 2, No. 4 (1964) pp. 551-64. Quotes from Fischer.
3. Sir Lincoln Evans, at *3rd World Congress of ICFTU*, Stockholm 1953, Report p. 398.
4. Sir Vincent Tewson, at *4th World Congress of ICFTU*, Vienna 1955, Report pp. 347-8.
5. Quoted Fischer, op. cit., p. 157.
6. *1953 ICFTU Congress Report*, p. 510.
7. J. Patrick, *What is a Trade Union?* Government of Kenya, 1952.
8. Cuban delegate, *1953 Congress Report*, p. 400.
9. Quoted in *International Free Trade Union News*, AFL-CIO, New York, August 1958.
10. *American Federationist*, March 1960.
11. *TUC Congress Report*, Blackpool 1959, p. 209.
12. ICFTU: *Report of First African Regional Trade Union Conference*, Accra, 1957, p. 55.
13. Quote from R. Schachter-Morgenthau: *Political Parties in French-Speaking West Africa*, O.U.P., 1964, p. 199.
14. Fischer, op. cit., p. 135.
15. Sydney Lens, 'Lovestone Democracy', *The Nation*, 5 July 1965.
16. G. C. Lodge, *Spearheads of Democracy – Labor in the Developing Countries*, Harper and Row, 1962.
17. G. E. Lichtblau, 'Current Trends in the International Labour Scene', *Year Book of World Affairs*, 1963, p. 216.
18. M. Roberts, 'Africa's Divided Workers', Chapter 5 in C. Legum, *Pan Africanism*, Pall Mall, 1962, p. 86.
19. ibid., p. 87.
20. Ghana, Guinea, Egypt, Mali, Morocco, Algeria and the Nigerian IULC. Membership figures culled from U.S. Department of

African Trade Unions

Labor, Bureau of Labor Statistics: *Directory of Labor Organisations*, Africa, 1962, p. xiv.

21. T. Mboya, *Freedom and After*, Deutsch, 1963, p. 254.
22. Quoted: Clive Jenkins, 'Trend', *Tribune*, 6 August 1965.
23. Lodge, op. cit., p. 158; following quote from p. 144.
24. A. Zack, *Labour and Training in Developing Countries*, Pall Mall, 1964, p. 151.
25. ibid., p. 103.

10 Labour and Economic Development

The small proportion of wage-earners in the total population and yet the strategic importance of the industries in which they operate are perhaps the two crucial economic facts in the role of African trade unions. That unions can acutely embarrass governments and yet are unable in the main substantially to affect political policy follows directly from these facts. It is certainly not surprising that many governments have found it convenient to 'contain' the unions which, with the armed forces, represent the only nation-wide organizations cutting across ethnic or regional boundaries and so posing a potentially serious threat to political power. But this strength is limited precisely because the unions do not yet represent a 'mass movement' of any dimensions; the 'mass' is still the peasantry, and with the peasantry the unions have little or no direct contact. As has been suggested, the wage-earners constitute less of a new social class or (in a narrower form) a privileged *élite* than the first products, of a major social revolution; but in their relations with government, they seem to represent vested interests that threaten the basis of national economic development.

The new governments of Africa are acutely aware that capital accumulation is essential to development, and they attempt to direct the fruits of productivity increases towards this end. They are therefore opposed to any sharp rise in wages which may lead to an increased demand by workers for consumer goods and a tendency to limit investment. In the absence of substantial heavy industry on which to build, most African countries have few consumer industries of their own, and any increased demand for consumer goods is likely to produce a heavy drain on the balance of payments. Furthermore, even at the level of the present meagre wages in Africa, some consumer goods are necessary, and governments are obliged to finance economic development by inflation; most union efforts are then in turn directed not to increasing the real level of wages, but simply to maintaining the purchasing power of wages steadily reduced in value by inflation.

The most important question then becomes – What is the minimum wage necessary for existence in an African country, while massive efforts are being made to industrialize? This introduces the equally important issue of the distribution of wealth among various sectors of the population. Because wage-earners possess some representative machinery and are based on towns which already possess the bulk of social services and facilities, they are likely to add to the problems of government by urging an even larger slice of the national wealth at the expense of peasants, the unemployed and the casually-employed. The governments, therefore, have always to be on guard against the development of the wage-earners as a privileged class. It is only necessary to draw attention to a multitude of statements by Presidents Nyerere, Senghor, or Nkrumah to show that this is already one of the main themes of African industrial relations. But in Zambia the complete reversal of the 'integration' policy prevalent in pre-independence days shows the complications that can be introduced if companies and governments agree to peg African wages to prevent the growth of a privileged class.

The wages of Africans in the Zambian mines were always far below those of the whites, and throughout the 1950s the African mineworker's organizations and the political parties campaigned for equal pay and equal job opportunity at all levels. In 1952–3, after an arbitration award by C. W. Guillebaud, wages were substantially increased and the principle of higher wages was accepted by the companies, so that wages went up by between 55 per cent and 60 per cent from 1956 to 1964. At the same time attempts to accelerate African advancement resulted in various agreements in 1955, the introduction of some training for African skilled workers in 1956, and the opening of fresh negotiations in 1959 to find a permanent solution. But after the mineworkers and the companies had failed to agree over the major question of wage differentials, the most serious strike in the history of the

Copperbelt took place in the first half of 1962. Although the government set up a commission under Sir Ronald Morrison to examine the advancement issue, very little came of it, and discontent continued to simmer throughout 1962. In June 1963 the companies (which by now had some 100 Africans in 'White Job' categories) put forward proposals to the (white) Northern Rhodesian Mineworkers Union for turning the union into a Staff Association and putting the African Staff Employees on the same terms of service as the whites though with lower rates of pay. The white 'closed shop' was abolished, so opening the way for more Africans to enter higher job categories, and intermediate positions of responsibility were created for Africans in addition to the top-level ones. But at the same time the companies stressed that African wages must be in keeping with the level of economic development in Zambia, while non-Africans had to be paid in accordance with overseas standards. Therefore, in spite of the increased responsibilities enjoyed by Africans, they would not be paid at the current high rates, and all appointments in the future would be at much lower levels. Although Africans were being offered increased chances of promotion and responsibility, the principle of equal pay for equal work was accordingly abandoned, and two levels of wage, 'expatriate' and 'local', were established. One of the consequences of this change in policy has been to double the gap between the lowest white wages and the highest African ones. Moreover, at the same time as the mining companies were reorganizing the wage-scales in the industry, the Hadow Commission was recommending a similar policy for the civil service, with two completely separate scales, one white and one African.

These changes would seem to be inevitable if the distribution of wages and earnings among different sectors of the African population in Zambia is to be kept equal in any way, though the gap between wages and agricultural earnings is widening and seems likely to widen further however efficient farming is forced to become. (Current British agricultural workers earn around £13 a week, compared with a national weekly average of nearly £19.) But there are two major disadvantages in the dual wage structure that may have far-reaching repercussions. By maintaining low wages for the middle-range skilled worker, the mining industry may be making it less attractive for African students to take up technical training; administration, teaching or even office work is much more attractive, and it is difficult to see how the industry will be competitive enough. But even more important, the reduced wages paid to Africans will almost certainly make the companies eager to replace white with African labour as soon as possible, and it is difficult to see the workers accepting that their increased efforts mean simply an increase in company profits, most of which leave the country. Unless the companies are prepared to redirect a great deal more of their profits into providing better housing and welfare services (and there is no sign of this), the government will be pressed by the workers themselves to correct the balance.

The alternative danger is that the government, backed by a growing bureaucratic and commercial class, will deny increases in wages and services while at the same time swelling the power, privileges and earnings of the dominant economic groups. In such countries as Nigeria, the Ivory Coast, Morocco and South Africa, the emergence of powerful economic and political interest groups has produced wide discrepancies between *élite* living standards and the depressed condition of both wage-earners and peasants. The revolutionary potential of such societies does not need to be stressed.

But beyond such additional issues, the conflict between increased consumption and capital accumulation is real enough, and therefore the tendency for governments to seek some measure of control over the unions is understandable. The strength of the unions therefore depends on the extent to which they are able to develop their own kind of relationship with the ruling party and the civil authorities, and the type of settlement procedures introduced by the government for labour disputes. That the government has assumed some control over a central trade union federation does not, of course, eliminate labour disputes, nor does the absence of formal links between ruling party and trade union mean that the administration does not control industrial relations by other means. In fact the distinction between government control over industrial relations and party control over the political affiliations and pronouncements of unions is a very important one. In virtually *every* African country the government, inheriting the machinery of the colonial administration, has very wide powers for supervising labour disputes, and in this sense a form of 'guided democracy' in labour matters is found everywhere. In many instances the strike as an industrial weapon is made nearly impossible by the existence of arbitration procedures which must be exhausted (under legal penalties) before a strike or lock-out can be called. In part this comes from the economic predicament of countries which cannot afford a large number of costly disputes (although, as the Nigerian Minister of Labour pointed out in 1959, one public holiday cost the country 100 times more in productive loss than the total number of strikes in the previous year.)[1] But also there is the well-established African tradition of solving disputes by discussion. Some of the industrial settlement procedures recently enacted fit into attitudes which accept the *palaver* as a method of arriving at an agreement, rather than a conflict requiring a judgement. It is therefore possible that, free of the long industrial battles that have characterized union history elsewhere, some African states may evolve systems of joint committees, labour courts and conciliation procedures which are close to local traditions and produce peaceful industrial relations. It does seem, however, that such a solution is less likely in states that are going through a process of rapid industrialization, and certainly today the conducting of industrial relations by *palaver* is more commonly found in the less-developed countries, like parts of French-speaking Africa or Ethiopia (though elements occur in all systems).

The main characteristic of nearly all the established settlement procedures for industrial disputes is the use of compulsory arbitration. And out of a wide variety of types, two main categories of arbitration can perhaps be traced. On the one hand is a group of countries which impose legal penalties (normally under civil law) for breach of agreements and where the arbitrators become in fact the bodies responsible for encouraging good labour relations. The power of the law and the personalities of the judges or members of the arbitration boards are of supreme importance, and a form of 'guided democracy' through the legal

African Trade Unions

system tends to take precedence over the free play of market forces or indeed any control by the political party. In such states the borderline between the limitation on union powers and 'guidance' can become very thin indeed, with the initiative of either employers or unions crushed under the all-powerful supervision of the court. Most of the former French colonies seem still to fall into this category. On the other hand, there are countries – like Ghana or Senegal – where a complex arbitration procedure exists at the top but where considerable room is left for collective bargaining at industrial and plant level. The distinction here may again be between countries which have a relatively high level of industrialization and those which do not. An industrializing country like Egypt or Ghana may try to prevent serious industrial disturbances by making strikes virtually impossible, but still permit some settlement of disputes through normal procedures of collective negotiation. The extent to which such an arrangement will in fact prevent industrial (or political) unrest depends on whether the machinery allows for rapid settlement and wages rise quickly enough at least to match increases in the cost of living. Several industrial disputes have become serious precisely because the settlement machinery was too slow and cumbersome or because wages had failed to match living costs. For example the 1960 demonstrations by commercial workers in Ghana were directed primarily against the tardy arbitration procedure; the Nigerian strike in 1964 emphasized the rapid rise in living costs beyond wage increases; and in 1965 the Tunisian labour crisis was partly due to union unrest at the staggering gap between the cost of living increases over nine years and the relatively meagre rise in wages. There may also be disputes over increased Africanization or the public ownership of industries, but these will largely be decided in direct confrontation with government and will not necessarily be manifested in routine disputes with employers. But, of course, if a major European firm appears to be going slow in its Africanization programme, strikes may be directed against it, even though general policy may be dictated by the government. Some of the strikes on East African plantations in 1958–62 and the 1962 Copperbelt strike in Zambia seem to have been of this character.

Labour and Economic Development

But whatever the form that industrial relations take in African countries, the government remains the most important factor. By giving the judiciary or arbitration boards absolute powers to determine wages and working conditions, many governments hope to ease the transition to an industrial society and limit the areas of friction. And everywhere by stressing the productive nature of unions, labour departments aim to create a sense of national purpose, accelerate the development of a coherent labour force, and raise the level of output. In addition to this, governments may, as in Ghana, Guinea, Kenya or some of the Equatorial French-speaking territories, introduce forms of compulsory or communal labour, in an attempt to use the labour surplus and accelerate the construction of roads or housing. Community developments on the one hand and Labour Brigades on the other are methods of using the available labour material at minimum cost, so involving a sometimes reluctant population in the task of developing the country. As a nation sets out to industrialize, such 'illiberal' measures are likely to become increasingly frequent, and the danger to any form of democratic society is obvious; but it is very doubtful whether such policies are any less 'liberal' than the appalling waste of human resources and the beggarly working conditions of Britain or Germany in the nineteenth and early twentieth centuries. In many respects the attempt to control working conditions and the continuing emphasis on the need to build 'classless' societies show that African governments are making a more determined effort to ease the transition to industrialization than Western Europeans with their merciless *laissez-faire* attitudes ever did.

For the unions, of course – created as they were out of nationalist struggle, with institutions and ideas largely borrowed from the imperial homelands – the challenge of survival is paramount, and it is in the context of economic change that they see their salvation. Unlike European or American unions, the African ones were created *before* large-scale industrialization; but once created, they have a surviving interest in continued industrialization. Unions therefore campaign for increased industrial effort, for the modernization of the economy and for the stabilization of the work-force. In this respect they can be

African Trade Unions

closer in objective to the government than to the rest of the population, who may resist greater industrialization because of its tendency to disrupt the traditional social and economic patterns. It is accordingly not surprising that many unions see their future in alliance with the fortunes of government (or where, as in Morocco and Nigeria, the government seems to be a perpetuation of the *status quo*, in competition). By negotiating for places in party councils or a seat in the Cabinet, for the closed-shop or the 'check-off' agreement or increased nationalization, many unions come to see their role as a spur to the government in the promoting of an industrial society. They therefore accept the stress on productivity with greater willingness than do unions in the more developed states. But whether or not they are accepted as government partners, depends in the end on the agreement of ruling *élites* to see rapid industrialization as a necessary aim and to consider the unions as suitable colleagues in such an effort. Both of these attitudes depend in turn on the political ideologies of the ruling parties, the extent of external pressure on their régimes, and the political-economic risks in granting unions such power that wage increases and social benefits (in societies that have such a small industrial sector) arouse the hostility of other sections of the population or jeopardize the hope of greater capital accumulation.

In fact, and despite the lip-service paid to productivity, most governments have been reluctant to recognize unions as a major element in the drive towards economic development, and this reluctance has broadly been shared by international agencies (though it is perhaps to the credit of the ICFTU that it has, though somewhat belatedly and under African pressure, changed its attitude). The first reason is political. Many one-party governments, only recently established in power, are wary of encouraging the growth of bodies which might easily become major challengers to their supremacy. By maintaining unions under control and denying them facilities for organization, they hope to maintain their power whole and restrict the possibilities of political unrest. As long as countries remain overwhelmingly unindustrialized, there is probably some chance that such tactics will succeed (though 'palace' revolutions, peasant revolts

Labour and Economic Development

or military *coups* with trade union support are always possible). But in the long run, for countries embarking on industrialization such a policy is likely to defeat itself, as various Latin American states disastrously show. The second major reason is connected with economic control by foreign companies. Many governments fear the effect on foreign investment if unions, sufficiently well-organized, prove too powerful to resist in campaigns for higher wages. This argument, though holding some force since African industries must not price themselves out of the market, overlooks the possibility that African workers, without effective organization, may resort to illegal strike action or sporadic acts of violence in efforts to better their condition. It is instructive that many investors, seeing the orderly way in which the Nigerian general strike of 1964 was conducted, concluded that the country was a good investment risk rather than the contrary. If they want economic development and industrial peace, African governments have not only to see that unions possess the facilities for collective bargaining and other methods of solving disputes, but that they are sufficiently effective in handling disputes to gain and retain the confidence of their members. In this context open support for the unions as well as the provision of negotiating machinery is essential.

What forms should support take? The experiences of African unions to date suggest several ways – none of them without difficulties – in which various governments have attempted to aid the growth of unions. The most important is financial. Governments are never in a position to aid the unions by grants of money (and to do so would place the unions themselves under intolerable pressure); but in many instances they have introduced laws obliging the employer – under stated conditions – to deduct union dues from wages and accept the closed-shop principle. Such measures immediately give unions the financial stability – and hence independence – which is normally lacking in developing countries, and for this reason many unions have come to see their future as dependent on obtaining such agreements. But the difficulties that unions face with the introduction of the check-off should not be underestimated. Employers fear the possession of large sums by unions – sometimes for legiti-

African Trade Unions

mate reasons. Union officers have been known to abscond with funds, to use them for non-union purposes, or generally to waste money, while, as Hunter quotes one employer, 'the thought of £200,000 in the hands of a single union with inexperienced leadership and in an explosive political situation is a little frightening.'[2] But these legitimate fears are often submerged by other motives, with employers aiming to produce manageable 'company unions'. Employers often claim after the check-off has been granted that it is unnecessary for union officers to visit the workplace. In a report on the operation of the check-off in Tanganyika, an observer has remarked:

I favoured the idea of the check-off until I saw how it was operated in East Africa. I examined a number of cases, and in each one the employers had imposed stringent, restrictive clauses. It seemed that they were willing to accept trade unionism and to enable it to be financially supported so long as unions renounced part of their primary function. In other words the check-off appeared to be used as a means of controlling and containing trade union development.[3]

In the light of such practices, unions must make sure that governments are sufficiently vigilant in maintaining the independence of the unions from employer control.

The fear of 'inexperienced leadership' is, of course, real enough, and may again lay the union wide open to employer interference. In some instances employers provide training for union officers, but this is very doubtful expedient which unions are wise to resist. The problem of union training remains. Because of language and education barriers the unions are not necessarily getting the best men. Some of their most able leaders have been siphoned off into government and management posts. But unions made financially viable by check-off agreements should be able now, in collaboration with government, to develop training courses and create labour colleges providing instruction for all levels of union work. If unions are given some responsibility for craft training, the government can be made to see the economic importance of such ventures.

It is not enough, however, for governments to provide the unions with check-off and closed-shop facilities, and establish

Labour and Economic Development

training schemes; they will only be able to make full use of the trade unions if they see them as having a positive role in economic development. In a recent attack on the recommendations of the UNs' Economic Commission for Africa, Reuben Mwilu, Director of the Kampala Labour College, suggested that unions should be included in all development programmes.[4] He pointed out that most of the development in East Africa had come from external capital rather than from the intensive use of labour, and that this had had the result of depressing the productivity of African workers, maintaining the gap between high-income and low-income groups, and aggravating the unemployment problem, particularly among young people. African governments, in their drive to increase industrialization, have been prepared to encourage foreign capital through fiscal incentives, but have made little effort to stimulate the use of manpower. Mwilu complained that the potential of trade unions in helping to organize and train labour had been ignored by the ECA as well as by many governments. But as some countries are discovering, the unions *can* be a major asset in economic development. They are – in addition to governments, industry and the universities – an important source of manpower training, almost the only organization on the horizon that can command the confidence necessary to create a viable work-force, and politically can play a crucial part in transmitting ideas and easing the transition to an industrial society.

Therefore, apart from training schemes and laws simplifying financial procedures, governments can lessen their problems, with those, of the unions, by encouraging union participation in economic development, by allowing the unions to develop commercial activities of their own, and by introducing forms of worker management in state-owned factories. In private industry, 'package deals' with unions on wages and productivity should also allow local workers' committees a greater say in the implementation of agreements and ultimately in the management of the enterprises. In an increasing number of countries such solutions are being debated for the overwhelming problems of operating without enough skilled management; individual enterprises in Ghana and Mali, the self-management committees of

African Trade Unions

Algeria, and the growth of union-directed cooperatives in Tunisia and Kenya demonstrate the possibilities. They also suggest the drawbacks. In particular, Algeria displays the dangers of having to move too quickly without either adequate training machinery or a comprehensive mass organization. But the potential for a major break-through in new union-management relations is there; it requires only a conscious and determined effort by government and unions together.

To build up their strength, the unions are having to examine the quality of union leadership and their methods of recruiting members. In pre-independence days, most union leaders came from the white-collar workers, who were almost the only people with knowledge of large-scale organization or the ability to converse in European languages so necessary for contact with government and management. The type of training scheme introduced by foreign union centres, the growth of nationalist parties and the centralized structure of the unions all tended to accentuate the difference between this union *élite* and the mass of the workers. Since most workers were migrant, and the unions were faced with enormous problems of membership turnover – problems which would daunt even the most established and powerful of European or American unions – the power of the few white-collar workers in control was inevitably reinforced. Then, with independence and the introduction of many such leaders into senior political, administrative or management posts, the unions were often faced with collapse. The responsibilities of management to encourage labour stability and of governments to provide adequate guidance for union growth were made all the stronger. The governments were presented with the alternative of encouraging new leaders and the growth of more responsible and representative unions, or containing them at the level of near breakdown.

In a few countries (but large ones – Nigeria, Sudan, Morocco, the Congo), the unions can hardly expect much support from governments because of multi-party or authoritarian constitutions which do not allow much scope for collaboration. Here the problem of growth will remain the unions' own. But everywhere the unions are faced with the problem of political identity, of creating institutions that will allow all workers to participate in the decisions affecting their daily lives, and of providing the incentives to produce union leaders who will have the confidence of members. African unions – in spite of contrary European and American pressures – have always concerned themselves with wider social questions than unions have traditionally done elsewhere. Because they have been present to welcome industrialization, they see their role as debating all issues of social concern – whether industrial or not – because workers moving into industry are as puzzled and frustrated by the social environment of towns and plantations as by the conditions found at work. Indeed, the problems of social adjustment are much greater than those of adjustment to a new type of work. Either in the single-party context (where they represent the industrial *avant-garde*) or in the multi-party one (where they may bear the responsibility for creating a worker's opposition), the unions are learning that 'unity (has) a real meaning by taking up all manner of issues – housing, accommodation, educational facilities, medical provisions, the quality of food as well as wages and working conditions.' The functions of the union are as wide as the communities in which the workers live.[5] This important social sense of African unions – a condition of their survival – promises to challenge trade union thinking throughout the world.

Chapter 10: Notes

1. T. M. Yesufu, *An Introduction to Industrial Relations in Nigeria*, O.U.P., 1962, p. 55.
2. Hunter, *New Societies of Tropical Africa*, O.U.P., 1962, p. 219.
3. V. L. Allen, 'Trade Unionism in East Africa', *Free Labour World*, 143, May 1962, pp. 164-6.
4. Reuben M. Mwilu, 'We would be glad to help', *Free Labour World*, 169-70, July-August 1964, pp. 17-19.
5. V. L. Allen, op. cit., p. 166.

Further Reading

Although the amount of useful material on African trade unions is scanty, some of the most valuable is in academic and trade union journals and often inaccessible. To help readers who may wish to take the subject further I have listed some of those books, pamphlets and essays which I have found particularly useful. Occasionally I have also included titles which were not specifically used in this book but which provide essential reading for certain perspectives on the subject. Where an article has appeared both in French and English I have quoted the English source: this also applies to *Présence Africaine* which publishes a French and English edition.

GENERAL

The most comprehensive bibliography on the subject is William H. Friedland, *Unions, Labor and Industrial Relations in Africa: an annotated Bibliography* (Center for International Studies, Cornell University 1965) which should be consulted for additional material. Histories and accounts of trade unions throughout Africa are scarce and very selective, but the most useful general introductions to labour conditions as a whole are still the two volumes published by the International Labour Office, the *African Labour Survey* (1958) and the *Labour Survey of North Africa* (1960). The only attempts to provide a general survey of trade unions are J. Meynaud and Anisse Salah-Bey, *Le Syndicalisme Africain*, (Payot, Paris, 1963) which concentrates on political relationships, and Mario Murteira, *Sindicalismo e Evoluçâo Social na Africa ao Sul do Sahara* (Estudos de Ciêncas e Socias, Lisbon, 1960) which pays some attention to the influence of European countries on African labour movements. B. C.

African Trade Unions

Roberts in *Labour in the Tropical Territories of the Commonwealth* (London School of Economics and Political Science, 1964) provides some useful material on many African unions and the policies of the British Colonial Office, the TUC and the international organizations, but suffers from legal preoccupations and a failure to recognize the major sociological differences in the role of unions in developing countries. More useful in outlining the social problems of African labour is *Présence Africaine's* early collection of articles *Le Travail en Afrique Noire* (Editions du Seuil, 1952), and J. Clyde Mitchell's *An Outline of the Sociological Background to African Labour* (Ensign Publishers, Salisbury, 1961). There are several books covering labour in developing countries and providing insights or reports on African situations. The most useful include: Bruce H. Millen, *The Political Role of Labor in Developing countries* (Brookings Institution, Washington, 1963); W. Galenson, (ed) *Labor and Economic Development* (John Wiley, New York, 1959) which contains important essays on Egypt and French West Africa; Everett M. Kassalow, (ed) *National Labor Movements in the Postwar World* (Northwestern University Press, 1963); Subratesh Gosh, *Trade Unions in Underdeveloped Countries* (Bookland, Calcutta, 1960); Sidney C. Sufrin, *Unions in Emerging Societies: Frustration and Politics* (Syracuse University Press, 1964) with a lengthy annotated bibliography including many references to Africa; and H. A. Turner, *Wage Trends, Wage Policies and Collective Bargaining: the Problems for Underdeveloped Countries* (C.U.P. for University of Cambridge Department of Applied Economics, 1965) which provides essential analysis for economic role of unions but was unfortunately published too late for discussion in this book.

Of the many books on African politics and social change which provide some comparative material on trade unions, the most important are: Guy Hunter, *The New Societies of Tropical Africa* (O.U.P., 1962); J. Woddis *Africa – The Lion Awakes* (Lawrence and Wishart, 1961) almost half of which is a discussion of trade unionism in Africa prior to independence; Thomas Hodgkin, *Nationalism in Colonial Africa* (Muller, 1956), in many respects the essential introduction to African social changes at the time; J. Coleman and C. G. Rosberg, (eds) *Politi-*

Further Reading

cal Parties and National Integration in Tropical Africa (University of California Press, 1964) which includes a valuable essay by Elliot J. Berg and J. Butler on Trade Unions; and P. Worsley, *The Third World*, Weidenfeld and Nicolson, 1964. Frantz Fanon's *The Wretched of the Earth* (MacGibbon and Kee, 1965) provides an incisive account of trade union dilemmas in independent Africa.

A few publications in pamphlet form make useful summaries of the major issues, either for Africa alone or as part of the Third World. William H. Friedland's *Unions and Industrial Relations in Underdeveloped Countries* (New York State School of Industrial and Labor Relations at Cornell University, 1963) is perhaps the most systematic and sympathetic: Walter Bowen's *Colonial Trade Unions* (Fabian Society, 1954) is interesting for its curiosity value as representative of British Labour thinking on the problem during years when British Fabian opinion was almost equivalent to government policy. From a different perspective S. A. Dange's report to the fourth WFTU Congress, *Trade Union Tasks in the Fight Against Colonialism*, (WFTU Publications, 1957) is equally instructive. In the same year the first meeting of the African Regional Organisation of the ICFTU produced its report on labour conditions in Africa: *Report of the First African Regional Trade Union Conference* (ICFTU, 1958).

Two reference books provide some necessary statistics on Union membership and working conditions. The U.S. Department of Labor, Bureau of Labor Statistics, in its *Africa – Directory of Labor Organizations* (1962) gives a country-by-country breakdown of unions including national centres, number of affiliated unions, officers and membership figures. Julius Braunthal and A. J. Forrest (eds) *Yearbook of the International Free Trade Union Movement*, Volume Two, 1961–2 (Lincolns-Praeger, 1961–2) includes a section on African ICFTU activities and affiliates.

STUDIES OF INDIVIDUAL UNIONS AND COUNTRIES

There are still very few published full-length studies of individual unions or the industrial relations procedures in particular

African Trade Unions

African countries. The most important (apart from essays and articles which are referred to in the chapter-by-chapter bibliographies) are:

R. Poupart, *Première Esquisse de l'evolution de syndicalisme au Congo*, (Institut de Sociologie Solvay, Brussels, 1960).

W. A. Warmington, *A West African Trade Union* (O.U.P., 1960) development and organization of the Cameroons Development Corporation Workers' Union.

T. M. Yesufu, *An Introduction to Industrial Relations in Nigeria*, (O.U.P., 1962).

H. A. Tulatz, *Die Gewerkschaftsentwinklung Nigerias* (Verlag für Literatur und Zeitgeschehen, Hanover 1963), a detailed account of Nigerian trade union affairs up to 1961.

M. Horrell, *South African Trade Unionism: A Study of a Divided Working Class.*(South African Institute of Race Relations, 1961).

Ivan L. Walker and Ben Weinbren, *2000 Casualties: A History of the Trade Unions and the Labour Movement in the Union of South Africa* (SACTU, 1961).

Saad ed din Fawzi, *The Labour Movement in the Sudan, 1946–55* (O.U.P., 1957).

Willard A. Beling, *Labor and Modernisation, A study of Tunisia* (Pall Mall-Praeger, 1965) not published before this book was completed.

A. L. Epstein, *Politics in an Urban African Community* (Manchester U.P. 1958) half of which studies the role of the African Mineworkers Union in Zambian mining towns.

In addition, the U.S. Department of Labor's Bureau of Labor Statistics has published short monographs on Sudan (1961), Congo (1959), Nigeria (1963), Liberia (1960), Morocco (1959), Libya (1958), Egypt (1955). Ghana (1958) and Tunisia (1958).

There are two regional studies: J. I. Roper, *Labour Problems in West Africa* (Penguin Books, 1958); and Elliot J. Berg, 'French West Africa' in the volume edited by W. Galenson mentioned above.

Further Reading

ADDITIONAL MATERIAL FOR INDIVIDUAL CHAPTERS

Chapter 1: Economic Development and the Changing Social Structure.

The most important source for information on the growth of a money economy in Africa is still the United Nations report, *Enlargement of the Exchange Economy in Tropical Africa*, 1954, but several other studies have brought the picture up to date. Guy Hunter's *New Societies of Tropical Africa* is perhaps the most wide-ranging, and Melville J. Herskovitz's *The Human Factor in Changing Africa* (Routledge and Kegan Paul, 1962) the liveliest. Herskovitz and Mitchell Harwitz have also edited the very useful *Economic Transition in Africa* (Routledge and Kegan Paul, 1964). An early classic by an economist is S. H. Frankel's *The Economic Impact on Underdeveloped Societies* (O.U.P., 1953) which includes some details on the concentration of European economic activity in Africa. Other studies on monopolies include P. Joye and R. Lewin, *Les Trusts au Congo* (Société Populaire d'Editions, Brussels 1961); Michael Barratt-Brown, *After Imperialism* (Heinemann, 1963), especially Chapters 8 and 9; while various official reports – for example the East African High Commissions *Reported Employment and Wages in Kenya, 1948–60*, Nairobi 1961 – give many valuable statistics.

On traditional African land ownership and the implied social structure, there is a useful summary in Denise Paulme, 'Traditional Systems of Land Tenure in Negro Africa', *Présence Africaine*, Vol. 20, No. 48, pp. 91–115 and Chapters 5 and 7 in Herskovitz and Harwitz (op. cit.). Ivan Potekhin, 'Land Relations in African Countries', *Journal of Modern African Studies*, Vol. 1 No. 1, pp. 57–8 provides a Russian view of African feudalism. Claude Meillassoux, 'Essai d'interpretation du phénomène économique dans les sociétés traditionelles d'autosubstance'. *Cahiers d'Etudes Africaines*, No. 4, December 1960, makes some shrewd comments on the Economic basis of communalism in African village life. For the adaption of traditional community methods to modern agricultural production see René Dumont, *L'Afrique Noire est Mal Partie*, du Seuil

African Trade Unions

1962 and W. Allen, *The African Husbandman*, Oliver and Boyd, 1965.

On Forced labour under colonial rule Hailey's *African Survey* and the ILO *African Labour Survey* provide the most comprehensive general reports. Other sources are mentioned in the footnotes but some extra material on Portuguese policy is found in Perry Anderson, 'Portugal and the end of ultra-colonialism', *New Left Review*, Nos. 15-17, 1962. The most useful introductions to labour migration are the CCTA report *Migrant Labour in Africa South of the Sahara* (Abidjan, 1961) and a bibliography on migrant labour by Hans Panofsky in *Journal of Modern African Studies*, Vol. 1 No. 4, pp. 521-30. Some of the problems of unemployment in modern Africa are traced in the CCTA *Symposium on Unemployed Youth* (Dar-es-Salaam, 1963), and in Gus Edgren, 'Unemployment in Africa', *East African Journal*, July 1965.

Chapter 2: The Colonial Experience

The most comprehensive introduction to British colonial labour policy is B. C. Roberts (op. cit.), but Woddis (op. cit.) and Meynaud-Salah-Bey (op. cit.) also give useful insights and a very different perspective. A pioneering essay on aspects of British and French colonial labour policy was Georges Fischer, 'Trade Unions and Decolonisation', *Présence Africaine*, Vols. 6-7, Nos. 34-35, pp. 121-69. Clues to British policy can also be found in several official documents, especially the reports by G. St John Orde-Browne on East Africa (1946), Northern Rhodesia (1938), West Africa (1941) and Tanganyika (1926), all published by H.M.S.O. The Colonial Office also produced periodical reports on labour problems of which *Labour Administration in the Colonial Territories* (1950) and *Labour in the United Kingdom Dependencies* (1957) are probably the most useful.

French colonial labour policy is briefly dealt with in Meynaud-Salah-Bey (op. cit.) and in the essay by Elliot J. Berg in Galenson (op. cit.). Legislation is listed in the 'Code du Travail dans les territoires d'outre-mer', (*Présence Africaine*, 1960) while Pierre Chauleur's *Le régime du travail dans les territoires d'Outre-Mer* (Encyclopédie d'Outre-Mer, Paris, 1956) gives greater detail and

Further Reading

commentary. The most useful general introductions to French colonial policy are Stephen H. Roberts, *The History of French Colonial Policy* (1870–1925), (1929, reprint Cass 1963); J. Suret-Canale, *L'Afrique Noire occidentale et centrale, 1900–1945* (Paris 1959); and Robert Cornevin, *Histoire de l'Afrique* (Paris 1956).

Early Belgian colonial policy is documented in E. D. Morrell, *Red Rubber* (Unwin, 1906); Ruth Slade, *King Leopold's Congo* (O.U.P., 1961); and Basil Davidson *The African Awakening* (Cape, 1956). E. Bustin 'The Congo' in G. Carter (ed), *Five African States*, (Pall Mall, 1964) is a useful introduction with an excellent bibliography of recent events and Belgian policy. Labour policy is discussed in A. Doucy & P. Feldheim, *Problemes du travail et politique sociale au Congo* (La Librarie Encyclopedique, 1952); in Poupart (op. cit.); and in P. Joye & R. Lewin (op. cit.).

Chapter 3: Industrialization and Race in South Africa

The most useful summaries of economics in South Africa are D. H. Houghton, *The South African Economy* (O.U.P., 1964); C. W. de Kieweit, *A History of South Africa, Social and Economic* (O.U.P., 1941); and a conservative view, W. H. Hutt, *The Economics of the Colour Bar* (Deutsch, 1964). Sections of Leo Kuper's *An African Bourgeoisie* (Yale, 1965), published too late for consideration in this book, provide sociological perspectives of economic developments.

Apartheid labour legislation and its consequences are discussed in G. J. Doxey, *The Industrial Colour Bar* (O.U.P., 1961). The pioneer study of African labour is S. Van Der Horst, *Native Labour in South Africa* (O.U.P., 1942) which has not been replaced by any single book for its range of information and analysis. E. Roux, *Time Longer than Rope* (Gollancz 1949) is the outstanding book on South African labour history, providing an inside account of African labour events between the two wars. I. L. Walker and B. Weinbren (op. cit.) provide an account of trade union history from the viewpoint of White union officials and M. Horrell, *Racialism and the Trade Unions* (SAIRR, 1959) a dispassionate analysis of the effects of apartheid. E. S. Sachs, *Rebel Daughters* (MacGibbon and Kee, 1957) is the account of

African Trade Unions

the Garment Workers' Union by its general secretary. An analysis of the Nationalist party's attitude towards trade unions is found in Chapters 2 and 13 of Brian Bunting, *The Rise of the South African Reich* (Penguin, 1964). The effect of government's industrial relations policies on the morale of unions is discussed in Garfield Clack, 'Industrial Peace in South Africa', *British Journal of Industrial Relations*, Vol. 1, No. 1, February 1963, pp. 94–106.

Chapter 4: The Rise of Trade Unionism in Africa

There is no single source for the material used in this chapter, the footnotes providing the more obvious ones, other material deriving from the individual studies on unions listed earlier in this bibliography. D. C. Savage's unpublished paper, 'Labour Protest in Kenya: the Early Phase, 1914–39' (*Proceedings of the East African Institute of Social Research conference*, June 1963) is one of the very few attempts to put together the material on the origins of unions. Other unpublished evidence of a comparable nature is found in William H. Friedland, 'Institutional Change: A Study of Trade Union Development in Tanganyika,' Ph.D. dissertation, University of California, 1963; David R. Smock, 'From Village to Trade Union in Africa', Ph.D. dissertation, Cornell University, 1964, a study of the Nigerian Coal Miners Union; and Elliot J. Berg, 'Recruitment of a Labor Force in Sub-Saharan Africa', Ph.D. dissertation, Harvard University, 1960.

Sections of James Coleman, *Nigeria – Background to Nationalism*, (C.U.P., 1958) provides information on the early political role of unions in Nigeria.

Chapter 5: Trade Unions and Political Commitment before Independence

The essay by Berg and Butler on 'Trade Unions', in Coleman and Rosberg (op. cit.) is a useful introduction along with Chapter 3 of Meynaud-Salah-Bey (op. cit.). On Ghana two essays document the growing political involvement of the unions: Lester Trachtman, 'The Labour Movement in Ghana: a study in political unionism', *Economic Development & Cultural*

Further Reading

Change, Vol. 10 No. 2, Part 1, January 1962, pp. 183-200; and Douglas Rimmer, 'The New Industrial Relations in Ghana', *Industrial and Labour Relations Review*, Vol. 14 No. 2, January 1961. W. Friedland, 'The Institutionalization of Labor Protest in Tanganyika', *Sociologus* (Berlin) Vol. 11, No. 2, 1961, pp. 133-47, discusses the political role of the TFL. In his autobiography, *Freedom and After*, (Deutsch, 1963) Tom Mboya discusses at length the relationship between the unions and the nationalist movement in Kenya, and Virginia Thompson's Chapter 'Dahomey', in G. Carter (ed) (op. cit.) provides a useful summary of the situation in that country. A well-documented but highly-coloured view of the political role of unions in former British Africa is found throughout J. Woddis (op. cit.).

Chapter 6: Towards an African Working Class

Among the reports on productivity of African workers, the most useful are: the CCTA reports, *Human Factors of Productivity in Africa* (1960), and *Absenteeism and Labour Turnover* (1961); M. E. Morgaut, *Un dialogue nouveau – l'Afrique et l'industrie* (Arthème Fayard, Paris, 1963); R. Poupart, *Facteurs de Productivité de la main-d'oevre autochtone* (Solvay Institute, Brussels, 1962); and P. Kilby 'The Productivity of African Labour', *Economic Journal*, No. 17, June 1961, pp. 273-91.

Some details on the growth of an urban working class in Morocco are found in Robert Montague, 'Naissance du proletariat marocain', *Cahiers Afrique et d'Asie*, III, Paris 1952; and André Adam, 'Le "bidonville" de Ben Msik à Casablanca', *Annales de l'Institut d'etudes Orientales*, VIII, 1949-50, Paris. Some material on urbanization is also found in the UNESCO survey, *Social Implications of Industrialisation and Urbanisation in Africa South of the Sahara* (1956). Among the more ample material from South Africa, some of the most relevant is, P. Meyer, *Townsmen or Tribesmen* (O.U.P., 1961); B. A. Pauw, *The Second Generation* (O.U.P., 1963); Leo Kuper (op. cit.); University of Natal, *The African Factory Worker* (O.U.P., 1950); Monica Wilson & Archie Mafeje, *Langa* (O.U.P., 1961); S. Van Der Horst, *African Workers in Town* (O.U.P., 1964).

For discussion of some of the literature on class relationships

African Trade Unions

in Africa see Kenneth W. Grundy, 'The Class struggle in Africa', *Journal of Modern African Studies*, Vol. 2, No. 3, 1964, pp. 379–93. Peter Worsley, *The Third World* (Weidenfeld and Nicolson, 1964), contains a useful analysis of the changing social structure in Africa.

Chapter 7: Trade Unions and Governments: (i) In Opposition

Some material on Morocco is found in D. Ashford, 'Labour Politics in a new nation', *Western Political Quarterly*, Vol. 13, No. 2, June 1960, pp. 312–31, and D. Ashford, *Political Change in Morocco*, Princeton U.P., 1960. See also I. William Zartman, *Problems of New Power: Morocco*, (Atherton Press, N.Y., 1964). But the best source for Moroccan union affairs is the UMT's monthly journal, *L'Avant Garde* and the series of special reports published periodically by the union.

Background information on Nigeria can be found in Yesufu (op. cit.) Tulatz (op. cit.) and Richard Sklar, *Nigerian Political Parties*, Princeton U.P., 1963, but for the Nigerian general strike and its political and economic setting, the Nigerian daily papers, especially the Lagos *Daily Times*, and the London weekly paper *West Africa* (each issue from 6 June to 4 July 1964) are basic reading. The U.S. Department of Labor's *Labor in Nigeria* (1963), is a useful summary of trends just before the strike.

Chapter 8: Trade Unions and Governments: (ii) Socialism and the One-Party State

Apart from sources mentioned for earlier chapters, some of the particular studies of countries and unions since independence include relevant material on party-union conflicts. Aristide Zolberg's *One-Party Government in the Ivory Coast*, (Princeton U.P., 1964) and Ruth Schachter-Morgenthau, *Political Parties in French-Speaking West Africa* (O.U.P., 1964) provide basic material on the relationship of unions to the leading parties. F. J. Tomiche, 'Le mouvement syndical dans l'Egypte actuelle', *Temps Modernes*, July 1959, pp. 107–23, and M. F. Ameen, *L'histoire du mouvement syndicale et legislation ouvriers en Egypte* (Maison de livres Almal-Kutob, Cairo, 1961) provide different

Further Reading

perspectives on Egyptian labour to that found in F. Harbison, 'Egypt', in W. Galenson (op. cit.).

East African trade unions problems are discussed in Roger D. Scott, 'Labour legislation and the Federation Issue', *East African Journal*, November 1964, and Hassan O. Kifile, 'Labour Relations in Tanganyika', *International Labour Review*, No. 88, October 1963, pp. 345-65.

There is some material on labour politics in Algeria since 1962 of which Juliette Minces 'Autogestion et lutte de classe en Algerie', *Temps Modernes*, No. 229, June 1965, pp. 2204-31, is the most coherent. From the ample Algerian sources, the Government publication *Documents sur l'Autogestion* (1963), is particularly useful as are also some issues of the main journals, *Revolution Africaine*, *El Moudjahid*, and the now banned Communist paper, *Alger Republicain*. Gerard Challiand's *L'Algerie – est-elle socialiste?* (Maspero, 1964) gives some documentations and a somewhat cursory account of Ben Bella's labour policies.

Chapter 9: The Politics of International Trade Unionism

It would be invidious to mention the host of bad literature on international trade union affairs, but as introductions L. L. Lorwin's *The International Labor Movements* (New York 1953) and J. P. Windmuller's *American Labor and the International Labor Movements* (University of Cornell, 1955) are less misleading than most. But Georges Fischer (op. cit.) is the best beginning and Sidney Lens, 'Lovestone Democracy', *The Nation*, 5 July 1965, a good follow up. On the role of the British TUC see D. I. Davies, 'The Politics of the TUC's Colonial Policy', *Political Quarterly*, Vol. 35, No. 1, 1964, pp. 23-34; and B. C. Roberts (op. cit.) Chapter 5. The Congress reports of WFTU, ICFTU and AATUF give some idea of what went on, but G. E. Lichtblau, 'Current Trends on the International Labour Scene', *Year Book of World Affairs* Vol. 17, 1963, pp. 105-218 gives a brief account (pro-ICFTU) of the trends. On WFTU policy Lichtblau has also written 'The Communist Labour Offensive in Former Colonial Territories', *Industrial and Labor Relations Review*, Vol. 15, No. 3, April 1962, pp. 376-401. Some details on activities in Africa by union centres of Communist countries are given in Z.

African Trade Unions

Brzeziński, *Africa and the Communist World*, (O.U.P., 1964), and the programmes of ICFTU affiliates are outlined in Arnold Zack, *Labour Training in Developing Countries* (Pall Mall, 1964). A summary of the main issues in the division between the ICFTU and AATUF is given in M. Roberts, 'Africa's Divided Workers', Chapter 5 in C. Legum, *Pan-Africanism* (Pall Mall, 1962).

Chapter 10: Labour and Economic Development

Among the few competent introductions to the economic role of unions in developing countries, two essays are particularly perceptive: Paul Fisher, 'Unions in less-developed countries: a reappraisal of their economic role', in E. Kassalow (ed) op. cit.; and H. A. Turner (op. cit.). Also useful is 'The evolutions of labour disputes settlement procedures in certain African countries, *International Labour Review*, Vol. 91, No. 2, February 1965, pp. 102–20.

An interesting assessment of African Labour philosophies is found in W. H. Friedland and C. G. Rosberg (eds) *African Socialism* (O.U.P., 1965), and for considerations of industrial democracy in developing countries see: Nabagopal Das, *Experiments in Industrial Democracy* (Asia Publishing House, 1964); and Albert Meister, *Socialisme et Autogestion* (du Seuil, 1964) on Yugoslavia. An interesting discussion of Ghana's unions along these lines is D. Guerin, 'Trade Unionism and Socialism in Ghana', *Présence Africaine*, Vol. 23, No. 51, 1964, pp. 16–25.

Glossary of Abbreviations and Terms used

AAPO All-African Peoples Organisation. Set up at first All-African Peoples Conference at Accra in 1958. Dedicated to anti-colonialism, African understanding and the creation of a United States of Africa, created OAU (q.v.) at Addis Ababa Conference, 1964.

AATUF All-African Trade Union Federation.

Action Group. Founded in 1951 by Chief Obafemi Awolowo. Until 1962 the ruling party of the Western Region of Nigeria.

AFL American Federation of Labour. Federation of predominantly craft unions merged with CIO (q.v.) to form AFL-CIO (q.v.) in 1955.

AFL-CIO American Federation of Labour-Congress of Industrial Organisations created in 1955 out of the two major American trade union federations the AFL (q.v.) and the CIO (q.v.).

AFRO African Regional Organisation of ICFTU, formed in 1960 with headquarters in Nigeria.

ANC African National Congress, Zambia. Founded in 1948 by Godwin Lewanika, subsequently led by Harry Nkumbula. Lost support to UNIP (q.v.) after 1959.

AOF Afrique Occidentale Française, French West Africa.

APP All People's Party. Opposition party in Sierra Leone led by Siaka Stevens, former trade unionist and Minister of Mines, Land and Labour in 1953.

ATUC African Trade Union Confederation.

AWF African Workers' Federation, Kenya.

CATC Confédération Africaine des Travailleurs Croyants, African regional organization of CISC (q.v.) formed in 1956.

CATU Confederation of Arab Trade Unions, formed in Cairo in 1956 with affiliates in North Africa and the Middle East.

CCTA Commission for Technical Co-operation in Africa South of the Sahara. Research organization established in 1950 by colonial governments, now with twenty-five members from Europe and Africa. Formed an Inter-African Labour Institute in 1952. Re-formed as Scientific, Technical and Research Commission of OAU (q.v.) at Addis Ababa Conference, 1964.

African Trade Unions

CFTC Confédération Française des Travailleurs Chrétiens, until its reorganization in 1964 the pro-Catholic French trade union centre. Affiliate of CISC (q.v.).

CGT Confédération Générale du Travail. Pro-Communist French trade union federation.

CGTA Confédération Générale des Travailleurs Africaine.

CGT-FO Confédération Générale du Travail, Force Ouvrière. Pro-SFIO (q.v.). French trade union federation, created 1949 after split in CGT (q.v.).

Check-off. Method of union dues-paying by which employer automatically deducts contributions from wages on behalf of a trade union.

CIA Central Intelligence Agency, United States of America. Internationally active political secret service organization. Activities described in D. Wise and T. B. Ross, *The Invisible Government*, Cape 1965.

CIO Congress of Industrial Organisations, industrial rival to AFL (q.v.) created in 1936, merged with AFL to form AFL-CIO (q.v.) in 1955.

CISC Confédération Internationale des Syndicats Chrétiens. Pro-Catholic trade union international, dominated by French and Italian affiliates.

Closed Shop. System in which all employees in a trade or industry are obliged to belong to a trade union.

CNTG Confédération Nationale des Travailleurs Guinéens.

CPP Convention Peoples' Party. Founded by Kwame Nkrumah in 1949, the leading nationalist party in Ghana before independence and the governing party since.

CPSA Communist Party of South Africa. Formed in 1922 and banned in 1950 under the Suppression of Communism Act.

CSC Confédération des Syndicats Chrétiens. Belgian pro-Catholic trade union federation.

EATUC East African Trade Union Congress.

FLN Front de Liberation Nationale. Formed in 1954, acted as the main political organization in the war against the French; since independence in 1962 has acted as the ruling political party.

FOFATUSA Federation of Free African Trade Unions.

GTUC Ghana Trades Union Congress.

Histadrut. Central Labour Federation in Israel.

ICFTU International Confederation of Free Trade Unions, formed after split in WFTU (q.v.) in 1949 led by American and British trade union centres. Strongly anti-Communist in character.

ICU Industrial and Commercial Workers Union of Africa, South Africa.

Glossary

IFCTU International Federation of Christian Trade Unions. English title of CISC (q.v.).

ILO International Labour Office. Labour department of United Nations Organisation, originally created in 1919.

Istiqlal. The Independence Party of Morocco, formed in 1944, led struggle against the French during 1950s; government party of independent Morocco from 1956 to 1960.

ITS International Trade Secretariats. International trade union federations representing unions in one occupation or industry; each ITS is affiliated to ICFTU (q.v.).

JAC Joint Action Committee of Nigerian Trade Unions.

KADU Kenya African Democratic Union. Created by Ronald Ngala and Masinde Muliro in 1960, mainly on Masai, Nandi and other tribal opposition to KANU (q.v.); formed minority administration in 1961; in opposition 1962–5; merged with KANU in 1965.

KANU Kenya African National Union. Formed in 1960 by Tom Mboya, Oginga Odinga and James Gichuru; rapidly became the leading nationalist party in Kenya under presidency of Jomo Kenyatta; after independence the Kenya governing party.

KFL Kenya Federation of Labour.

KLGWU Kenya Local Government Workers Union.

Kwame Nkrumah Institute. Ideological training centre of the CPP in Ghana (q.v.).

Labour Party (South Africa). Formed in 1909, originally an all-white party, allied with Nationalist Party (q.v.) in government of 1924; changed policy in 1930s and supported Smuts war-time government; came out with unequivocal support for non-whites in 1946; lost all parliamentary seats in 1958.

Landsorganisationen. Swedish central labour federation.

Lumumba Institute. Ideological centre established in Kenya in 1963.

National(ist) Party. Originally formed by General Hertzog in 1915 to redress the wrongs done in the 1902 Boer War, became militantly racialist party gaining power in 1924 and in 1933 in coalition with first the Labour Party (q.v.) then the South African Party of General Smuts. Split in 1934, its militant wing led by Dr D. F. Malan emerging as winners of the 1948 general election, and has been in power ever since.

NCNC National Council of Nigeria and the Cameroons. Formed by Herbert Macaulay and Nnamadi Azikwe in 1944 to gain independence for a united Nigeria; suffered after creation of Action Group (q.v.) and NPC (q.v.) but emerged at independence as governing

African Trade Unions

party in Eastern Region and junior partner in federal coalition government.

Neo-Destour. Formed in 1934 by Habib Bourguiba, led struggle against French and emerged as single party government in 1955, since when it has been continuously in office. Renamed the Socialist Destour Party in 1965.

NLC Nigerian Labour Congress.

NFL Northern Federation of Labour, Nigeria.

NLM National Liberation Movement, Ghana opposition party between 1954 and 1957.

NPC Northern Peoples' Congress. Formed in 1951, supported by Northern Nigerian emirs, became the governing party in the Northern Region and the senior party in the federal coalition.

NRTUC Northern Rhodesia Trades Union Congress.

NTUC Nigerian Trade Union Congress.

NUTA National Union of Tanganyikan Workers.

NWC Nigerian Workers Council.

OAU Organization of African Unity.

PAI Parti Africain de l'Indépendence.

PDCI Parti Démocratique de la Côte d'Ivoire. Ivory Coast section of interterritorial party the RDA, led by Felix Houphouet-Boigny; severed relations with French Communist Party in 1950; emerged as governing party of independent Ivory Coast.

PDG Parti Démocratique de Guinée. Guinea section of the interterritorial party the RDA (q.v.); led by Sékou Touré after 1952; the governing party of independent Guinea.

RDA Rassemblement Démocratique Africain. Created with Communist support in 1946 as a mass movement for the whole of French West Africa, fostered parties in all French West African states. Broke ties with Communists in 1950. RDA parties eventually led colonies to independence in all of French West Africa except Senegal.

SACTU South African Congress of Trade Unions.

SAFTU South African Federation of Trade Unions.

SAMWU South African Mineworkers Union.

SATUC South African Trade Union Council.

SEATO South East Asia Treaty Organisation.

SFIO Section Française de l'Internationale Ouvrière, the French Socialist Party led since 1951 by Guy Mollet.

SGWTUF Sudan Government Workers Trade Union Federation.

SRATUC Southern Rhodesian African Trade Union Congress.

SRTUC Southern Rhodesian Trade Union Congress.

Glossary

SWTUF Sudan Workers Trade Union Federation.

TANU Tanganyika African National Union. After 1953 the leading nationalist party in Tanganyika under its President, Julius Nyerere; since 1961 the governing party.

TFL Tanganyika Federation of Labour. Dissolved by government order in January 1964 and replaced by NUTA (q.v.).

TUC Trades Union Congress, United Kingdom. Only trade union federation in Britain, industrial wing of the currently ruling Labour Party.

TUCSA Trade Union Congress of South Africa.

UAC United Africa Company, African branch of Unilever.

UDD Union Démocratique Dahoméenne.

UGTA Union Générale des Travailleurs Algériens.

UGTAN Union Générale des Travailleurs d'Afrique Noire. Inter-territorial trade union federation created in 1956 by Sekou Touré out of former CGT (q.v.) affiliates in West Africa.

UGTCI Union Générale des Travailleurs de la Côte d'Ivoire.

UGTM Union Générale des Travailleurs Marocaines.

UGTT Union Générale des Travailleurs Tunisiens.

ULC United Labour Congress of Nigeria.

UMT Union Marocaine du Travail.

UNFP Union Nationale des Forces Populaires, left-wing party in Morocco, formed in 1960 after split in Istiqlal (q.v.).

Union Sudanaise. Established as section of the RDA (q.v.) in French Sudan in 1946, emerged as major party in 1957, fused with Senegalese UPS (q.v.) in 1959 to create Federation of Mali, which broke up a year later, Soudan (under Mobido Keita) becoming the Republic of Mali.

UNIP United National Independence Party, nationalist party in Zambia led by Kenneth Kaunda, formed in 1959 and now the governing party of independent Zambia.

UNSTD Union Nationale des Syndicats des Travailleurs du Dahomey.

UNTCI Union Nationale des Travailleurs de Côte d'Ivoire.

UPS Union Progressiste Sénégalaise, formed in 1958 by Leopold Senghor out of two Senegalese parties formerly related to SFIO (q.v.); currently the government party in Senegal.

UPTC Union Pan-Africaine des Travailleurs Croyants. Pan-African trade union federation established by CATC unions (q.v.) in 1959.

USTT Union Syndicale des Travailleurs de Tunisie.

Wafd. Major political party in Egypt from 1919 to 1952.

WAA Workers' Affairs Association, Sudan.

WFTU World Federation of Trade Unions. Originally formed in 1945

African Trade Unions

by Communist and non-Communist unions, after creation of ICFTU (q.v.) in 1949 became predominantly Communist-directed with headquarters in Prague.

ZAPU Zimbabwe African Peoples Union. Led by Joshua Nkomo, one of the two major African nationalist parties in (Southern) Rhodesia.

Index

References to African unions and political parties are found under the name of country; no names of individual African unions or national union federations are included in the Index

Abboud, General Ibrahim, 141
Achour, Habib, 165-7, 205, 209
Adebola, A. H., 84, 128, 146
African Timber and Plywood Co., 116
African Trade Union Confederation, 158, 206-7
Agriculture, 16-20, 22, 23; *see also* Cash-Cropping, Land-ownership, Peasants
Ahomadegbé, Justice, 105
Akainyah, Judge, investigation of, 128
Algeria, 19, 43, 45, 60, 76, 122, 170, 203, 229-30; trade unions in, 96, 98, 102-3, 180-85, 192, 197-8, 200, 206, 207
All-African Peoples' Organization, 197, 203
All-African Trade Union Federation, 161, 173, 197, 200, 203-7, 210
Allen, V. L., 148; quoted, 115, 228, 231
American Federation of Labor, 194-5, 201
American Federation of Labor – Congress of Industrial Organisations, 65, 195-7, 201-2, 206, 207-9, 215
Anderson, Perry, quoted, 135
Angola, 16, 21, 203
Apithy, Souron-Migan, 105-7
Appiah, Joe, 177
Ashford, D., quoted 139
Awolowo, Chief Obafemi, 82
Azikwe, Nnamdi, 82

Balandier, G., 74
Ballinger, W. G., 60
Bechuanaland, 16
Beck, Mayoa, 199
Becu, Omer, 207-8
Ben Barka, Mehdi, 139-40
Benbella, Ahmed, 180-85
Ben Salah, Ahmed, 165-6, 205
Ben Seddik, Majoub, 200, 205
Berrada, Hamid, 140
Borha, L. L., 84, 146
Bouabid, Abderrahim, 139
Boumedienne, Hourari, 182, 185
Bourguiba, Habib, 165-6, 171, 205; quoted 204
Brandie, J. S., 41
Britain, labour conditions and trade unions in, 37, 54, 167
Bulloch, John, quoted 127-8
Buganda, 19, 127, 130-31
Bunting, S. P., 57

Cameroon, 18, 42, 46, 130; trade unions in, 96, 138, 199
Camille, Gris, 90, 158, 198
Cash-Cropping, 18, 114, 119, 129-31
Central African Republic, 130
Central Council of Soviet Trade Unions, 189
Central Intelligence Agency, 201
Chad, 129
Cissé, Alioune, 154
Citrine, Walter, 189
Class Structure, development of, 114-32, 144-6, 222

251

Index

Colonial Development and Welfare Act, 1940, 39
Colonial Economic Policies, 24–6, 31, 46, 49, 54
Comhaire-Sylvain, J, 74
Commission for Technical Co-operation in Africa South of the Sahara, 115
Commonwealth Labour Conferences, 188
Communism, 55–8, 60–63, 77–8, 89, 93, 198; suppression of, 60, 62, 64, 66–7, 69, 95, 201–3, 207–9; *see also* World Federation of Trade Unions, Confédération Générale du Travail
Communist Party of the Soviet Union, 55, 61
Confédération Africaine des Travailleurs Croyants, 154, 156–7, 204
Confédération Française des Travailleurs Chrétiens, 44
Confédération Générale du Travail, 44–6, 88–9, 106, 153, 189, 193, 197–200, 201
Confédération Générale du Travail – Force Ouvrière, 45–6, 89, 193, 197, 201
Confederation of Arab Trade Unions, 161, 200
Congo (Brazaville), 33, 122, 129–30; trade unions in, 107, 149
Congo (Leopoldville), 16, 21, 23, 24, 28, 42, 47–9, 123, 125, 189, 199, 203; trade unions in, 48–9, 138, 149, 150, 207, 230
Congress of Industrial Organizations, 189
Cresswell, Capt., 58

Dahomey, 126, 130; trade unions in, 104–7, 138, 149, 154, 158
Danquah, J. B., 177
Deakin, Arthur, 190
de Gaulle, Charles, 154
Denise, Auguste, 156

Development projects, 18
Dia, Mamadou, 155
Diallo, Abdoulaye, 89, 198 203
Diop, Majemout, 155
Dumont, René, quoted 20

East Africa, 17, 36, 38, 49, 215, 224, 228, 229
Economic Commission for Africa, 229
Economies, government control of, 31, 33; 46, 49, 54, 65–70, 219 ff.
Edusei, Mrs Krobo, 128
Egypt, 19, 170, 224; trade unions in, 153, 158–61, 164, 203–4, 205
Elkan, Walter, quoted 26–7, 119
El Sheikh, Shafia Adhem Ahmed, 141–2, 197
English Working Class, 124
Ethiopia, 19, 207, 223

Fabian Society, 169
Favrod, E. H., quoted 126–7
Fawzi, Saad ed din, quoted 91, 92
Feudalism, 19, 126
Fiankan, Gaston, 90
Fischer, Georges, quoted 40, 198
Foster Commission 1940, quoted 73
France, labour policy in, 44–5
Franchon, Benoit, quoted 191
Freetown Strike Inquiry Report 1955, quoted 80
French-speaking Equatorial Africa, 16, 24, 46, 98, 107, 149, 199, 225; social differences in, 126–7, 129–30
French-speaking West Africa, 19, 46, 75, 204, 223; trade unions in, 84–90, 93, 96, 153–8, 164, 189, 198–9, 205, 207; social differences in, 126–7, 129–30
French Sudan: *see* Mali

Gabon, 126

252

Index

Galvin, Miles E., quoted 137
Gambia, 75, 189
Gezira scheme, 18, 28, 90
Ghana, 16, 20, 24, 28, 46, 75, 77, 81, 107, 123, 127–9, 170, 224, 225, 229–30; trade unions in, 96, 108–10, 111, 125, 138, 174–80, 189, 196–7, 200, 202–4, 224
Gompers, Samuel, 201
Goodluck, Wahab, 84, 147; quoted 146
Grant, Marcus, 79
Guèye, Abbas, 154, 198
Guillebaud, C. W., 220
Guinea, 20, 85, 89, 107, 112, 130, 170, 199, 225; trade unions in, 87–8, 96, 154, 171–4, 202–3

Hached, Ferhat, 165, 190–92
Harbison, F., quoted 161
Harris, Charlie, assassination of, 62
Hassan II, King, 139–40
Hertzog, Albert, 62
Hertzog, Gen. J. B. M., 58, 59
Histadrut, 170, 210
Hobsbawm, E. J., quoted 124
Houphouet-Boigny, Felix, 89–90, 156–7, 198; quoted 198
Hunter, Guy, 228

Ibrahim, Abdallah, 139
Ikoku, S. G., quoted 179–80
Ikoli, Ernest, 82
Imoudou, Michael, 81–2, 84, 146, 147, 203
India, 15, 38, 39, 188–9
Indirect rule, 19
Infra-structure, development of, 24–5
International Aid and Training Programmes, 209–16
International Confederation of Free Trade Unions, 45, 49, 65, 100, 102–3, 106, 110, 141, 143, 147, 158, 167, 168, 191–7, 201–13, 215–16; report quoted, 25;
African Regional Organization of, 203–6
International Federation of Christian Trade Unions, 45, 49, 143, 158, 193, 204, 206
International Labour Office, 32, 35, 37, 49, 100, 188, 209, 215
International Socialist Journal, quoted 147–8
International Trade Secretariats, 209, 212–14
International Trade Union Organizations before 1945, 188–9, 201
International Workers of the World, 57
Investment, European and American, 16, 20, 23, 24–5, 229
Ivory Coast, 28, 76, 85, 126–7, 130, 177, 222; trade unions in, 89–90, 96, 106, 154, 155–8, 199

Jamela, Reuben, 102
Johnson, Chief J. M., 146
Johnston, Sir Harry, 19
Jones, Ivon, 57

Kadalie, Clemens, 57, 59–61
Kamaliza, Michael, 110, 161–2; quoted 164
Kampala Labour College, 163, 207, 210–12, 229
Katanga, 21, 27, 47–8, 115–16
Katilungu, Lawrence, 97
Kaunda, Kenneth, 97
Kawawa, Rashidi, 110, 161
Kenya, 16, 19, 23, 24, 27, 36, 41, 43, 60, 75, 76, 80, 107, 127, 225; trade unions in, 76–9, 96, 98, 99–101, 167–71, 193–5, 205, 206, 207, 212, 230
Kenya Labour Department 1950 Report, quoted 77
Kenyatta, Jomo, 101
Khayam, Sidi, 148
Kibisu, Peter, 101, 168
Kilby, Peter, 115

253

Index

Kwame Nkrumah Institute, 178, 179

Labour, forced, 26, 32–6, 225
Labour, migrant, 21–3, 25–9, 47–8, 67, 80, 114–25, 230
Labour policies of African Governments, 118, 137–9, 152–3, 219–30; international comparisons, 135–7
Labour policies of colonial powers, general, 49–50; Britain, 34–43, 76–80, 84, 90–93, 109, 189; France, 33–4, 39, 43–6, 76, 80, 81, 84–7, 93, 189; Belgium, 32–3, 39, 47–9, 189
Labour-Nationalist pact in South Africa, 54, 58
Labour Party of Britain, 38, 124
Lamine-Guèye Law 1950, 43–4, 86
Land, colonial seizure of, 16–20
Landownership, 16–20, 22, 90, 124–7, 130–31
Landsorganisationen, 189, 210, 215
Latin America, 68, 125, 227; trade unions in, 137, 201
Lebret, Father, 155
Le Proletaire, quoted 87
Liberia, 24, 28, 207
Libya, 19
Lodge, George, quoted 202, 208–9
Lovestone, Jay, 201
Lubembe, Clement, 168; quoted 170

Macaulay, Herbert S., 82
Madeley, Walter, 61
Maga, Hubert, 105–7
Malagasy Republic, 199
Magrheb: *see* North Africa
Malawi, 16, 19, 21, 42, 78
Mali, 20, 129–30, 155, 170, 199, 229–30; trade unions in, 88–9, 96
Maluleke, J. T., 102

Marx, K., quoted 15
Mass Society, idea of, 23
Mauretania, trade unions in, 158
Mboya, Tom, 99–101, 110, 167–9, 194–5, 205; quoted, 100, 101, 167–8
Meany, George, quoted 207
Mezerna, Ahmed, quoted 122
Micaud, Charles A., quoted 166
Mkello, Victor, 162
Mohammed V, King, 139
Monopolies, marketing and production, 24, 33; political importance of, 24, 220–22, 228
Morgan Commission on Wages and Salaries, 1964, Report, 127, 143–6
Morgaut, M. E., 115
Morocco, 19, 43, 60, 76, 121–2, 149, 222, 226; trade unions in, 96, 138, 139–40, 142, 149, 150, 192, 197–8, 200–201, 207, 230
Morrison, Sir Ronald, 221
Mozambique, 21
Mwilu, Reuben, quoted 229

Nasser, Gamal Abdel, 161
Negro Improvement Association, 60
Ngo, Blaise Yao, 156–7
N'gom, Jacques, 199
Niger, trade unions in, 130, 154, 158
Nigeria, 19, 24, 28, 42, 49, 75, 77, 98, 107, 123, 125, 126–8, 149, 222, 226; trade unions in, 81–4, 93, 96, 97, 106, 138, 142–8, 150, 189, 203, 204, 205, 207, 224, 227, 230
Nkomo, Joshua, 102
Nkrumah, Kwame, 108, 197, 220
Nkumbula, Harry, 97
Nock, Ibrahim, 145, 146
North Africa, 19, 55, 79, 189, 200
Northern Rhodesia: *see* Zambia
Nyasaland: *see* Malawi

254

Index

Nyerere, Julius, 220; quoted, 110, 163–4
Nzeribe, Gogo Chu, 146; quoted 84, 148

Oldenbrook, J. H., 196
Orde-Browne, Granville St John, 39
Overseas Territories Labour Code 1952, 44, 46, 86–7

Parry, Edgar, 79
Patrick, James, 41; quoted 194
Peasants, 19, 114, 126, 129–31, 180–81
Poll Tax, 26, 35–6
'Poor Whites', 54, 85
Poupart, R., 115
Présence Africaine, quoted 131–2
Productivity of African Workers, European attitudes to, 26, 35–7, 75–6, 115–20

Quaidoo, P. K. K., 177

Railway density in Africa, 21
Rand Rebellion, 57–8, 59
Roberts, B. C., quoted 178
Rwanda and Burundi, 47

Saillant, Louis, 45, 190–92; quoted 191
Self-management, 179–85, 229–30
Senegal, 44, 49, 85, 123, 126–7, 130, 177, 224; trade unions in, 89, 106, 154–5, 206
Senghor, L. S., 89, 164, 220; quoted 150, 155
Sierra Leone, 41, 75, 98, 107; trade unions in, 79–80, 106, 138, 149, 189, 199
Smuts, Jan Christian, 55, 58, 62
Solod, Danil, 173
Somalia, 24
Soumah, David, 155

South Africa, 16, 19, 21, 22–3, 47, 53–71, 75, 79, 116–18, 203, 222; migrant labour and, 21, 22–3, 27–8, 117–18; racial policies of, 23, 53–4, 58, 62–70; trade unions in, 53–71, 189, 197
Southern Rhodesia, 16, 19, 21, 24, 76, 78, 79; trade unions in, 99, 101–2, 104, 207
Stevens, Siaka, 79, 106
Stewart, Charles H., quoted 122
Strikes, 39, 56, 57, 58, 63, 67, 75, 77–8, 79–80, 81, 82–4, 86, 90, 92, 95–6, 100, 105, 108, 110, 111, 127–9, 140, 141–2, 143–8, 149, 157, 161–2, 168, 177, 185, 220–21, 224; suppression of, 42, 49, 56, 58, 77, 81, 95–6, 141, 156, 159, 162, 176, 223
Sudan, 19, 24, 28, 107, 149; trade unions in, 90–93, 106, 138, 140–42, 197, 205, 230
Swaziland, 16
Suret-Canale, Jean, quoted 126

Tanganyika/Tanzania, 16, 18, 21, 23, 36, 43, 76, 107, 123, 211; trade unions in, 96, 110–11, 158, 161–4, 204, 207, 212, 228
Tanoh, Amon, 156
Tawney, R. H., quoted 37
Tettegah, John K., 108–9, 174–5, 197, 200, 203, 205, 206; quoted 174–5
Tewson, Sir Vincent, 101, 195
Thompson, E. P., quoted 124
Tlili, Ahmed, 165–7, 205, 209
Togo, 46, 130
Tomlinson Commission, 22, 28; quoted 117
Touré, Sekou, 45, 87–9, 97, 104, 153–4, 171–2, 196, 198–9; quoted 172
Trade Unions in Africa, Origins of, 15, 38, 40, 42, 55–60, 72–112, 122, 124–5

255

Index

Trades Union Congress of Britain, 38, 39, 40, 44, 46, 55, 56, 59, 64, 65, 109, 188–9, 193–6, 201, 209, 215; Report on South Africa, quoted 64; 1959 Congress Report, quoted 196

Traditional Economies, 23–4, 125–6

Tribes and trade unions, 72–5, 97–8

Tumbo, C. K. S., 162

Tunisia, 19, 43, 46, 76; trade unions in, 96, 138, 165–7, 170–71, 190–92, 196–7, 200, 204, 205, 206, 209, 214, 224, 230

Turcson-Ocran, E. C., 108

Uganda, 41, 78, 97, 119–20, 126, 211; trade unions in, 119, 207, 211

Unemployment, 29, 57, 78, 121–3

Union Générale des Travailleurs d'Afrique Noire, 90, 97, 104–6, 153–8, 172–3; training college at Conakry, 172, 210

Union Minière de Haut-Katanga, 24, 47–8, 116

United Africa Company, 24, 83, 108, 109–10

Upper Volta, 28; trade unions in, 130, 158, 177

Venture, quoted 169

Wage-labour, growth of, 21–9, 32–7, 47, 53–4, 57, 67–8, 79, 81, 85, 114–25, 219

Wages, 26–7, 36, 44–9, 57, 66, 68–9, 78, 80, 81, 85–7, 92, 119–21, 122, 126–8, 130–31, 143–5, 150, 155, 163, 219–22, 224

Warmington, W. A., quoted 42–3

Webb, Sydney, colonial labour dispatch of, 38

Welbeck, N. A., 176

Wells, F. A., quoted 116

West Africa, 16, 24, 28, 49, 75, 79, 80–81

West Africa, quoted 146, 147

West Indies, 38, 39

White Settlers and African Labour, 76, 86, 98–104, 180–81, 220–22

Wilson, Woodrow, 201

Windham, Mr Justice, 101

Witwatersrand Native Labour Association, 21

World Federation of Trade Unions, 45, 103, 141, 189–92, 197–200, 209, 210, 213, 215–16; Labour College at Budapest, 210

Yacé, Philippe, 156–7

Yesufu, T. M., quoted 72–3, 74

Zack, Arnold, quoted 211

Zakaria, Ibrahim, 141, 197

Zambia, 19, 24, 39, 47, 75, 76, 78, 120–21, 123, 220–22; trade unions in, 73, 97, 138, 189, 207, 221, 224

Zanzibar, 207